Praise for *Citizen You*

"*Citizen You* is a refreshing, sparkling challenge to all of us to seize the day and do something to change the world. You can't read this book without feeling inspired, energized, and motivated to get engaged in your school or your community, in issues local and global, in what it takes to help build a future worth dreaming about."

—*Jacqueline Novagratz, CEO of the Acumnen Fund*

"*Citizen You* inspires readers to get involved in a way that's right for them—whether in their own community or a village on the other side of the world. Now more than ever, it's important to recognize that philanthropy takes many forms and that every person has something to contribute."

—*Pierre Omidyar, founder and chairman of eBay, and Pam Omidyar, cofounder of the Omidyar Network*

CITIZEN
YOU

CITIZEN YOU

DOING YOUR PART TO CHANGE THE WORLD

Jonathan M. Tisch
with Karl Weber

Foreword by
Mayor Cory A. Booker

Crown

New York

Published in the United States by Crown Publishers,
an imprint of the Crown Publishing Group,
a division of Random House, Inc., New York.
www.crownpublishing.com

CROWN and the Crown colophon are registered trademarks
of Random House, Inc.

Library of Congress Cataloging-in-Publication Data

Tisch, Jonathan M.
  Citizen you : doing your part to change the world / Jonathan Tisch
and Karl Weber.—1st ed.
      p. cm.
  Includes index.
  1. Social action.   2. Social change—Citizen participation.
  3. Social service.   I. Weber, Karl, 1953–   II. Title.

HN18.3.T57 2010
361.2—dc22   2009053438

ISBN 978-0-307-58848-7

Printed in the United States of America

Design by Donna Sinisgalli

1   3   5   7   9   10   8   6   4   2

First Edition

For Lizzie, Charles, Henry, and Mason . . .
Your love and support have allowed me to
pursue more than I ever dreamed possible.
Thank you for doing your part
to change my world for the better.

Contents

It is time to recapture that sense of a common purpose: I am my brother's keeper, I am my sister's keeper. I'm tired of hearing about how America is on the wrong track—I want us to come together to put it on the right track. I'm tired of hearing about red America and blue America—I want to lead a United States of America. I'm tired of talking about what we can't do, or won't do, or won't even try—I want all of us to stand up and start reaching for what is possible.

That's what history calls us to do. Because loving your country shouldn't just mean watching fireworks on the Fourth of July; loving your country must mean accepting your responsibility to do your part to change it. And if you do stand up, I promise you that your life will be richer, and our country will be stronger.

—PRESIDENT BARACK OBAMA

Freedom and responsibility,
Liberty and duty,
That's the deal.

—JOHN W. GARDNER, FOUNDER,
COMMON CAUSE AND INDEPENDENT SECTOR

Foreword

America is a great nation because generation after generation has put forth new ideas to face an increasingly complex and challenging world. Our generation can be no different. Today, we are facing unprecedented challenges, from a worldwide economic slowdown and global climate change to health care and education systems that are failing to serve the genius of our children and prepare them for our twenty-first-century economy. It is time for the next generation of Americans to embrace new ideas, approaches, and innovations to address our problems and seize the profound opportunities before us.

Citizen You is a book for these times. My friend Jonathan Tisch has long been engaged at the crossroads where business, government, philanthropy, and civic activism meet. He has been a leader of the travel and tourism industry, a socially responsible business leader, an advocate for the poor and disadvantaged, a supporter of many of New York's (and America's) most important charitable efforts, an outspoken voice for progressive politics, and a practitioner of creative public-private partnerships. Jon knows the seriousness of the problems our society faces, and he understands our need to search for new solutions. *Citizen You* is his latest contribution to that effort.

In these pages, Jon and his coauthor Karl Weber have gathered the stories of some of today's most remarkable citizen activists. They come from every walk of life—students who are using their classroom learning to shape innovative approaches to social problems; businesspeople who are finding ways to serve both profit and human needs; social entrepreneurs who are creating new kinds of organizations that empower citizens to improve their lives and their communities; and government officials who are breaking through bureaucratic rules to improve services while cutting costs and promoting individual freedom.

I'm inspired by stories like these. I know they're real because we're transforming life for the people of Newark through similar alliances among business, government, nonprofit groups, and citizen alliances. Our public-private partnership, GreenSpaces, has brought public parks within reach of thousands of our citizens for the first time in decades. We've made basic health care and prescription drugs available to hundreds of families through Newark Rx and Newark Health Plus, two more partnerships between the private and public sectors. And with the help of local law firms, venture philanthropists, and a national think tank, we've developed innovative programs that are helping ex-offenders build new lives and contribute to their communities.

In times like these, we can't afford to waste a single mind. Everyone has something to contribute to solving the daunting challenges we face. *Citizen You* is a powerful introduction to some of the many ways individuals are changing our world for the better. I hope it will be read by people all over our country, and the planet, and that many will be inspired, like me, to join the movement it describes so eloquently.

Cory A. Booker,
mayor of Newark

|| 1 ||

Social Mindstorms

*Fresh Thinking Shakes Up
the World of Civic Activism*

We're living in an extraordinary moment in history—a time when the world is calling out for a new corps of citizen activists who are prepared and willing to tackle the global challenges we face. In response, we're seeing the birth of a new model of civic engagement—a model of *active citizenship,* being shaped by thousands of individuals and organizations that are exploring new ways of addressing social problems.* It's an exciting explosion of practical creativity that is already demonstrating how seemingly intractable problems can be set on the path to solution through innovative thinking that breaks free of old constraints.

The emergence of this new activism couldn't be happening at a better time. We live in an era when millions of people are eagerly

---

*In this book, we'll be using the terms *active citizenship, civic engagement,* and *social activism* in more or less interchangeable fashion. In our usage, all these terms refer to a way of life in which participation in civil society in many forms—not simply through voting but also through activities on and off the job, in schools, and in the broader community—is considered the norm for all citizens, not just for a select few. And we define such participation, in turn, as including any activity whose primary purpose is the betterment of society as a whole, as opposed to personal profit or other forms of individual or family benefit. The descriptions, examples, and stories in this book are designed to illustrate these definitions.

searching for new sources of meaning and purpose in life. These questing individuals include young people, the estimated seventy-six million members of the Millennial Generation who are coming of age in a troubled world and are filled with the idealism of youth, yet lack the clear political and economic purposes that motivated early generations of Americans; members of the middle cohort, Generation X, who are struggling to find their role in a world where the economy is struggling, resources are scarce, and rewards seem to be restricted to a lucky few; and the vast numbers of baby boomers, now nearing retirement, who are looking back on their turbulent, promising early days in the 1960s and 1970s and won-dering what happened to their dreams of reshaping the world.

Each in its own way, these generational groups are all looking for opportunities to apply their restless energies to the pressing needs of society. For many, the new activism may hold the answer.

•   .   •

The story of Scott Harrison offers a vivid example of the power of ac-tive citizenship to transform lives—the lives of those who find new meaning in service to others, as well as the lives of the less fortunate who are benefiting from today's new spirit of civic engagement.

Next to the air we breathe, water is surely the most basic of human necessities. In the developed world, we take for granted the availability of clean, safe water for drinking, cooking, and washing. But more than 1.1 billion people in the global south—one-sixth of the world's population—lack access to clean water. The result is epidemics of disease, tens of thousands of deaths *every week* (many from conditions that may seem trivial yet are often deadly, like se-vere diarrhea), and the destruction of countless lives from the an-cillary effects of water shortages. Those effects range from warfare over water supplies to the inability of millions of children to attend school because they must spend their days gathering water for their families instead—for example, hiking up to three hours to get to the nearest well or, in some cases, a dirty riverbed where they fill a bucket with water swirling with mud and raw sewage.

Solving this global problem is obviously an enormous challenge, far too big for one person or even one organization. But three years ago, a young man named Scott Harrison decided to find out what kind of impact a single individual could have on the lives of millions of thirsty people around the world. The answer has amazed even him.

Harrison's organization, known as charity: water, has become one of the fastest-growing nonprofit groups in the world. In its short lifetime, it has attracted fifty thousand donors from two hundred countries who have contributed over $10 million, which has gone to fund more than thirteen hundred water projects in fourteen developing nations. These projects, managed by local nongovernmental organizations (NGOs) with proven track records of integrity and efficiency, like the International Rescue Committee and Living Water International, are modest and human scaled. Rather than massive dams or desalinization plants, charity: water funds wells, village clinics, and filtration systems for local ponds in countries like the Central African Republic, Bangladesh, and the Ivory Coast. The individual projects are small, but taken together, their impact is huge. So far, almost a million people have been provided with potable water through the efforts of charity: water . . . and if Scott Harrison has anything to say about it, this is just the beginning.

Yet almost as remarkable as the humanitarian impact of Harrison's work is Harrison's own story. The creation of charity: water represents not the first but the second personal transformation this thirty-three-year-old New Yorker with the shy smile and the hipster style—jeans, black sweater, scraggly beard—has experienced in his young life.

"I was raised in a very religious home," Harrison recalls, "and my mom was severely disabled due to an autoimmune disorder. She had to wear a face mask, stay in rooms where the windows were shielded with tin foil, and couldn't even take a ride in a car. Everything from air conditioning to the electromagnetic field created by a TV set might make her sick. My dad and I spent years caring for her. Because of her illness, her life was incredibly restricted—and so was mine."

When Harrison turned eighteen, he decided to change his lifestyle—not a little, but by 180 degrees. He moved from the New Jersey suburbs to New York City, enrolled in film classes at NYU, began spending his evenings checking out the downtown music scene, and wound up creating a career as a nightclub promoter and party planner. Harrison remembers:

> I was throwing events for some of the hottest magazines, hosting parties in the trendy clubs in the city, and traveling around the world for fashion week celebrations. I was selling drinks for sixteen dollars and bottles of Absolut for three hundred and fifty dollars, and watching bankers dancing on tables with pretty girls and spraying champagne around the room. It was fun, going to work at ten o'clock and coming home at five in the morning. But it was also a radically unhealthy lifestyle, not just physically but psychologically and spiritually.

For ten years, Harrison worked his way up the social food chain, rising in jet-set circles, dating a string of models, and amassing a personal Rolodex with the private phone numbers and e-mail addresses of fifteen thousand of the most beautiful and pampered young people in the country. He stayed in touch with his parents mainly through brief messages bragging about his glitzy new lifestyle: "Hey, I'm in Paris for the weekend, flying down to Rio next week . . ."

But all the while, an inner voice from his boyhood was whispering a message that he couldn't completely ignore—a message that this life of luxurious selfishness wouldn't satisfy him forever.

That simmering inner conflict bubbled to the surface during a three-week getaway in South America. One morning, hungover after a night of partying with fireworks and champagne, Harrison pulled out the book he'd brought along for the trip—an inspirational tome titled *The Pursuit of God* by pastor and self-taught theologian A. W. Tozer. Harrison started to read, and got hooked. The next thing he knew, he'd decided to start rereading the Bible he'd abandoned ten years earlier. For the first time in his life, he began thinking about issues like faith, community, and service from the perspective, not of a child, but of an adult.

Harrison became convinced that it was time to change his life again. And once again, he decided to take a 180-degree turn. Eager to shift from a life of self-indulgence to one of service, and remembering stories from his boyhood about the good works of religious missionaries in places like Africa, he began researching charitable organizations that sought to help the poor in the developing world.

Harrison lacked any skills that would be of obvious use to such a group; he wasn't a doctor, a nurse, an engineer, or a schoolteacher, and there's not much call for party planners at organizations like CARE or Oxfam. His first attempts to find a useful role were fruitless. But then he learned that Mercy Ships, a global charity that sends floating hospitals staffed by medical volunteers to serve poor people in the developing world, was looking for a photographer to record and publicize their work. Although Harrison had never done any professional camera work, he talked them into giving him the assignment. As for salary, Harrison paid *them* $500 per month from his savings to cover his own expenses.

His stint with Mercy Ships was eye-opening. In war-torn Benin, he saw a crowd of seven thousand poor, desperate people lined up outside a stadium, hoping to be among the fifteen hundred lucky people selected to receive free surgery to treat life-threatening tumors and horrendous deformities. He visited a leper colony in Liberia and accompanied doctors on their rounds in villages with no electricity, no sanitary facilities, no drinking water. All the while, he was snapping photos and sending some of them home, via e-mail, to his party-loving friends back in the States. Some were repulsed and asked to be taken off Harrison's e-mail list. But others were moved and asked, "How can we help?"

When Harrison returned home to New York, an old friend from the nightclub business told him, "Scott, these photos you've been taking are important. Our group needs to see them." The friend helped to organize an exhibition at a gallery on Eighteenth Street called the Metropolitan Pavilion. Within nine days, visitors drawn largely from Harrison's personal trove of names and addresses donated $96,000 to benefit the work of Mercy Ships.

Harrison had found his calling. He couldn't help the suffering the way a doctor or a nurse could, but he was a gifted marketer—the years he'd spent luring New York's beautiful people to visit the clubs and parties he promoted had demonstrated that. Now he would apply those same skills to a more vital mission. After several months of research to determine where the greatest need and opportunity existed, Harrison founded charity: water, and his life's work truly began.

Although Harrison claims not to be much of a manager—he recently hired a chief operating officer to manage the dozen employees and assorted unpaid interns who now work at charity: water—he has used his communications skills and his instinctive creativity to build the organization into a highly effective outreach tool. He travels constantly, visiting sites in Africa and Asia where water projects are under way so that their stories can be vividly, compellingly told on the organization's website. He has introduced innovative ways of connecting donors to their beneficiaries—for example, granting naming rights to wells and providing links to

Google Earth's satellite images that allow donors to actually see their projects being constructed. And he devised what he calls the "100 percent model," under which a separate group of donors agrees to cover all of charity: water's operating expenses, so that everyone else can be assured that every penny they give will provide direct benefits to the poor people of the world.

Obviously, the nearly one million people in the developing world who are gaining access to the life-giving water they need through the work of charity: water have seen their world transformed by Scott Harrison. Harrison's personal transformation has been just as great. When he left behind the party scene, he quit smoking (something he'd tried and failed to do twenty times previously), quit using drugs, and got his drinking under control. He's married to a young colleague from charity: water with whom he expects to work on humanitarian causes for decades to come. And in an amazing and happy confluence of events—whether you choose to call it a miracle, as Harrison does, or just a wonderful turnaround—even Harrison's disabled mom has recovered after twenty-eight years of suffering. They recently had dinner together in a restaurant for the first time in their lives. And although Scott has not returned to the traditional, conservative religion of his boyhood, he definitely sees his new life of service as a response to a spiritual calling.

Scott Harrison's journey is an extreme example. He went from a life of total self-indulgence to one of complete dedication to the needs of the least fortunate. But his actions have also engaged the lives of thousands of others whose devotion is less extreme. Through his photographs, the videos on his website, his newspaper and TV interviews, and the speeches he gives in schools and churches, Harrison has helped educate countless Americans about the problems faced by the "bottom billion" in Africa and Asia. And through the work of charity: water, he has enabled thousands to help shoulder the responsibility for alleviating that suffering, giving ordinary citizens, most of modest means, the opportunity to make the world a better place, one village well at a time.

Not everyone who chooses to become involved in the new activism will find his or her life transformed as Scott Harrison did. For many, active engagement in the needs and challenges of society will simply be a rewarding new element in a life that's already busy and productive. For others, it will bring new meaning to an existence that may have felt humdrum or uninspired. But for everyone who chooses to contribute in ways large or small, there will be the satisfaction of knowing that their gift to the community can have a multiplying effect, giving hope to others and helping to spread the enlivening spirit of shared citizenship throughout our entire society.

·   ·   ·

Today's new activism is emerging at a time when a fresh definition of citizenship is sorely needed—a time of unprecedented challenges on the national and world stage, when citizen engagement is not a choice but a necessity.

Within the last generation, the cold war ended and the fear of nuclear annihilation receded. Today new technologies are enabling cross-cultural connections and business opportunities that were never before possible, and expanding economies like those of China, India, and Brazil have lifted millions of poor people into middle-class status. But growth in the developing world has worsened global pollution, increasing the risk of disastrous climate change, and age-old problems from terrorism to racial and religious hatred to poverty and disease have continued to defy solution. Now a worldwide financial and economic crisis threatens to reverse the gains of recent decades and return millions to lives of desperate poverty.

Here in the United States, a generation of young people is on the rise that is better educated and better equipped for the future than any in our history. Having largely shed old forms of bigotry—racism, sexism, homophobia, xenophobia—they are eager to play their part in helping to solve the great challenges of our time. And in 2008, they took a momentous step in that direction by helping to elect our first "citizen activist" president—Barack Obama, a former community organizer who harnessed the power of idealism and citizen engagement to create what many have called the best-run, most innovative, and most broadly inclusive political campaign in our nation's history. But today's youth also face challenges more daunting than any since the Second World War—economic collapse, looming environmental disaster, crumbling infrastructure, dysfunctional health and educational systems, and festering international tensions.

Rarely has the world been faced with such momentous opportunities and dangers. The election of a smart, charismatic young president is a hopeful sign. But the problems we confront are too enormous to be solved by any one person or even by the massive powers of government alone. The question is: Will we the people dare to reshape the social, political, and intellectual structures that have confined us, making it all but impossible for us to make the right choices for our world's future? Or will "old thinking" doom us to repeating the same mistakes that made the twentieth century an era of both enormous technological advancement and horrific human suffering?

The new activism holds a possible hopeful answer to this fateful challenge.

•   •   •

Today, newly engaged citizens are busy on dozens of fronts experimenting with new ways to solve long-intractable problems. In particular, they are exploring ways of transforming old models of civic activism into new ones that may have the power to create more meaningful, far-reaching change. In the process, they are also transforming their own lives, becoming not just engineers, lawyers, or teachers, but citizen engineers, citizen lawyers, and citizen teachers—models of the kind of engagement to which everyone can and should aspire.

Today's new activism is transforming old ways of thinking about citizenship and social change in the following seven ways.

From Volunteerism to Active Citizenship

For millions of concerned citizens, the old model was about volunteering—"giving back" a portion of your time and resources as a way of expressing gratitude for the blessings you enjoy and, perhaps, of improving the lives of those who are less fortunate. Volunteerism is a proud American tradition, but its impact is inherently limited.

The new model is about active citizenship—taking part in the life of the community, not out of noblesse oblige but because you care about the health of the society in which you live and share a responsibility for its future with every other citizen. Active citizenship doesn't just mean giving time to the local soup kitchen on a Saturday night (although efforts like that may be helpful, even admirable); it also means examining the root causes of problems like hunger and considering the entire range of actions you can take as a citizen to help eliminate those causes. Where volunteerism tries to alleviate the symptoms, active citizenship strives to cure the disease.

From Charity to Social Entrepreneurship

In the old model, affluent individuals and companies who cared about the welfare of society were urged to donate money and other resources (time, talent, goods, services) to benefit the needy. Those who contributed received nothing in return other than a sense of personal virtue and, perhaps, a tax deduction. And when their generosity ran out, or the stock market took a dip, the donations would usually dry up, often leaving the poor worse off than ever.

In the new model, problems like poverty, hunger, homelessness, and disease are tackled by self-sustaining organizations run according to sound business principles and designed to generate revenues even as they help those in need. Powerful examples of social entrepreneurship include Bangladesh's Grameen Bank, which turns a profit even as it provides small loans to millions of rural poor, helping them earn their way out of poverty, and the Clinton Foundation's UNITAID initiative, which has brought medications at affordable prices to 750,000 AIDS sufferers while enabling pharmaceutical manufacturers to make a reasonable profit on each sale.

From Targeted Philanthropy to Systemic Change

In the heyday of traditional philanthropy (approximately 1920 to 1985), major donors like the great foundations would award financial grants to individual not-for-profit organizations, which would use the money to support programs aimed at alleviating specific effects of social dysfunction. These efforts helped reduce human suffering and fostered incremental improvements, but they usually did little to bring about large-scale, lasting change.

In the new model, activist leaders are stepping back to examine entire social structures, looking for the organizational problems that prevent them from serving human needs. The goal, however, is not heavy-handed "social engineering" like something out of the Soviet era, but rather a search for leverage points at which a realistic investment of resources can trigger broader, positive change. Consider, for example, the Harlem Children's Zone project, which targets kids in a sixty-block area of New York for a broad array of interventions, from parenting workshops and pre- and postschool programs to charter schools and job training, all aimed at reshaping the future for an entire generation of inner-city youth.

From Helping a Few to Building to Scale

In the old model, a relative handful of lucky beneficiaries were helped by charitable programs. Often the founders of these programs hoped that their successful efforts would become models for more widespread campaigns—but this rarely happened.

No longer content with piecemeal improvements, today's citizen activists are taking seriously the challenge of building successful change efforts to scale. They are involving global corporations from Walmart to Procter & Gamble to apply their systems-building expertise to the problem to finding ways to bring needed goods and services to entire countries, even continents. And a younger generation of philanthropists, led by high-tech billionaires like Bill Gates and Pierre Omidyar, are sponsoring programs designed to alleviate suffering among hundreds of millions of people using simple, practical, scalable techniques like inoculations, water safety programs, and microcredit.

From Lobbying Governments to Energizing the Private Sector

It was once assumed that only national governments (or international agencies) had the financial clout and political influence required to address major social problems. That assumption has largely fallen by the wayside.

With the collapse of most former communist regimes, the scaling-back of socialist systems in Western Europe, and the downsizing of government programs in the United States, more and more people are realizing that the private sector—including for-profit businesses, nonprofit organizations, universities, and other institutions—must carry the main burden of most future efforts to improve society. Thus, in recent years, the major turning points of social progress have involved not the launching of government programs but private efforts, from the launching of health-care programs by the Gates Foundation to the peacemaking and democracy-building efforts of the Carter Foundation. And leadership in global citizenship is being exercised not by presidents or prime ministers but by private individuals from many walks of life—inspiring figures like Al Gore, Bono, Nelson Mandela, and Warren Buffett.

From Modest Reforms to Entirely New Models

Citizen activists once contented themselves with encouraging government, business, and individuals to undertake small improvements in the way they conducted "business as usual." For example, they might urge corporations to donate funds to help the poor, or to provide products at discount prices to those in dire need.

Today, the greatest energies are being focused on creating entirely new models in both the public and private spheres, often blending social activism, business systems, and government support in novel ways. For example, the private initiative known as One Laptop per Child (OLPC), founded by experts at the MIT Media Lab and funded by high-tech companies, is building powerful, low-cost computers for sale to school systems in such developing-country markets as Brazil, Cambodia, and Pakistan. It's a way of bridging the "digital divide" that combines the best capabilities of business, academia, and government in a way never seen before.

From Paternalism to Community-Based Action

Finally, the new activists have learned the pitfalls of traditional top-down, paternalistic forms of social change. They've seen how massive aid programs like those administered by the World Bank and other global institutions often fail to meet their goals due to a lack of real understanding of conditions on the ground and the needs of local people.

Today's smartest citizen activists are partnering with individuals and groups who were once relegated to the role of passive recipients, from Native Americans to indigenous peoples of Africa to inner-city youth in the United States, drawing upon their insights, needs, and preferences when designing programs to foster social progress.

• • •

There are so many incredible opportunities for determined, creative individuals to literally change the world—sometimes in giant leaps, more often in small yet significant steps. Scott Harrison discovered his niche. But additional, equally inspiring examples are all around us.

For example, there's Will Allen, the famed "urban farmer" who has taught thousands of inner-city residents how to grow nutritious, delicious, natural foods in vacant lots. Son of a South Carolina sharecropper, Allen played pro basketball briefly in the ABA, then settled down with his wife and kids on a small plot of land in the suburbs of Milwaukee. Like many others, Allen became aware of the phenomenon of "food deserts" in America's cities—neighborhoods where there are fast-food outlets, convenience stores, and liquor stores aplenty, but no places to buy fruits, vegetables, and other healthy foods. But Allen didn't just fret about the problem or hope for a solution from city hall. He founded Growing Power, which has created farms in Milwaukee and Chicago and training sites in five other states, each creating neighborhood jobs and producing tasty, good-for-you produce that's available in local markets, schools, and restaurants. Allen's programs are improving the nutrition of some ten thousand people and providing a practical model of reform that he hopes to spread to locations around the country. "Chicago," he tells a visitor with a grin, "has seventy-seven thousand vacant lots." Imagine how many malnourished people could be fed with the produce of seventy-seven thousand block-size urban farms! Will Allen and his supporters are working to make it happen.

For a very different image of an active citizen, there's Alex Green, a twenty-year-old high school graduate from Topeka, Kansas, whose mom pushed him into signing up for the National Civilian Community Corps. NCCC is a federal program that provides young people with a modest stipend ($80 per week, plus $4.50 per day in food money) in exchange for essential services—disaster relief, nature conservation, infrastructure repair, and the like. In his two years working for the NCCC, Green has built houses in communities destroyed by Hurricane Katrina, cleaned up after floods in West Virginia, and cleared fallen timber that blocked hiking trails in a state park in Maryland. Perhaps equally important, Green has grown on the job. As a teenager, he'd experimented with drugs and drinking, and he'd had some scrapes with the law. "I saw community service as a punishment," he admits. Now he's become a team leader, supervising a crew of other service volunteers that includes college graduates with business degrees. Green has turned his life around and is busy helping others do the same, while contributing his time, talent, and energy to making America a better place to live.

Or consider Paula Lopez Crespin, a fifty-year-old Latina and former banking executive who rose from teller to vice president of marketing—then abandoned her business career to join Teach for America (TFA), the program that trains aspiring educators for jobs in some of the country's toughest and most demanding inner-city schools. (Maybe you think of TFA as being tailored specifically to new college graduates. That's the common assumption—yet currently over 80 percent of TFA applicants are either graduate students or would-be career changers.) Inspired to take this leap by her own daughter, who joined TFA after graduating from the University of Colorado, Crespin passed the program's grueling admissions process (which accepts fewer than one applicant in eight) and, in June 2009, completed her first year as a math and science teacher for third and fourth graders at Cole Arts and Science Academy in a troubled Denver neighborhood. Her typical workweek stretches to sixty hours. Adding to the challenge, Crespin's husband has recently changed careers as well, leaving the business world to pursue a master's degree in social work. The family income has shrunk a bit. But Crespin says, "It hasn't really bothered us. We are happier than we were."

As these examples and many others like them suggest, you don't have to be a millionaire or a CEO to contribute something unique to the betterment of our society. You don't have to be particularly religious, high-minded, or idealistic. You don't need the unique talents of a music superstar like Bono or the world renown of a statesman like Bill Clinton. The fact is that *everyone* has a role to play in the emerging world where active citizens are the driving force for social progress.

Students, teachers, and academic researchers can launch or support programs for social change in their local communities or in needy areas around the world, using their research methods and technological savvy to promote innovative ideas with an immediate positive impact on human problems.

Business managers, executives, and entrepreneurs can apply the resources and talents of their companies to community needs, as the workers and managers of Walmart did when they led the disaster recovery effort in the Gulf States after Hurricane Katrina, or as the people of Procter & Gamble are now doing with its Pur water treatment product.

Leaders, workers, and volunteers at nonprofit organizations, NGOs, charities, and foundations can use their experience in tackling social problems to help them develop creative new partnerships with government, business, and citizens' groups that can do far more in combination to solve humanity's greatest dilemmas than any single sector could do alone.

And government employees, legislators, and elected officials can put their considerable clout behind the active citizenship movement, providing seed money and other forms of support for promising new programs as well as clearing regulatory and legal hurdles that might otherwise stymie efforts at change.

We hope that everyone who reads this book will be inspired to ask, "What can I do to help make our world a better place?"—and then to devote at least a portion of his or her life to discovering the answer.

Today, the opportunities for individuals to make a real difference are more numerous and varied than ever. When a terrible earthquake devastated Haiti in January 2010, the island country's neighbors responded with remarkable speed and creativity. President Obama asked Americans to take advantage of new technology by texting their donations to the relief effort. Within a week, users of a single phone network (Verizon) had contributed three million dollars, ten dollars at a time, and the Red Cross reported receiving more than ten million dollars through texting. Dozens of nonprofit organizations rushed to the scene with medical supplies, food, water, tents, blankets, and rescue equipment. Corporations jumped into the fray: employees at Cargill packaged 20,000 meals for earthquake victims; UPS sent members of its logistics emergency team to set up a supply distribution center in the Dominican Republic; Florida-based Seacor dedicated a construction team to rebuilding Haiti's largest port to facilitate food and medical shipments; and tech companies from Google and Intel to Apple provided equipment, set up emergency communications networks, and lent experts to help repair damaged infrastructure. And countless ordinary Americans—doctors and nurses, construction workers and firefighters, school teachers and psychologists, engineers and clergy—put their personal lives on hold to rush to the scene and offer help.

Are you ready to begin exploring some of the amazing new ways that your fellow citizens are responding to the challenge of civic engagement? Our journey begins on the next page.

‖ 2 ‖

A New Breed of Leader

*A Generation of Change
Agents Ready to Hit
the Ground Running*

Of all the countries in Central America, Guatemala has had perhaps the most troubled history. Just a decade ago, it emerged from a devastating civil war among left-wing insurgent groups, right-wing paramilitary organizations, and an authoritarian government, which lasted thirty-six years and produced more than two hundred thousand deaths, horrendous human rights abuses, and a number of acts of genocide directed by the government against the country's indigenous peoples.

Sadly, the United States has played an inglorious role in this tragic story. For decades in the early twentieth century, the U.S.-based multinational United Fruit Company dominated Guatemala economically, controlling the railroads, electrical monopolies, and telegraph system, and deliberately stifling any development that did not benefit the company directly. In 1954, a military coup supported by the CIA overthrew the democratically elected president Jacobo Árbenz, paving the way for the decades of civil war that began in 1960, in which Guatemala became a victim of the cold war rivalry between the United States and Communist rebels supported by the Soviet Union and Cuba.

Most Americans know very little about this history, although it sheds much light on the uneasy relations that have long existed between the United States and our neighbors to the south. Those who do know about it have mostly absorbed the knowledge from history books or a college course. But it's quite another thing to learn about the civil war of 1960–1996 firsthand, by seeing its devastating impact on men, women, and children living in the villages of rural Guatemala.

That's the experience that Tufts University student Krista Grace Morris had when she spent a summer living on a cooperative coffee farm run by ex-guerrilla fighters who are trying desperately to save the local people from becoming dependent on the only lucrative industry currently active in rural Guatemala—the trade in illicit drugs. And the shocking insights she developed during that sojourn to the dark side of human history have reshaped her academic and career plans in a way you might find surprising. Rather than study international relations with a special emphasis on Latin America, as she had originally intended, Morris came home from Guatemala determined to attend law school in the hopes of improving the legal controls on pseudoephedrine, a drug that is ravaging communities across America.

As a college junior, Morris's personal and professional journey is obviously still in its formative stages. But it has already taken some unpredictable twists, thanks to the kind of mind-opening collision between academic learning and real-world experience that students at Tufts University's Tisch College of Citizenship and Public Service are uniquely positioned to experience. As a result, students like Morris are graduating with both a remarkable firsthand understanding of social problems and an impressive determination to devote their considerable knowledge and talent to bettering the human condition. In effect, they leave the university campus as newly minted active citizens, ready not only to build careers but also to change the world—for the better.

The latest stage in Morris's personal evolution began, like many journeys at Tufts University, with an amazing course taught by a dynamic teacher. In this case, the course was titled The Anthropology of War and Peacemaking, and the teacher was Jennifer Burtner, a youthful Ph.D. from the University of Texas at Austin. Burtner herself has spent a lot of time in Guatemala and other Latin American countries, studying the impact of poverty, war, political oppression, and violence on local peoples. In Burtner's class, Morris learned all about the tragic history of Guatemala and made the decision to pursue a research project in the country. But when she arrived "in country," she discovered that no amount of classroom study could adequately prepare her for the realities on the ground:

> There I was, living on a coffee cooperative with a community led by ex-guerrillas from the civil war, people who are really trying to support themselves and build their society legitimately. But the government is providing them with none of the services or support they need, and their coffee plantations were practically destroyed by Hurricane Stan in 2005. Meanwhile there are violent street gangs everywhere, most of them making huge profits off trafficking in cocaine that travels up from Columbia through Guatemala on its way to Mexico and ultimately the United States.
>
> I couldn't help thinking, "If these coffee growers would just switch to growing cocaine or marijuana, their economic problems would be solved." All the incentives are set up the wrong way, as I described in the research paper I wrote after my trip.
>
> But it took me a while to figure all of this out. At first, I was sitting there interviewing people in the village and asking questions that were very history-book-oriented: "What

can you tell me about the United Fruit Company?" Only later did I realize that these were not the right kinds of questions to ask men who'd been sleeping in mountain hideouts for thirty years with AK-47 rifles by their sides.

In the end, I discovered that the legacy of the civil war was all about violence. In the 1980s, the government adopted a scorched-earth policy in their war against the insurgents. They would go into a village where the indigenous farmers lived, and put up a list of ten names. Then they'd announce, "We think these ten people are sympathetic to the guerrilla insurgents. You have fifteen hours to show us their corpses. Otherwise we will kill everyone in your village." It was a way of pitting people against one another that I learned goes all the way back to the way the Spanish enforced slavery in the New World, using indigenous people as tools to extend colonial power.

After four decades of this kind of fighting and killing, it's not surprising that the generation that has grown up after the 1996 peace accords is so violent and so caught up in gang warfare and drug dealing. It's an entire society suffering from post-traumatic stress disorder. Soldiers and guerrillas returned from the fighting and were unable to reintegrate themselves peacefully into society. They beat their kids, and those kids would leave home and go out in the streets looking for a substitute family. And that's how the violent gangs that rule the society today were born.

Meanwhile, the police who are supposed to keep the peace are the same police who were committing human rights violations during the war, armed with the same guns. And making it all worse is the fact that no one in the country wants to talk about it. Kids aren't learning about the civil war in school. University students aren't being taught about it. There's no discussion about what happened, what it means, or how to prevent it from happening again in the future.

Krista Morris's story makes it clear that, for her, "research" means a lot more than referencing articles on Google or even studying documents in an archive somewhere. It's about immersing herself in a true-life history lesson being acted out in real time several thousand miles from the peaceful suburban campus of Tufts.

It's easy to imagine a student reacting to an experience like this one in various ways—perhaps by becoming disillusioned about human nature, angry at governments here and abroad that fail to prevent such evils, or deeply relieved at having the opportunity to escape from such traumas by retreating into a comfortable middle-class life in the security of North America.

But Morris is choosing none of these paths. Instead, she is planning, first, to spend a year in Madrid digging still more deeply into the historic roots of Latin America's centuries-old turmoil. ("I want to see the Spanish perspective on everything that has happened. Do they feel they were the catalyst for the way the history has unfolded? Can we blame the Spanish for Guatemala, or the French for Algeria? Where do things like this really start?") Then she plans to go to law school, though not with the purpose of practicing international law as she once planned. Instead, Morris is turning her sights back on her home country and the needs and attitudes of Americans like herself:

> It's funny. Everyone at Tufts talks about being active in our communities, and we pride ourselves on being aware, educated, and empowered. And a lot of us have studied things like the Guatemala civil war and the problems of Latin America, which is all important and good. But sometimes

we forget that things like this are happening right here in our country too.

So I want to practice law here in the United States, focusing on U.S. drug policy and in particular on the problem of methamphetamine. Meth, I've learned, fundamentally alters the brain in a way that's astounding, rewiring the circuits to crave the drug. This makes recovery from meth addiction very difficult. Guatemala led me to recognize the problem of narco-trafficking, and this in turn led me to recognize that the problem of meth addiction originates in the United States. So after I become a lawyer, I hope to work on the problem of how we control the substance pseudoephedrine, which is used to manufacture meth. It's a transnational problem, but one with roots here in America.

To me, this feels like a better way to help the world than to go back to the coffee cooperative in Guatemala and encourage them to keep growing coffee.

Obviously, this is a very personal choice for Krista Morris—not *the* right thing to do, but the right thing *for her*. And that seems to be one of the important life lessons she is learning at Tufts: that there's a sweet spot in life for practically everyone, a spot where intellectual challenge, social conscience, career goals, and personal passion intersect. For each individual, that sweet spot is different. But it exists, somewhere, for everyone—and there's no life quest more important than discovering it.

•   •   •

The ideal of active citizenship is one with a long lineage, both in Western culture and around the world. For thousands of years, it was at the heart of mainstream concepts of education, going back to Aristotle's notion that "the excellent citizen" was the ultimate product of learning. But in the last two hundred years, it has been eclipsed at most centers of higher learning by competing values, such as scientific objectivity, "pure" academic research, and professionalism conceived of as disinterested technical skill. Today, a handful of colleges and universities are working to revive the old concept of raising citizens rather than merely training workers. Among the leaders of this movement is my alma mater, Tufts University, and its Tisch College of Citizenship and Public Service.

Tufts has had a long tradition of encouraging active citizenship on the part of its students, faculty, and alumni. One small personal example: Back in the spring of 1976, when I was a senior at Tufts, the university helped arrange an internship for me at WBZ-TV in Boston, where I got the chance to learn the techniques of television production and apply those skills to creating public affairs news stories. Even then, Tufts was known as an institution that encouraged its students to be deeply engaged in the life of the community. It's a value that has remained with me and influenced my life ever since.

The Tufts board of trustees decided in 2000 to expand their commitment to this value by creating what was then known as the University College of Citizenship and Public Service. Generous grants from two Tufts alumni—Pierre Omidyar (class of 1988), the founder of eBay, and his wife, Pam (class of 1989)—made the new college possible. The Omidyars regarded their gifts as "seed money," hoping that, if the concept was successful, others would come along to advance the cause. The then president of Tufts, John DiBiaggio, often described the University College as central to the future of the institution, a conviction that I and many other members of the board of trustees came to share. In 2006, after I made a gift of my own earmarked for the University College, Tufts did me the honor of renaming the college.

It's worth noting that my friend Pierre Omidyar remains the largest single donor in the history of Tufts University. His gifts include a $100 million donation to start the Omidyar-Tufts Microfinance Fund, which is invested solely in providing small, low-cost loans to entrepreneurs in the developing world. This unique enterprise is a model of creative philanthropy, since it benefits society in at least two ways—first by offering vital self-help money to people who are working hard to lift themselves out of poverty, and then by channeling the profits from the lending operations to help support the educational mission of Tufts. Following in Pierre's footsteps as a supporter of Tisch College is itself an honor for me.

And under the guidance and leadership of visionary educators like Larry Bacow and college dean Rob Hollister, Tisch College is striving to offer "the gold standard in civic education." Its program has four unusual features:

• *Replacement of the traditional "college center" model with integration across the university, and in every school, discipline, department, and corner of the curriculum.* The result? Active citizenship now infuses every facet of Tufts's work. Public service and community engagement become not a task, but a *way.* Before they graduate, 80 percent of Tufts students take at least one course with an active citizenship component.

• *Connecting active citizenship with academic rigor and learning outcomes.* Most colleges promote the idea that students can learn from their service experiences—but very few insist on documenting that learning and using the results to improve future programs. Even fewer support faculty research that deepens our understanding of the nature and importance of civic engagement. Tisch College does both.

• *Focusing not on symptoms, but on root causes.* Students are asked to approach their service work not only with their hearts but with their minds; they are given the analytical tools to assess the root causes of societal problems, to devise practical solutions, and to drive deep positive change. Faculty research shares the same focus.

• *Making active citizenship open to everyone.* The school's goal is to prepare active citizens for leadership in a diverse range of communities. That means it needs to reach students who reflect those communities, extending beyond the affluent neighborhoods and schools that normally feed elite universities like Tufts. It's a profound challenge in times of economic uncertainty, but one the university is determined to meet.

Some of today's youngest change makers, like Krista Morris, are students at Tisch College who have developed remarkable community-building projects as part of their training in the arts of active citizenship. And a new generation of academics—some of them faculty fellows at the Tisch College—are applying methods from the social and physical sciences to real-world social issues, from the problems faced by Pakistani immigrants as they try to assimilate into American culture to the challenges of making veterinary medicine more environmentally sustainable. Teachers like these are demonstrating to graduate and undergraduate students that academic research can be deeply relevant to the needs of society, and that the citizen-scholar, too, has a vital role to play outside the "ivory tower" in the age of the new activism.

Under Rob Hollister and his colleague, Nancy Wilson, Tisch College makes its influence felt all over the Tufts campus by working with every school and department to ensure that as many courses as possible include an active citizenship component. Today, more than a hundred undergraduate courses have been enriched with a citizenship element. The college also provides seed grants and other forms of funding to faculty members from every department who want to pursue research interests that link with the concept of active citizenship. And through the Citizenship &

Public Service Scholar program, students develop local community projects with advisers and site supervisors, and meet regularly for skills workshops, retreats, and debates over the problems and challenges they face.

The infusion strategy is an unusual way to structure a college within a university. But it's a very deliberate one, designed with several objectives in mind.

One is to embody the very notion of "engagement." If the ideal of active citizenship means anything, it means that people in *every* walk of life need to consider the social impact of their daily decisions and actions—that civic life is *not* just a once-a-year activity on election day, or even a once-a-week action like volunteering at the local soup kitchen. Making Tisch College a spiritual partner with every other school and department at Tufts rather than a separate "citizenship ghetto" is a natural extension of this idea.

As Tufts president Larry Bacow puts it, "Citizenship is part of the DNA here." Tisch College is the primary carrier of that piece of the genetic code.

Another goal is to avoid any sense of competition for resources or attention with other units of the university. It would be deadly if people in, say, the chemistry department or the theater department developed the idea that "those citizenship people" were draining money, space, faculty slots, or any other valuable commodity away from their educational mission. The whole point is that active citizenship *complements* and *enhances* all the other work done on campus rather than detracting from it.

And still another goal is to foster rich, rewarding interactions among practitioners of many different disciplines at Tufts, something that is surprisingly rare in the silo-ridden world of contemporary academia. Many Tufts faculty report that having the opportunity to work with colleagues from different departments on Tisch-sponsored initiatives is a uniquely rewarding experience for them—as when professors and students from the engineering, biology, and nutrition faculties collaborated to design and build an energy-conserving green roof atop the library building.

Tufts has long been a leader in civic engagement among universities. In 1990, Jean Mayer, then president of Tufts, convened a conference of twenty-two university leaders in Talloires, France, to address the burgeoning issue of environmental sustainability. The result was the founding of University Leaders for a Sustainable Future and the issuing of the Talloires Declaration, setting forth principles of environmental stewardship by which all the member institutions agreed to abide. Today, more than three hundred college and university presidents in forty-nine countries have signed the declaration. And Tufts continues to lead in the environmental field by example: In a recent study of America's fifteen greenest colleges and universities, Tufts ranked ninth.

The Talloires concept has also produced other offspring. For example, Tufts is now a leader of the Talloires Network, a consortium of twenty-eight universities from twenty-three countries that meets periodically to share ideas on civic engagement. The universities in the network also collaborate on specific projects, such as a global literacy initiative.

Tufts is just one of the many colleges and universities around the country and the world that take the challenge of civic engagement seriously. Citizen students like Krista Morris are the result.

•   •   •

Maybe it's not too surprising that a course titled The Anthropology of War and Peacemaking could help shape the social conscience of a student like Krista Morris. As we've seen, the class led Krista to travel to Guatemala, where her experiences challenged her understanding of the world and led her toward a potential new career path.

But what about a course titled The American Musical? How likely is it that this class, taught by Drama and Dance Department chair Barbara Grossman—author of a biography of Fanny Brice, Broadway's original "funny girl"—would lead to a similar life revelation for another socially engaged student?

Not too likely, perhaps—but that's exactly what happened to Tufts University senior Stephanie Coplan.

A philosophy major, Coplan is typical of many Tufts students in that she spent her college years engaged in several forms of civic engagement and volunteerism. She worked twelve hours a week as a volunteer at a local preschool on behalf of a nonprofit called Jumpstart, helping kids develop their social skills and basic literacy. As a resident assistant in South Hall, she created the ResLife Music Series, which brought local performers from the surprisingly vibrant Somerville music scene into the dorm each week. She even became a one-woman lobbying team to convince her friends to switch to Fair Trade coffee after taking a class titled Politics of Coffee offered by Daniel Hoagland, a community health advocate at Tufts.

But Coplan's most unusual and creative act of civic engagement was devising a way to kindle a love of musical theater, along with an appreciation for its broader cultural and social significance, among a group of disadvantaged middle-schools kids from West Somerville, the working class neighborhood bordering the Tufts campus.

The idea was triggered when Coplan took Barbara Grossman's class on the American musical. You might assume that a course focusing on an art form whose heyday was in the 1930s, 1940s, and 1950s would struggle to attract students on a campus in the 2000s, among members of a generation raised on hip-hop. But no—Grossman's reputation is such that overflow crowds of seventy-five to a hundred students regularly attend her classes. (One student felt compelled to warn those who might expect her course to be easy, writing online, "Prof. Grossman is serious about her art—literally. It's no slacker class, but the material is so fun you won't mind.")'

Grossman's class is much more than just a nostalgic romp through the classic tunes of the American songbook. It's also an analysis of musical theater as a reflection of larger social forces. "When we listened to *South Pacific* and *The King and I*," Coplan explains, "we debated how the shows reflected the lure of exoticism in the age of the American Dream, and how Broadway gave middle-class people an imaginary vision of what life might be like halfway around the world—and what that meant for the way the United States related to other countries."

Coplan is a lifelong musician, a pianist; as a high school senior, her college choices came down to one of the Ivy League universities, Julliard, and Tufts. She found Grossman's perspective on musical theater eye-opening and fascinating. So when she realized that West Somerville Neighborhood School, a small kindergarten-to-eighth-grade school "literally around the corner" from Tufts, had only a scanty music program and *no* theater program at all, she decided to do something about it.

Coplan's plan was one of nineteen active citizenship projects developed by undergraduate and graduate students at Tufts to receive special funding during the 2008–2009 academic year. (Others ranged from BookMatch, a competitive after-school reading program created by students Emily Scott and Patricia Letayf for fourth- and fifth-grade pupils in the Medford public schools, to Portuguese 101 for Dental Health Providers, an initiative devised by students Todd Walker and Spencer Wilson that offered weekly language classes to help Tufts Dental School students do a better job of serving the large Portuguese-speaking community in the area.)

Coplan's project was called Broadway2Broadway, its name inspired by the fact that the Somerville main drag bears the same name as New York's Great White Way. She recruited fellow students at Tufts to help develop her program, luring volunteers with an ad on the TuftsLife student website headed, "Do People Call You Artsy?" Coplan's artsy recruits accompanied her on her visits to the West Somerville school to present programs on any theater-related topic they had a passion for—dancing, singing, songwriting, acting, filmmaking, improvisation. "It was cool because it was interdisciplinary," Coplan observes—but as far as the kids from Somerville were concerned, just having something this different and entertaining to do after school was amazing, "interdisciplinary" or not.

Actually, gathering an audience for Broadway2Broadway wasn't easy at first, as Coplan recalls:

> I went to the lunch period for the sixth, seventh, and eighth graders, and I went from table to table, asking, "Hey, do you like dancing? What about singing?" I avoided the words "musical theater," because I knew it would turn people off. These are kids who've never done a school play. They never heard of *Guys and Dolls*. They have no idea who Rodgers and Hammerstein are. If they're watching TV and there's a reference to anything theater-related, they can't pick up on it. So I just talked about singing and dancing, and that really attracted people.

In the end, Coplan signed up ten kids for Broadway 2Broadway—not bad when you consider that the three target grades at the West Somerville school only have a total of sixty students. And the group was half boys, half girls, another testimony to Coplan's considerable salesmanship.

Coplan described one of her favorite Broadway2Broadway programs:

> Two Tufts students, Caroline Berliner and Michelle Wilson, came to Somerville with me one day. They're actors,

dancers, and singers, and they chose to do a lesson on *My Fair Lady*. So we started the afternoon by showing the opening scene of the movie, where Rex Harrison as Henry Higgins is bragging about how he can tell where anyone in London is from based on their accent. You remember the song he sings about it—"Why Can't the English Teach Their Children How to Speak?"

And then we paused the DVD and explained to the kids about the socioeconomic breakdown of London. We showed them a map of the city and pointed out where the better areas were and also the slums where someone like Eliza Doolittle would live. So it was much more than just a fun movie scene. It was a lesson about class, economics, and social barriers—something really relevant to their lives.

We let the movie continue. After a while, we got to the point where Professor Higgins is working on vocal exercises with Eliza, the scene where they sing "The Rain in Spain." And then we paused the movie again and had the kids stand in a circle and chant a bunch of diction exercises like the ones theater actors do—things like repeating, "Red leather, yellow leather" or "Unique New York" one hundred times, really fast. And the point of that was to help them discover that, when you're speaking on a stage, it's not like talking face-to-face with your friends—it's a special form of communication that requires technical skills.

After breaking for English teatime, we did a choreographed dance lesson set to the tune, "I Could Have Danced All Night." The kids loved it!

As you can probably tell from her account, Stephie Coplan had a wonderful time that afternoon, too. But the big payoff for her came a week later, when the next Broadway2Broadway class was held, and Carlos's mom came to pick him up afterward.

Carlos was the smallest, shyest, quietest kid in the group—an adorable twelve-year-old with wild, curly hair who was so tiny he could have been eight. When Coplan signed up participants for the program, she'd had each of the kids name a particular theatrical interest—singing, acting, whatever—but Carlos had declined to name one, and he rarely spoke during class. So she'd been wondering all semester, *Why is he here?*

But now, a week after *My Fair Lady,* Carlos's mom sought Coplan out.

"Are you the counselor who runs the Broadway program?" she asked.

"Yes," Coplan replied.

"Well, you have done something to my little Carlos. Because after last week, he came home and he just wouldn't stop singing that song—'I Could Have Danced All Night'—over and over again! You know, I never heard him sing before. And he has a beautiful voice! I actually cried to hear him sing."

Coplan was amazed—to learn that shy little Carlos had this in him. But what shocked her even more was when Carlos's mom went on to say, "Now he's decided what he wants to be when he grows up—an opera singer!" In subsequent weeks, Coplan learned that Carlos's newfound talent had impressed his friends; she noticed his self-confidence increasing and his shyness vanishing.

Will Carlos really grow up to be an opera singer? Who knows? The odds are long, after all. But what matters most is that, for the first time, he has a goal that connects his life as a twelve-year-old in Somerville with the life he may someday live as an adult in the big world. He is beginning to think, for the first time, about the classes he needs to take, the skills he needs to develop, the kind of higher education he needs to pursue to make a dream come true.

That way of thinking will serve Carlos well no matter what his ultimate career may be.

Maybe Carlos will be a professional singer; more likely, he may have a career in some other field and be someone who simply loves and enjoys music. Either way, he may well remember Stephie Coplan and her Broadway2Broadway program as the spark that ignited a flame that would burn for decades to come.

As for Coplan herself, she is now working as a litigation case assistant at the prominent law firm of Goodwin Procter as well as donating her time and talent to the New England Innocence Project, a nonprofit initiative that works to exonerate wrongfully convicted criminals through the use of DNA evidence. Like Krista Morris, she has made a significant discovery: Getting involved in a social cause that truly engages your passion is likely to change *you* as much as—or more than—it changes the world. It seems safe to predict that whatever else America's rising generation of active citizens accomplishes, they will enjoy lifetimes of continual self-discovery and self-creation. It's not a bad future to look forward to.

•   •   •

The idea of building a university's identity around the concept of active citizenship is a timeless one, with roots that go back to the civic ideals of ancient Greece. But it's also a particularly timely one in these early years of the twenty-first century. Today's college youth are members of a generation—often called the Millennials—for whom the notion of civic engagement is especially meaningful and attractive.

A lot has already been written and published about the Millennials. Born (according to one widely used definition) between 1978 and 2000, the Millennial generation currently includes around ninety-five million young people. Over the next few years, as the

U.S. population in this age cohort grows through immigration, it is expected to become the largest generation in American history, even bigger than the previous record holders, the baby boomers.

According to a number of studies, these young Millennials are unusually politically and socially engaged. In recent polls, college freshmen and other groups of young people report far higher rates of interest, conversation, and activity around political and social issues than among previous generations. Voter turnout among the young also appears to have risen steadily since 2000, and by some measures it appears that the strongly pro-Democratic vote among Millennials in 2008 played a major role in swinging the presidential election to Barack Obama. Many studies also show a steady increase in rates of volunteerism among young people over the past three decades, with new highs among the Millennials. As Lee Coffin, Tufts's dean of undergraduate admissions, puts it, "The kids I meet who will be tomorrow's entering freshmen are not jaded. They have a wonderful idealism about them. They write essays saying, 'I'm going to go to college and learn how to save the world'—and they say it like they really mean it!"

No one has a crystal ball, so it's impossible to know how the civic values of today's youth will play out in the decades to come. But I'm convinced the potential is there for the Millennials to make some unique contributions to the future of our nation and the world—provided it's nurtured by a society that offers its young people abundant opportunities to be civically engaged.

Few experts know as much about young Americans and their emerging social consciousness as Peter Levine. He's the director of CIRCLE, a nonpartisan research center, based at Tufts, that studies young civic engagement and civic education. Levine has examined the role that active participation in civil society plays in the lives of young people. Among other things, he has found that civic engagement is not so much a reflection of students' personalities as it is a vehicle for shaping, deepening, and enriching them. It's a counterintuitive truth revealed, as Levine explains, by long-term studies of civically engaged youth:

> Although values do not cause people to participate, participation changes people's values and habits. When we compare participants who appeared similar *before* a civic opportunity, we often find that they behave quite differently afterward. A similar gap emerged between comparable people who did and did not participate in the Freedom Summer [civil rights] campaigns [in the Deep South] of 1964. Such profoundly moving and terrifying work might be expected to leave a lasting mark. But the same is true to a lesser extent of young people who participate in student government or school newspapers. Even forty years later, they remain more civically engaged.

That's why the efforts of Tufts and other colleges and universities that are promoting active citizenship are so important. As a society, we need to do all we can to nurture and encourage the civic commitment of our young people. In a real sense, our future may depend upon it.

•   •   •

Americans aren't the only ones to be caught up in the Millennial spirit. Young people around the world share much of the same visionary passion for civic engagement as their counterparts in the United States—and many have inspiring stories to tell.

Malek Al-Chalabi came to Tufts from Dubai. Yes, it's a long way to travel for college—Al-Chalabi had no special ties to the United States and had never visited the country before except on vacation. But it so happens that one of Tufts's staffers in the international admissions department was a graduate of the same high school as Al-Chalabi. (Talk about a small world.) And when we spent a day talking with a group of eight Tisch College students—including Malek Al-Chalabi as well as Krista Morris, Stephie Coplan, and others—about their experiences at Tufts, one member of the group was Stephanie Brown, a classmate of Malek's who'd met him a year before they'd started at Tufts . . . in St. Petersburg, Russia, of all places. Al-Chalabi and Brown were both attending a model United Nations conference there, and tied for first place in one of the scheduled parliamentary competitions—only to run into each other the following year on the tray-return line in one of the dining halls at Tufts, some 4,105 miles to the west. (As we said, it's a small world.)

As a civil engineering student, Al-Chalabi spent his years at Tufts not just mastering the scientific and technical aspects of his field but also exploring its social, economic, and political dimensions. Specifically, Al-Chalabi has been engrossed in studying the environmental aspects of civil engineering, a topic that should loom large in the careers of thousands of professionals in the decade ahead, as issues like global warming, shortages of energy and clean water, population growth, and economic stagnation make even straightforward engineering projects increasingly challenging.

Like many Tufts students, Al-Chalabi discovered several ways of exploring the social issues that fascinate him. He took courses on epidemiology and public health—yes, even health care has its engineering aspects—as well as courses like Water and Diplomacy (which explores the connections between engineering, sustainable land use, and public policy), Innovative Non Profits (which analyzes the business practices needed to create an effective nonprofit organization), and Education for Active Citizenship (which studies methods of transforming civic ideas into reality).

With the sponsorship of Tufts's International Center, he created the Tufts International Ambassador Program, which brought undergraduate students from countries around the world into local elementary schools to offer presentations about their countries of origin, discussing everything from climate and local food to political and cultural topics. And with a grant from the Tisch College Capstone Fund, he developed a documentary film titled *Path to Platinum* that examined how and why various organizations on three continents (in the United States, Australia, and the United Arab Emirates) made the decision to invest in green building projects. (The title refers to the platinum rating granted by the U.S. Green Building Council, the highest ranking for sustainability under the widely recognized LEED system.)

But the most important—and fascinating—civic activity that Al-Chalabi participated in was the Green Infrastructure Project, created with the help of Jen Lawrence, his community supervisor at Groundwork Somerville. This is a local organization that promotes sustainability through activities ranging from neighborhood cleanup days and farmers' markets to initiatives to expand bike/pedestrian paths and to improve the nutritional quality of school lunches.

The Green Infrastructure Project was an ambitious effort to show how engineering tools and knowledge can interact with public policy to promote specific, concrete improvements in the lives of ordinary citizens. It's the kind of real-world connection that some professionals are apt to ignore, but on which Al-Chalabi tries to focus:

> When engineers and policymakers try to work together, the communication often doesn't work. The engineer may be able to talk all day about the numbers on a given project—how you calculate them, the formulas underneath them—but he usually isn't prioritizing what they mean for policymakers in the long term. Once the numbers have been printed out, the engineer tends to say,

"Okay, my work is done." But in reality, his work is just beginning. The important stuff is what happens at the interface between engineering and policy, where people can
say, "Here are the numbers, and here's the policy, and
here's the human impact of the plan. Now what can we do
to make this work better for everybody?" That interface is
where I want to be.

The lack of clear communication across the human-technology
interface, Al-Chalabi has found, leads to concrete, specific problems. "If you go to a town's Department of Public Works," he observes, "and raise an issue like sustainability, the engineers there
may refuse to touch it. They're likely to say, 'Well, we just want to
fix the sewers.' Now, fixing the sewers is important. But *how* you fix
them can have a huge impact on the long-term sustainability of
the city, and to make the right decisions you need to have everybody involved, including community leaders, health experts, and
many others, sitting around the same table and speaking the same
language."

In an effort to help establish such a common language, Al-
Chalabi's Green Infrastructure Project made use of a modern
technological tool known as a geographic information system (GIS).
GIS is a complex, powerful technology that combines mapping
software enabled through remote sensing devices with information
derived from such older disciplines as land surveying, aerial pho-
tography, mathematics, and geography. In the hands of a skilled
practitioner, GIS can produce a sophisticated, interactive image of
a neighborhood, city, or region that reveals previously unrecog-
nized information about the environment and its social and economic impact.

Al-Chalabi used GIS to develop a detailed analysis of the
physical realities of Somerville—its infrastructure, resources, and

development patterns—together with their social and human implications:

> The software lets you show in a vivid, visual way the inequalities in a community, in areas from health and economics to housing. Our picture of Somerville showed all kinds of things that most people had never realized before. For example, you could see at a glance that virtually every park in Somerville is located in one of the more affluent areas of the town. This is something you might not notice just driving around, but when you take a bird's-eye view of the community, it's obvious. So a poor kid, in addition to the other disadvantages he or she suffers, probably doesn't have a playground near home to play in after school.
>
> For another example, we mapped all the major highways that cross Somerville, and we overlaid on each one a buffer zone of three hundred meters, because that's approximately the area that will be affected by the air pollution associated with a highway. When you pull back and look at the map of the community this creates, you discover that every single school in Somerville is subjected to air pollution because of the high population density, the grid of highways, and the locations of the schools. So all those kids are breathing polluted air when they are playing outside at recess or waiting to start their school day.

By providing a living, multidimensional map of a town or region, GIS can be an invaluable tool for city planners, local officials, and community groups. Combining his engineering know-how with his feel for issues such as sustainability, Al-Chalabi was able to demonstrate the value of GIS and put this tool for the first time in the hands of those best equipped to use it.

In May 2008, Al-Chalabi's GIS portrait of Somerville made its debut. The venue was a specially outfitted room in Tufts's Anderson Hall, home of the university's engineering school, where a so-called visualization wall is filled with a giant flat-screen projection-style TV, ideally suited for group demonstrations like this one. A group of Al-Chalabi's engineering classmates and professors were in attendance. But more important, Mayor Joe Curtatone and a collection of the most active Somerville residents—community organizers, government officials, and academics—were also present.

We asked Al-Chalabi how he managed to attract all the local movers and shakers to what some might have considered a mere "student project." The answer: It was all about the process. To develop the information database underlying his analysis of Somerville, Al-Chalabi had to spend time with each of the relevant community groups—organizers and administrators concerned with everything from health care and transportation to retailing and traffic safety. As he worked with each group to incorporate their data into his GIS presentation, he explained the project and got their buy-in to its potential importance. So when showtime rolled around, all the relevant people already had some degree of ownership in Al-Chalabi's project.

Al-Chalabi walked his audience through a detailed presentation about the geography and infrastructure of Somerville. For most, it was an eye-opening experience—the first time they'd understood the complex interactions among the various systems that serve their community, from water supply and the electrical grid to bus routes and sewer systems. Problems they'd never before recognized became obvious; assumptions they'd made about local needs were turned on their head.

The community leaders left the May 2008 presentation filled with ideas about how plans for future economic and physical development could be improved based on their new, deeper understanding of the town. A series of specific recommendations drafted by Al-Chalabi based on input from local activists was prepared for follow-up discussions beginning in September.

And then the recession hit. Local tax revenues and funding from state and federal agencies plummeted. Suddenly the priority of community nonprofits as well as local government agencies shifted from planning for the future to simple survival in the present. The big-picture analysis Al-Chalabi had presented took a backseat to hundreds of tiny, immediate decisions regarding employee layoffs, budget cuts, and emergency relief measures. A few initiatives triggered by Al-Chalabi's effort, such as a river cleanup day, will move forward, but for now most of them must be put on hold until the economic climate changes.

As you can imagine, Al-Chalabi is disappointed. But ups and downs are inevitable features of the life of an active citizen. It's too soon to say how his Green Infrastructure Project will ultimately impact the life of Somerville. As Al-Chalabi has already learned, the process of social change is more often measured in years than in days, weeks, or months.

Meanwhile, Al-Chalabi's personal quest for a career at the interface between engineering and public policy will continue. Today he is studying at Imperial College in London on his way to a master of science degree in environmental technology, with a focus on energy policy. "It's a program," he says, "that is built around linking science with policy." And then? The possibilities are limited only by the variety of real-world challenges posed by the complex interactions among technology, government, economics, and human needs—and for the foreseeable future, there's likely to be no shortage of those.

●　　●　　●

On the afternoon of April 21, 2009, Dean Robert Hollister of Tisch College convened a special gathering. It was the induction

ceremony for the 2009 members of the Honos Civicus Society—
the ninety-seven inaugural members of this new Tufts University
organization designed to honor graduating seniors who exemplify
the ideal of active citizenship.

The Honos Civicus honorees were a varied lot. The venues for
their civic activities ranged from Big Brothers/Big Sisters of America to the Somerville Arts Council, from the Massachusetts Council on Compulsive Gaming to the Harvard Square Homeless
Shelter, from the office of Massachusetts governor Deval Patrick
to the Romney for President campaign.

We spoke with several of the students, and each had a unique
story to tell. Tai Dinnan explained how her work with a sustainable
agriculture program in Tanzania shaped the understanding of nutritional issues that she later applied to helping schoolkids in
Somerville plant and harvest vegetables in a community garden.
Chase Webber, a premed student, talked about working at the
Language Bank, providing community members whose English
skills are poor with the translation help they need to deal with doctors, teachers, and government officials. And Michael Conroy, a
psychology major, described what he learned as a volunteer medi-
ator in small claims court—knowledge that should come in handy
in his potential future career as an international dispute resolution
specialist.

The only thing they all have in common is that they are, in
Dean Hollister's words, "practical visionaries," prepared to take the
insights, skills, and passions developed over four years at Tufts into
the larger world with the determination to make a real difference
at whatever they put their hand to. It's hard not to be optimistic
about the future of our country and our planet after meeting young
men and women like these.

Food for Thought, Seeds for Action

• *Bridging the classroom and the real world:* A crucial aspect of education for citizenship is drawing concrete, practical connections between classroom learning and the challenges of real life. Have you been able to draw such connections in your own life? If not, consider how you can do so now. Is there an academic program, full- or part-time, to which you can apply that might enhance your abilities to contribute to the life of your community? The possibilities are almost limitless, ranging from language lessons and writing or speaking classes (to enhance your communication skills) and classes in business, finance, or leadership (to improve your managerial skills) to classes in sociology, psychology, and the sciences, any of which can provide you with tools for tackling exciting new challenges in our complex world.

• *Supporting tomorrow's activists:* Educational institutions at every level, from elementary schools to universities, can benefit from partnerships with community organizations and concerned individuals. How can you reach out to a school in your hometown (or perhaps to your own alma mater) to help develop the civic engagement skills of its students? Options might include serving as a mentor to a group of student volunteers, linking your favorite charity or nonprofit group to a team of student supporters, and sponsoring a worthwhile student activity through the company where you work.

‖ 3 ‖

Social Entrepreneurship

*The Creative,
Results-Oriented Approach
to Social Change*

For most people, the opportunities we have to give time and talent to the communities in which we live seem terribly modest—helping out at the local community center, mentoring an at-risk student, driving an elderly neighbor to a medical appointment. In comparison with the vast social problems plaguing our country, such efforts may appear insignificant. But once in a while, a seemingly small step may open doors to a limitless future.

Take Eric Schwarz as an example. Working from a small, crowded office overlooking Boston Harbor, Eric Schwarz is now directing a national effort to create a cadre of "citizen teachers." Schwarz is shaking up education by bringing thousands of outsiders into classrooms around the country, "democratizing" education by redefining who is and is not a teacher. In the process, Schwarz hopes to revitalize many of our nation's most troubled schools and, perhaps, to save a generation of American kids from the fate too many millions have suffered: becoming high-school dropouts doomed to dead-end jobs and lives at the bottom of the social ladder.

An ambitious goal? Absolutely. But it grew from the smallest, simplest of efforts—a volunteer effort in a single classroom that sparked a creative idea whose growth continues to this day.

The path that led Eric Schwarz and his friend Ned Rimer to create what became the Citizen Schools movement began in 1994. Schwarz was a fellow at the Kennedy School of Government, a former executive with the City Year national service program, and a onetime investigative reporter and political columnist for the *Oakland Tribune* and Quincy (MA) *Patriot Ledger* newspapers. He was also restlessly casting about for his next personal challenge—some way to get involved in tackling one of the seemingly intractable social problems he saw festering around him.

Schwarz was drawn to education as a possible field of action. More than a decade earlier, the groundbreaking report *A Nation at Risk* had been published, launching what would become the modern school reform movement. The report had alerted Americans to the fact that their national education system was broken—that too many kids were failing to finish school, and that even those who graduated often lacked the basic skills necessary to help the country compete in an increasingly globalized world economy. "If an unfriendly foreign power had attempted to impose on America the mediocre educational performance that exists today," the report warned, "we might well have viewed it as an act of war."

Like countless others, Schwarz had been troubled by *A Nation at Risk*. But he wasn't a schoolteacher, an educational administrator, or a policymaker. What could he do to help promote the kinds of changes needed by America's schools?

Now, years later, Schwarz came up with an idea—a modest one, but one he personally found easy to get excited about. "Maybe I can find a few kids I can work with," he thought. "And I'll teach them journalism. After all, that's one thing I know how to do."

He called a principal he happened to know at the Paul A. Dever middle school in Dorchester, Massachusetts, and proposed the concept. Soon Schwarz found himself working with ten fifth graders whose teacher had identified them as good kids who were nonetheless struggling in class. The students were his for two hours a week for eleven weeks. Their shared mission: to publish a newspaper for the school, starting from scratch.

Schwarz is a soft-spoken, mild-mannered man with a shy smile, but his eyes light up when he describes what happens next:

> Every kid got a chance to write two or three different articles. We tried our hand at everything you'd find in a real newspaper—comics, sports, feature articles. We wrote and edited and drew pictures together and worked on layouts and design. The kids even sold four hundred dollars' worth of ads to cover the cost of printing. And then, the last week of the course, I rented a van and loaded the whole group into it for a drive to the printing plant in Chelsea. The kids got to watch their paper flying off an old offset web printing press, getting folded, stamped out, and wrapped in twine in batches of five hundred.
>
> We drove back to school, and the kids were practically jumping out of their skins with pride, running around and handing out copies of their paper. They'd developed writing skills, thinking skills, planning skills, organizational skills. What's more, they'd developed a sense of purpose and pride. They were school heroes! It was their first great taste of success, at the age of eleven.
>
> And I was hooked. I said to myself, "This is an awesome feeling. I've got to find a way to bring this experience to other people." And that was the start of Citizen Schools.

The next semester, Schwarz's friend Ned Rimer worked with another group of kids, teaching them a skill he happened to know—first aid. And like Schwarz, he found it a fun, inspiring experience—one he wanted to share with others.

Schwarz and Rimer weren't the first outsiders to find working as volunteers in a local school memorable. Countless parents and other caring citizens can recount similar memories of serving as math tutors, volunteer librarians, sports coaches, or chaperones on visits to museums, zoos, or aquariums. But they realized their one-time adventure could become the seed of a much bigger enterprise. They saw the possibility of making their experience into the foundation of a national program with the lofty goal of transforming American education. This difference is what makes Schwarz and Rimer exemplars of one of today's most significant global movements—*social entrepreneurship.*

Social entrepreneurship is usually defined as the application of business and management methods to social goals. More broadly, it describes the work of any individual, organization, or movement that develops and implements innovative ideas in an effort not merely to ameliorate social problems but to cure them. In some cases, programs that embody the social entrepreneurship ideal provide social benefits through for-profit businesses; in other cases, they apply business techniques to nonprofit enterprises, making them more efficient, innovative, and effective.

The phrase was coined in 1963 by Bill Drayton, then a twenty-year-old student at Harvard University. He used it to describe the work of people like Vinoba Bhave (1895–1982), the founder of India's Land Gift Movement, which sought to redistribute land more equitably to meet the needs of the untouchables and other poor people. As a young volunteer, Drayton joined Bhave's movement, which ultimately put seven million acres of land into the hands of the formerly landless, helping to lift many of them out of lifelong poverty.

Drayton became excited by the notion that creative, innovative thinking could be applied to solve seemingly intractable social problems. Along with other thinkers, such as Rosabeth Moss Kanter,

Charles Leadbeater, and Michael Young, Drayton promoted the idea of social entrepreneurship widely.

Today, social entrepreneurship is a widely recognized movement, supported and spread by organizations such as Ashoka (founded by Bill Drayton), the Skoll Foundation, and the Schwab Foundation for Social Entrepreneurship. The number and variety of social enterprises active around the world is truly astonishing. We could fill this book several times over with their stories. Just to give you a flavor of this burgeoning field, here is a sampling of a few notable examples:

• Mercy Corps, originally founded by Dan O'Neill in response to the Cambodian refugee crisis of the 1970s, today operates in thirty-five countries, helping people and communities recover from tragedies—the Indian Ocean tsunami, war in Afghanistan, massive food shortages in North Korea, ethnic conflict in the Balkans—while working to support civil society through programs that include microfinance, conflict management, environmental protection, and development of renewable energy sources.

• Apopo, a social enterprise founded by Belgian Bart Weetjens that—of all things—trains African giant pouch rats to sniff out land mines on former battlefields. Apopo carries out its mine-clearing efforts in war-torn areas like Mozambique and Africa's Great Lakes region while it develops plans for raising mission-supporting funds through for-profit operations—for example, using the rats' powerful sense of smell to provide cargo-inspection services to shipping companies and disease-detection services to cash-strapped hospitals that can't afford costly diagnostic tests.

• The Sekem Group, an Egyptian company founded by Ibrahim Abouleish to promote organic farming, herbal medicines, and economic development in his homeland. In addition to helping spread pesticide-free, nonpolluting agricultural methods through a network of eight hundred independent farmers, the company runs a school and a medical center for its employees.

• Witness, founded by musician Peter Gabriel in 1992, which uses video technology to document cases of human rights violations, gender violence, the use of children as soldiers, and other forms of abuse. Witness videos produced in countries ranging from Saudi Arabia to Burma, Mexico to Sierra Leone have been used as evidence in legal proceedings, to document reports by the United Nations and global human rights commissions, and as resources for news broadcasters and documentary filmmakers.

• D.light, a company with offices in Palo Alto, India, China, and East Africa, that produces affordable solar LED lamps designed to replace dangerous, polluting, and costly kerosene lights that are widely used by hundreds of millions of people in the developing world who live far from any reliable source of electricity. Founded by Sam Goldman, a former Peace Corps volunteer, who learned about the need for sustainable lighting solutions while serving in Benin, West Africa, D.light has developed several models of solar-powered lamps that sell for prices ranging from eight to thirty dollars.

Thanks to inspiring stories like these—and dozens more like them—social entrepreneurship has become a popular buzzword among both businesspeople and the general public. Today, Eric Schwarz and Ned Rimer are bringing the energy and creativity of this movement to their Citizen Schools initiative.

•   •   •

Reflecting on the success of their experimental teaching projects with the fifth graders from Dorchester, Eric Schwarz and Ned Rimer became excited about the potential for engaged outsiders—"citizen teachers"—to bring fresh creative energy into struggling school systems. And infused with the spirit of social entrepreneurship, they resolved to think big. They began looking for ways to make the citizen-teacher concept into the opening wedge of a movement to help fix what ails American education.

Efforts like Citizen Schools almost always begin with trial and error and experimentation that leads to gradual discovery of what works. The two friends tried a host of school-based activities, discarded some, and refined and enlarged the ones that worked best. In hindsight, Schwarz finds it easy to describe the several key principles that came to animate the emerging program. They include:

- *Expanding students' time for learning.* Between 1983 when the wake-up call of *A Nation at Risk* had been issued and 1994, the amount of money the United States invested in education had doubled, yet the results obtained had scarcely improved. The reason, Schwarz contends, is that our schools have largely stuck to the traditional schedule of short hours and long vacation breaks. "Kids are awake for five thousand hours a year," he observes, "but they're only in school for one thousand of those hours. It doesn't make a lot of sense to put 100 percent of our resources into those one thousand hours while ignoring the other four thousand." By developing after-school programs to stimulate and excite kids for up to fifteen additional hours per week, Citizen Schools has become one of the most important efforts to build learning opportunities into the out-of-the-classroom hours that represent the biggest wasted opportunity for millions of students.

- *Hands-on learning.* "Kids in public schools get very little opportunity to learn in real-world settings," Schwarz notes. "They sit in a chair alongside twenty-five or thirty other students, and even if the teacher is excited about what he or she is teaching, it's hard for the students to catch that enthusiasm." Citizen Schools aims to energize learning by using the age-old model of apprenticeship, by which professionals like lawyers and doctors traditionally mastered their craft. Working with local volunteers who love their work and enjoy teaching about it, students get to try their hand at activities ranging from designing a solar car to arguing a case in a mock courtroom to producing a video documentary about their neighborhood. Not only do they get a taste of real-world careers, they also begin to see—often for the first time—the relevance of classroom studies to work: how a veterinarian uses algebra, how an architect uses geometry, and how a magazine editor uses English grammar.

- *Democratizing teaching.* "It's crazy that we limit teaching to those with the willingness and opportunity to become full-time teachers," says Schwarz. "We need to find a way to bring more caring adults with passion and skill into the lives of our kids." Citizen Schools creates that opportunity. The goal is not to compete with or replace teachers with traditional credentials like education degrees; Schwarz himself has an education degree (from Harvard), which he pursued after launching Citizen Schools. Instead, the idea is to support and supplement the work of professional educators through the enthusiasm and energy of citizen volunteers. "You can't run a hotel or a hospital without a second shift of workers," Schwarz notes. "I don't see why we, as a country, think we can run an education system without a second shift, and with only a very limited pipeline of employees coming into the school system. At Citizen Schools, we want to expand the pool of educators so the learning day can grow from six or seven hours to nine or ten hours."

- *A comprehensive approach.* The apprenticeships taught by citizen teachers, exciting as they are, don't represent the whole Citizen Schools system. Students are engaged four to five afternoons per week and involved in a range of activities designed to enhance their overall school experience. They spend an hour or more every afternoon in a classroom where they tackle homework, work on special projects, or get tutoring in their toughest subjects. Thursday is Exploration Day, dedicated to outings that combine education and fun. (A trip to a laser-tag arcade includes a discussion of the science behind lasers led by an engineer or physicist.) Friday is spent on sports and exercise—activities most adults remember as routine parts of the school day that have been dropped from the programs of many cash-strapped and time-short public schools. And the 8th Grade Academy program includes field trips to ten colleges, which for many students is the first time they begin to draw a connection between their lives as twelve-year-old students and their potential futures, both in academia and in the world of work.

• *A targeted audience.* Citizen Schools focuses on middle-school students. This is no accident: plenty of research shows that most high school dropouts become disillusioned with learning during the middle-school years. Bored, resentful, and alienated, they resolve to leave the classroom as soon as they're legally able—and that's just what too many of them do. To short-circuit this destructive process, Citizen Schools works with school administrators to target at-risk students in the most troubled, underachieving schools in the communities and designs its programs specifically to engage and involve them. The goal is to give these eleven- and twelve-year-olds a renewed interest in learning and a sense that there are meaningful rewards—intellectual, personal, economic, and social—waiting for them if they work hard and graduate from high school.

It took several years for the Citizen Schools concept to take shape. But from early on, Schwarz was interested in more than just helping a few local kids and providing a memorable, rewarding experience for a handful of well-meaning volunteers. His goal was much bigger: to address specific, systemic weaknesses in the theory and practice of American education. This is what makes Citizen Schools a powerful example of the social entrepreneurship movement. Unlike traditional charities, social enterprises don't merely seek to alleviate chronic problems. They try to identify root causes and apply innovative, sometimes radical approaches to solving them.

Another marker of the social enterprise is its use of methodologies borrowed from nontraditional sources, especially business, to improve efficiencies and expand impact. Citizen Schools illustrates how this works. For example, like a business (but unlike many traditional charities and nonprofits), the organization uses statistical methods to track its results and determine the degree to which it is achieving its objectives. Beginning in 2001, Citizen Schools engaged the Washington, D.C.–based firm of Policy Studies Associates to examine the impact of its program through a longitudinal study that tracks participating students over a period of years and compares them with nonparticipating peers matched for other characteristics. The latest Policy Studies Associates report (January 2008) includes the following findings:

- "Citizen Schools participants are much more likely than their peers to enroll in top-tier college-track high schools" (59 percent versus 28 percent).
- "Students who participated in Citizen Schools in middle school continue to attend school at higher rates in high school."
- A higher percentage of participants earn A's or B's in English and math courses than nonparticipants.
- Participants do better than nonparticipants on so-called high-stakes tenth-grade exams in English and math— despite the fact that, on average, they did *worse* on similar tests in fourth grade, prior to participating in Citizen Schools.

Of course, these positive results are encouraging. But perhaps more important is the fact that Citizen Schools has submitted its efforts to rigorous evaluation by an impartial outside organization and is committed to releasing the outcomes publicly, whether favorable or not.

The comparison to business is instructive. One of the pillars of integrity underlying the free-market system is the variety of disclosure mechanisms, mandated by the SEC, FTC, and other agencies, that make it possible for investors and consumers to scrutinize the records of companies. The trend toward creating similar public disclosure systems for nonprofits is one of the real contributions of the social entrepreneurship movement.

Citizen Schools has also borrowed from business in its use of leadership techniques borrowed from the best practices of leading corporate managers. In their book *The Charismatic Organization,* Shirley Sagawa and Deborah Jospin describe how Eric Schwarz jump-started a new phase of organizational improvement for Citizen Schools in February 2005, using a process modeled on the ideas of strategy gurus Jim Collins (author of *Good to Great*) and John Kotter (*Leading Change*) as well as the innovation techniques pioneered by the design company IDEO.

A business planning council was appointed that met periodically over fifteen weeks to tackle such challenges as improving student success rates, engaging volunteers more deeply, and ensuring the long-term financial stability of the organization. In the end, the council produced a consensus plan that included ten specific recommendations, including increasing the emphasis on apprenticeships by offering two rather than one per week and eliminating the former "affiliate" structure in favor of managing sites directly from the organization's Boston headquarters.

Such a businesslike approach to growth is unusual in the nonprofit world. The stereotypical image of a nonprofit organization is of a loosey-goosey gaggle of "free spirits" where consensus is impossible to achieve, decisions take forever, and implementation is at the mercy of strong-willed volunteers who refuse to subordinate their preferences to the good of the organization as a whole. Citizen Schools defies the stereotype. Like other leading exemplars of the social entrepreneurship model, it combines the passion and idealistic spirit of a nonprofit with much of the rigor and discipline of a conventional business. The result is a well-run, sustainable organization that produces measurable results, rather than a mere collection of well-intentioned but ineffectual dreamers.

Although Citizen Schools has a long way to go when measured against its ultimate goal of reforming education for an entire generation of schoolkids, it has come a long way from its roots in a single classroom apprenticeship taught by Eric Schwarz. Today Citizen Schools is active at forty-four school sites in seven states, serving around four thousand students through the efforts of thirty-two hundred citizen teachers. Many more schools are eager to join the effort as soon as more volunteers and necessary funding can be mobilized.

It seems clear that the Citizen School model works. Now the challenge is bringing it into more communities around the nation where at-risk kids are in need of its benefits.

Food for Thought, Seeds for Action

• *Start small:* Although social entrepreneurs often have ambitious long-term plans for the programs they launch, social enterprises usually start small. Muhammad Yunus's Grameen Bank was founded when Yunus lent the equivalent of $27 from his own pocket to impoverished villagers in his native Bangladesh, enabling them to escape from the clutches of rapacious moneylenders. Citizen

Schools began with Eric Schwarz's ten-student journalism apprenticeship in a Dorchester middle school. Is there a modest need in your own community that you can fill through a simple, creative act? Go ahead! That's often how the social entrepreneurship spirit finds a new foothold.

• *Spread and grow:* Once you are involved in a small, local effort aimed at addressing some social need, the next question to ask is: How might it be possible to expand this program and thereby reach more people in need? For example, can you recruit more volunteers to provide a similar service to the one you are offering? Can you extend your efforts into additional locations or communities? Can you attract partners from business or the nonprofit sector to increase your outreach? Can you apply for support from an appropriate government agency or philanthropic foundation? Can you use traditional media (newspapers, TV, radio, public speaking) or new media (the Internet, social networking, blogging, Twittering) to spread the word about your program and encourage others to emulate it?

• *Apply your business skills:* Serving as a volunteer or part-time worker in a nonprofit social venture doesn't mean leaving your "other" life behind. Think about the skills, knowledge, and insights you use in your day job, and look for opportunities to apply them productively to your Citizen You activities. Are you an expert at marketing, advertising, or promotion? Do you have experience in crafting business strategies or financial plans? Are you a specialist in human resource development, legal issues in business, or logistics? Ask whether the community organizations you support can benefit from your talent.

In popular discussions of social entrepreneurship, the focus is often on the individuals who launch and build social enterprises. For example, in David Bornstein's excellent book, *How to Change the World: Social Entrepreneurs and the Power of New Ideas,* the author emphasizes the unique qualities of social entrepreneurs themselves, calling them "transformative forces" and describing them as

> . . . people with new ideas to address major problems who are relentless in the pursuit of their visions, people who simply will not take "no" for an answer, who will not give up until they have spread their ideas as far as they possibly can. (p. 1)

Like Bornstein, we have nothing but admiration for the most effective social entrepreneurs, who set an example to all of us in their persistence, creativity, and dedication. But overemphasizing the personal traits that mark the social entrepreneur may actually do a disservice to this important movement. Although it takes a special kind of person to devote his or her life to a social cause, social entrepreneurship isn't only the preserve of a unique cadre of obsessed or even saintly heroes. To us, the most exciting aspect of the social entrepreneurship movement is precisely that it breaks down barriers between aspects of life usually considered separate and unconnected: business and charity, personal profit and social benefit, material gain and spiritual fulfillment. Becoming involved in social entrepreneurship *doesn't* involve leaving behind everything you've learned and enjoyed in daily life; on the contrary, it's about bringing to a social cause everything you may have to offer, from social skills to leadership ability, from management know-how to artistic creativity, from organizational talent to the sheer ability to work hard.

And you don't have to be a genius to participate in the movement, nor independently wealthy, nor particularly gifted in any other way. All you need to become a part of the social entrepreneurship movement is a willingness to contribute—in your spare time, or your full time, according to your preference and circumstances.

Citizen Schools offers a vivid example of how almost anyone can become a part of the social entrepreneurship movement. "We now have thousands of citizen teachers," Eric Schwarz says. "They're scientists and engineers, architects and web designers, businesspeople and lawyers and homemakers. Each one has an incredible story to tell, and every one is different. The only qualification is being passionate about some topic and wanting to share your passion with our students."

The skills taught in Citizen Schools apprenticeships cover an amazing range. Some are related to the citizen teachers' day jobs, but others are not. For example, consider the three classes recently taught by ten employees at the biotech company Genzyme in Albuquerque (one of many corporations that has encouraged its workers to support Citizen Schools). One was a class in cytogenetics, which is their company's stock in trade. (The students learned to extract DNA from strawberries and analyze the chromosomes for mutations, an amazing activity for middle-school kids, and one that seems guaranteed to stimulate an interest in science.) But the other two classes were a creative writing workshop (led by a lab technician who is a novelist on the side) and a course in world cultures taught by three Genzyme staffers who happen to have lived everywhere from Japan to Saudi Arabia. As Eric Schwarz says, all you need is the passion.

Other recent apprenticeships taught at Citizen Schools around the country include a project to produce, taste-test, and advertise a brand-new breakfast cereal, led by a team of citizen teachers who work at General Mills; a community development project in which students created a new design for Boston's City Hall Plaza, led by a young real estate professional from the area; a CSI-like forensic science class, in which students used DNA testing and other high-tech methods to solve a fictitious crime, taught by a scientist from Merck; and a video-production class led by a team from Google in which students taped public service announcements on topics like reducing teen violence and environmentalism to be shown on YouTube. Ideas for future projects are limited only by the imagination of tomorrow's volunteers.

Most apprenticeships have a service element—a way in which the students can use their newfound knowledge to benefit their school, their families, or their communities. In some cases, this service is built on the "teach-back" concept, which holds that people fully master new skills only when they turn around and teach those skills to others. In one recent Citizen Schools apprenticeship, a citizen teacher who worked at Fidelity taught a group of students the basic principles of personal financial planning. As their service project, the kids selected a "client"—the school gym teacher, whom they all loved, and who was worrying about how he would be able to send his fifteen-year-old son to college. The students developed a personalized PowerPoint presentation that they used to teach the gym teacher about strategies for saving and investing, demonstrating the power of compound interest and showing how $100 a week invested in a balanced blend of high-yield and low-risk instruments could produce handsome returns over a four-year period. The kids mastered vital skills that will benefit them in their own lives, and, by teaching those same skills to their gym teacher, they helped out a friend—a classic win/win situation.

Citizen teachers often come up with ideas that no professional educator would be likely to conceive. Schwarz recounts the story of a woman who offered to teach a class based on her work at the Folsom Funeral Home in Roslindale, Massachusetts. His first thought was, *A class on embalming? Maybe this is one we want to go slow on.* But the funeral director had a very different idea in mind. "We're in the grief business," she explained. "Our job is to help people deal with the loss of a loved one. But we've found we're not very good at working with kids. So I'd love to teach a course about dealing with grief, where the kids and I could explore our feelings about loss and work together to figure out better ways for young people to cope with a death in the family." The class proved to be a powerful learning experience for everyone involved.

The citizen teacher volunteers aren't the only people who make Citizen Schools possible. There are also paid staffers with various professional and personal profiles. Some are full-time teaching fellows, mostly recent college graduates who spend two years working with students, leading the academic coaching, and organizing and mobilizing volunteers. Many attend classes part-time in pursuit of the world's first master's degree in education (offered by Lesley University) with a specialization in out-of-school-time learning.

In some cases, out-of-the-box thinking by the leaders of Citizen Schools has been required to develop job opportunities for potential staffers. "The Achilles heel of an after-school program is staffing," Schwarz observes, "because it's inherently a part-time job. How do you get high-quality people on a part-time wage and often with lower benefits?"

The solution: Citizen Schools adapted tactics like those used by employment agencies, matching their needs and those of their employees with opportunities elsewhere in the community. A bit of sleuthing uncovered local organizations like museums that also needed part-time help. Citizen Schools developed partnerships with these organizations, sharing talented people who were able to combine two half-jobs into the equivalent of a rewarding full-time position.

Another powerful attribute of Citizen Schools is the way it effectively combines resources from three disparate sectors—government, business, and private citizens—to produce results that would be impossible without such a partnership.

The government contributions include the access to space and other resources provided by local school districts; partial funding of staff salaries through grants from Americorps, the national service program; and grants provided through other streams of federal funds. Citizen Schools is hoping these government subsidies will increase in the near future as new funding sources come online, including the discretionary five-billion-dollar Race to the Top fund created in early 2009 by the Department of Education and the new social innovation fund being administered by the White House Office of Social Innovation and Civic Participation in the Obama administration.

The business contributions include grants from corporations like Bank of America, Fidelity, and Microsoft, as well as donations of time and talent by thousands of employees whose companies support their work as citizen teachers. And the private offerings to Citizen Schools include, of course, the contributions of the citizen teachers themselves, without whom the entire program would be impossible.

Many social entrepreneurship projects are built from similar cross-sector alliances. For example, author David Bornstein tells the story of Everyone's Reading in Africa (ERA), a program designed to promote adult literacy in South Africa, which was founded in 1991 by Beulah Thumbadoo, a former employee of Penguin Books in Johannesburg. Concerned about the millions of men and women who had been denied even basic education under the apartheid regime, Thumbadoo traveled the country experimenting with various techniques for teaching adults to read and encouraging them to develop a love of learning.

Eventually, she developed a comprehensive plan that included a business component (convincing five publishers to produce dozens of attractive, well-written and well-edited easy-to-read books designed especially for new adult readers), a government component (persuading the South African education minister to back ERA with promotional events, writing activities, and library campaigns), and a citizens' voluntary component (enlisting the help of volunteer teachers, African language translators, writers, and librarians to promote reading among poor South Africans). Traditional philanthropy is also involved; grants from corporations like the mining company Anglo Platinum have helped to make Thumbadoo's work possible.

Occasional skeptics have challenged the value of social entrepreneurship by claiming that the societal goals it serves should rightfully be the domain of government. They say that, by harnessing free-market forces, business methods, corporate donations, and citizens' efforts in the quest to make our communities better places to live, social entrepreneurs are providing a "safety valve" that reduces the pressure on government to fulfill its responsibilities to serve the needs of all citizens. Wouldn't it be better if citizens demanded that government do a better job, making citizen-run efforts superfluous?

Maybe there's some truth to this. Maybe, in a perfect world, our public schools would all be so good that there would be no need for a social entrepreneur like Eric Schwarz to create a cross-sector network like Citizen Schools to meet the unmet needs. But in the real world, we have two choices: to wait forever in the hopes that government will eventually figure out ways to educate at-risk kids, house the homeless, feed the hungry, and heal the sick, or to act on our own, as citizens, to pull together all the available resources in an effort to solve these problems *now*.

There's no doubt in my mind which choice is better.

•   •   •

As social entrepreneurship becomes more and more widespread, some of today's smartest thinkers are applying themselves to the next set of challenges—developing intellectual and organizational structures and systems to support the social entrepreneurship movement and lift it to the next level of effectiveness. Capitalism could never have become the world-changing, growth-stimulating, wealth-creating powerhouse it is without such fundamental concepts as double-entry bookkeeping, contract law, financial reporting systems, and the limited liability corporation. Now it is time for social entrepreneurship to develop a parallel set of concepts to help managers design and run social enterprises more efficiently and effectively.

One of today's leaders in this effort is Kim Alter. A successful founder and former manager of social enterprises, she now runs Virtue Ventures, the first management consulting firm focused on international social enterprise. Alter describes it as a "market developer" for social enterprises in the developing world. Alter also serves as a visiting fellow at the Skoll Center for Social Entrepreneurship at Said Business School at the University of Oxford in England, where she conducts research and teaches courses on social entrepreneurship.

Like most experts in the field, Alter has her own preferred definition of social entrepreneurship. "A social enterprise," she says, "is any venture created for a business/environmental purpose mitigating a social problem or a market failure and to generate social value while operating with the financial discipline, innovation, and determination of a private-sector business. It combines explicit social objectives and ethical values with revenue generation through market activities, thereby producing blended social-economic value." Alter adds, "For a social enterprise, the social problem *is* the business opportunity."

Because social entrepreneurship is still relatively new, the place of the social enterprise in the broader economic system is still somewhat unclear. Existing social enterprises may fit into any of several legal forms—they can be nonprofits, for-profit businesses, or hybrid combinations of related enterprises in differing legal forms. This in-between quality of social enterprise is gradually changing. In fact, one important trend that Alter has been tracking is the emergence of new structures for organizing social enterprises. These include new legal forms, such as the Low-Profit LLC (LC3), originated in Vermont, which is a new type of for-profit corporation organized specifically for "charitable or educational goals," and the Community Interest Company, started in the UK in 2006, "designed [as the new law states] for social enterprises that want to use their profits and assets for the public good." It seems likely that new business structures like these will spread to other jurisdictions, facilitating even more experimentation with new kinds of social enterprises.

The evolution of the field also includes new ways of financing social enterprises. Because social entrepreneurship has attracted such intense interest from the newest wave of corporate and personal philanthropists, including such well-known and powerful trendsetters as Bill Gates of Microsoft and Pierre Omidyar, cofounder of eBay, experimentation with new ways of launching, financing, managing, and growing social enterprises has boomed. These include what Alter describes as "mixed capital" (combining a variety of funding sources, from philanthropic contributions and foundation grants to venture capital and market-based revenues from sales), so-called soft loans (which earn below-market rates of return), patient capital (with highly flexible repayment plans), and quasi-equity stakes (in which donors receive, in exchange for their funding, a degree of influence over the business program that is comparable to ownership).

One of the most promising experiments in this area is the proliferation of social venture funds. These are organizations that play a role analogous to venture capital funds in the for-profit arena, identifying and vetting nonprofits with effective social-benefits models and channeling donor and investor money to them so as to finance their growth and expansion. It's one of those ideas that seems obvious once someone creates it but that, for decades, the world of social activism somehow had to limp along without.

Vanessa Kirsch runs New Profit Inc., one of the best-known and most successful funds specializing in what it calls "venture philanthropy." The concept came to her while she and her husband, Alan Khazei (founder of City Year, a kind of "domestic Peace Corps" that supports full-time volunteerism in cities around the United States) were undertaking a year of reflection, research, and travel shortly after they got engaged.

During their travels, Kirsch and Khazei met with more than 350 social activists, business leaders, and government officials in twenty countries. Kirsch came to realize that some of the problems with financing they'd observed among social entrepreneurs in the United States were mirrored around the world. "There's lots of startup money for nonprofit work," as Khazei once told Cheryl Dahle of *Fast Company* magazine. "There's lots of money for the really big, established groups. But there's almost no money for those organizations in between—those who need bridge money to sustain and to grow."

It was a problem Kirsch had personally experienced years earlier, when trying to raise money to expand her proven national service program for young adults, Public Allies. "[S]ome of the foundation people were saying to me, 'Vanessa, you're getting too successful. We can't fund you anymore.'"

Eric Schwarz of Citizen Schools points to the same issue. "There's something wrong with the way we scale success," he says. In the nonprofit world, great ideas are being born all the time, yet they rarely get the resources needed to grow. "In the for-profit world," Schwarz says, "a majority of the thirty biggest companies in America were launched in the last generation or two. But in the nonprofit world, the only organization in the top thirty that was founded in the last thirty-five years is Habitat for Humanity. All the others are a century old. And yet there are a million new nonprofits that were started in the last decade or two. This picture makes no sense."

(Actually, the top thirty companies in the Fortune 500 include quite a few old ones, including GE and IBM, alongside newer firms like Verizon, Costco, and Home Depot. But Schwarz is right about the top thirty charities: that list is indeed dominated by venerable organizations such as the Mayo Clinic, the Salvation Army, the YMCA, and the Red Cross. And of the more than two hundred thousand nonprofits that have opened in the United States since 1970, only 144 have reached $50 million in annual revenue. Growing nonprofits to scale does seem to be much harder than growing a for-profit business.)

Kirsch decided to help fill this gap. Working with Monitor Group, a respected management consulting firm based in Cambridge, Massachusetts, she developed a business plan and began raising money from donors seeking opportunities to support nonprofit organizations that promised both sustainable business models and quantifiable social benefits. The overarching goal: to take social programs offering proven benefits to ever-wider worlds of beneficiaries.

In 1998, Kirsch launched New Profit, investing some $2 million from sources like the John S. and James L. Knight Foundation and Mark Nunnelly of Bain Capital in three entrepreneurial nonprofits: Working Today (a union for freelancers), Jumpstart (a group that matches college-age tutors with at-risk preschool kids), and Eric Schwarz's Citizen Schools.

Today, an expanding New Profit supports a portfolio of seventeen organizations (with eight past investments), providing not just funding but also strategic reviews, coaching, leadership training, board development, and other valuable forms of intellectual capital. It also rigorously measures results, tracking the growth of the organizations it supports along two measures—annual revenue growth and annual growth in the number of "lives touched." (We see here the notion of "blended social-economic value" as described by Kim Alter.) According to New Profit's statistics, the current portfolio of organizations has achieved average growth of 44 percent on the revenue side, and 48 percent on the "lives touched." We can compare this to an average of just 3 percent revenue growth for all U.S. youth development nonprofits.

New Profit and a handful of similar organizations—including, for example, the Acumen Fund, which specifically targets global organizations aimed at improving the lives of the world's four billion poorest people—are playing an important role in the development of social entrepreneurship, bringing specific benefits to each side in the partnership they foster. To social entrepreneurs, they bring not just funding but also the validation of their imprimatur as recognized experts in evaluating nonprofit organizations based on clear, objective measurement standards. To the donors and "venture philanthropists" who provide the money, they bring a new degree of accountability to the world of charity, making it possible for foundations and other grantors to verify that their money is producing measurable benefits.

Yet experts like Kim Alter remain unsatisfied with the current intellectual, managerial, and organizational underpinnings of social enterprise. "The methodology used by social entrepreneurs needs to evolve further and faster," she says. To help find remedies to this problem, Alter has been leading an initiative funded largely by the Skoll Foundation whose goal is to craft an "integrated approach to social enterprise" by developing a methodological framework that blends business and social practices with approaches unique to social enterprise. Among the developments she has been helping to encourage:

- Creating Venturesource (www.venturesource.org), a free, open-content resource library that hosts a collection of

case studies, articles, and management tools, and provides a network platform for knowledge sharing among
social enterprise practitioners;

- Expanding the range of strategic tools used by social enterprises to include not just traditional business techniques but also approaches created by experts in
economic development and the social sector, which
have generally been neglected by social entrepreneurs,
as well as documenting original technical approaches
pioneered by practitioners;

- Improving the cross-fertilization of ideas among social
entrepreneurs working in various sectors (health care,
child poverty, water access, agricultural improvement,
and so on) who have tended to work in isolation from
one another; and

- Creation of new performance-measurement systems
that will make it easier for social enterprises to define,
quantify, and track their own accomplishments, spot
weaknesses, and institute and test improvements.

"Right now," Alter explains, "social enterprises are mostly limited to using traditional business measurement tools. These are
useful, but they're not enough, since they don't reflect the important differences between for-profit companies and organizations
whose primary goal is to produce social benefits."

Here's an example Alter cites:

A basic principle is that a social enterprise should *not* generate profits. It should be financially self-sustaining, but
whatever surpluses it creates through revenue-generating
activities should be invested in the social cause it supports
or in business growth to generate *more* social impact. So,
for instance, think about a coffee shop run on a typical

for-profit basis. The owner of the shop will probably hire employees at the lowest competitive wage—maybe at the legal minimum—and is likely to deliberately keep benefits as modest as possible, for example by hiring part-time workers so that health-care benefits and overtime wages don't have to be provided. The result would be larger profits and an improved bottom line.

This is normal, even understandable behavior for a profit-making company. But now imagine that same coffee shop being run as a social enterprise—for example, by an organization devoted to helping people with barriers to employments such as disabilities, to develop skills and obtain work. Now it no longer makes sense to keep employee salaries and benefits at a minimum. You want to pay "livable" wages that will allow the workers to rent apartments and pursue independent lives. You want to provide medical benefits so they can get the health care and counseling services they may need. The social enterprise may also provide costly additional supportive services to help their employees to be more successful at work: child care, job coaching, or soft-skills training in hygiene or interfacing with the public.

These are human resources expenses, but in the context of a social enterprise they are also what might be called socioeconomic costs. Most important, they are not just a drain on profitability, as they would be with a for-profit company. They reflect the mission of the enterprise. So while subsidies for social programs are an inherent cost of operating a social enterprise, social enterprises are a much more efficient social service model than charities, which operate at a 100 percent deficit.

So the social enterprise literally needs a different accounting system than the for-profit company—one that accounts for program costs, social subsidies, and mixed forms of capital—all leading to a triple bottom line that accurately reflects the social, environmental, and financial objectives of social enterprise. This is something we're now working to create.

In a similar fashion, social enterprises often have streams of income unlike any that typical for-profit companies enjoy—for example, cost-sharing arrangements with nonprofit partners, subsidies from government, or provision of resources at a discounted price by supportive for-profit organizations, as when a corporation provides equipment, office space, or legal services at a minimal cost. Traditional accounting systems have no way to accurately reflect these forms of income, which makes it harder for managers of social enterprises to figure out how to plan for using them intelligently and strategically. It's another conceptual gap that Alter and her colleagues at Skoll and elsewhere are working to fill.

• • •

The brilliance of social entrepreneurship lies in its power to unleash the creativity of millions of private citizens in addressing seemingly intractable social problems. Just as entrepreneurship in business leads to innovative products, services, and business models that generate much of the world's dynamism, growth, and economic opportunity, social entrepreneurship stimulates fresh thinking about deep-rooted social challenges whose solution has eluded government and traditional philanthropy.

There's a powerful inherent appeal to the concept of social entrepreneurship. It crosses political and ideological lines that represent barriers to the acceptance of some other forms of social activism. Because social entrepreneurship aims to improve the lives of the poor and disadvantaged, and to alleviate social problems like poverty, lack of health care, environmental degradation, and poor educational opportunities, it wins the admiration of people who consider themselves liberals. And because it uses methods pioneered by business, relies on free-market mechanisms, harnesses self-interest to social interest, and tends to avoid reliance on government support, it attracts applause from businesspeople and others who usually consider themselves conservatives. This combination makes social entrepreneurship a win/win, feel-good story that almost everyone is happy to support. Thus, it's tempting to think of social entrepreneurship as *the* solution to the world's problems, a "magic bullet" that can eliminate poverty, pollution, disease, ignorance, and homelessness just by unleashing the inherent creativity and idealism of humankind.

Unfortunately, it's unlikely that social enterprise—or any other single idea—has the power to solve all our problems by itself. There are some challenges that free-market solutions, no matter how clever, are unlikely to fully meet. As Kim Alter points out, not every social need can be addressed through self-sustaining, revenue-generating activities—otherwise, why wouldn't for-profit companies already be meeting those needs?

Let's consider the example of Muhammad Yunus's Grameen Bank, widely acknowledged as the world's most successful example of social entrepreneurship. Since 1995 it has been a self-sustaining business, taking customers' deposits, paying interest on these, and lending the funds to other customers in the form of microloans at reasonable interest (never higher than 20 percent, and often lower). In all these ways, Grameen Bank operates like a traditional financial institution. But to reach this point, it first had to pass through many years when it operated on a non-self-sustaining basis. Grants from the Ford Foundation and other philanthropic contributions were needed to prime the pump.

And even today, with Grameen's many years of experience as a role model, microcredit on the Grameen lines seems difficult to achieve. Many of the other large, successful microlending institutions in the world, such as Latin America's Compartamos, have helped thousands of families start or expand small businesses and improve their financial status—but they have done so while charging far higher interest rates than Grameen Bank, sometimes as high as 80 percent. The result has been intense controversy among development experts and other supporters of microlending as to whether such microcredit banks truly qualify as social enterprises— or whether, in some cases, they may even deserve to be considered predatory lenders taking advantage of the poor.

The point is that finding market-driven, self-sustaining solutions to social problems is far from easy, even in a case like that of microcredit, where a widely admired success story (Grameen Bank) exists to show the way. It seems likely that, for the foreseeable future, addressing the world's greatest social ills is going to continue to demand a wide variety of programs, including social enterprise but also including efforts by government, philanthropy, religious institutions, nongovernmental agencies, foundations, and charities, as well as social and political activism. And these disparate efforts will undoubtedly compete with, partner with, stimulate, encourage, inspire, and challenge one another, which is all to the good.

Nonetheless, there's little doubt that social entrepreneurship represents a genuinely new and significant approach to civic activism, one with tremendous potential to produce promising new solutions to the challenges we face. As David Bornstein notes, social entrepreneurship represents an important change in the way social problems are addressed by society:

> Around the world, this work has been dominated by centralized decision making and top-down, usually governmental, institutions. It has been managed a little like a planned economy. This makes sense from the perspective that governments are responsible for translating the will of

the citizenry into public policy and public goods. But governments are often not the ideal vehicles to carry out the social R&D, just as they are not the ideal vehicles to create new businesses. As in business, advancing new ideas and creating new models to attack problems require an entrepreneur's single-minded vision and fierce determination, and lots of energy and time. It is the kind of work that flourishes to the extent that society successfully harnesses and nurtures the wide-ranging talents of millions of citizens.

This kind of flourishing is now happening in more and more countries, involving more and more citizens from every walk of life. In the history books of the future, it seems likely that the explosion of social entrepreneurship will be viewed as one of the most important global developments of our time.

Food for Thought, Seeds for Action

• *Stepping up to the plate:* You don't have to be a gifted entrepreneur to help build the social entrepreneurship movement. Every social enterprise can benefit from the support of volunteers whose main contribution is their passion for the cause. Identify the mission you feel most strongly about—whether it's improving education, reducing poverty, providing health care, cleaning the environment, or any other worthwhile cause—and find a social enterprise that is at work on the front lines. Chances are great that there's a valuable role for you to play.

• *Partnering across sectors:* Social entrepreneurs excel at creating partnerships for addressing social problems among concerned individuals, businesses, and government agencies. Think about a social challenge that interests you. Is there an organization in *any* sector that is currently tackling that challenge using a promising approach? If so, can you imagine how resources from organizations in other sectors could expand the program, enhance its effectiveness, or improve its efficiency? Perhaps you can play a role as a bridge builder, helping to promote partnerships across sectors that can lead to powerful new solutions to today's social ills.

• *Supporting social venture funding:* Organizations like New Profit and the Acumen Fund are providing reliable channels for charitable donors who are seeking proven, effective ways to invest their money in community-building, socially beneficial causes. Do you play a role in allocating charitable funds? (For example, you may serve on the board of a church, synagogue, or mosque; help run a community chest or other local organization; or work for a company that makes grants or matching donations to charitable causes.) If so, you may want to consider investing some of those monies in a social venture fund, where donations produce measurable benefits based on careful analysis and rigorous, business-like evaluation.

‖ 4 ‖

Engaged Professionals

*Redefining Work with
Social Goals in Mind*

A handful of occupations are commonly granted the dignity of being considered "callings." The word implies a special status on the part of those who labor in a particular field, as if they have been "called" to the work they do by some power greater than themselves. We apply it to people who do work that is clearly devoted to the well-being of others rather than being motivated by the hope of personal gain—members of the clergy, for example, or health-care professionals who spend their careers caring for the underprivileged or neglected. Think of Mother Teresa, sharing the poverty of AIDS and tuberculosis patients in Kolkata as she struggled to alleviate their suffering; Albert Schweitzer, who gave up the comfortable life of a physician and musician in his native Alsace to minister to the sick and helpless in Gabon; or Florence Nightingale, a wealthy woman who took up nursing in order to improve the scandalous conditions experienced by the desperately poor in the workhouses of London. It's obvious that there is something special about people like this, which is why some of them become legends, revered the world over for their near-saintly qualities.

Unfortunately, the existence of uniquely devoted individuals like these leads many people to make a serious mistake in thinking about their own lives and work. It's easy to look at the Teresas, Schweitzers, and Nightingales of the world and conclude that work with a social objective is the special privilege of a small handful of people. And if the idea of emulating these heroic figures should ever cross our own minds, it's easy to dismiss it as unrealistic. After all, very few of us are saints, or even want to be saints! Unlike Mother Teresa and her few peers, we have needs, desires, and dreams that are self-oriented and all too human. We have families to nurture, mortgages to pay, and retirements to finance. And while helping others has its appeal, we also want to enjoy our share of the good things in life—a nice home, a new car, an occasional vacation. Self-sacrifice for the benefit of one's neighbors is a special road reserved for only a few.

As a result, most people set aside the idea of serving others when it comes to planning their careers. They focus instead on more mundane goals: financial success, power, status. There's nothing wrong with these things. But for millions of people, they aren't enough. A lifetime spent in pursuit of purely self-oriented goals leaves many feeling unsatisfied. They aren't ready to abandon "normal" life and follow the self-sacrificial path of a Schweitzer or a Nightingale, but they wish they could feel as though they are doing more to improve the world than they can manage with a couple of hours of volunteer work at the local soup kitchen or an occasional weekend pounding nails with Habitat for Humanity. Surely, they say, there's a way to experience both the everyday rewards of work and the special satisfaction that comes from pursuing a personal calling.

Actually, there is. It's a path that is being opened up today by pioneers in the world of work—men and women who are showing that careers can be designed to benefit both the individuals who practice them and the society in which they live. For these pioneers, life as a socially engaged professional offers fascinating challenges as well as psychological rewards that go way beyond the monetary. They're creating a new way of thinking about work that satisfies the desire for self-advancement and personal benefit as well as the latent idealism so many people have learned to suppress or ignore.

It's true that very few of us were born to be Teresas, Schweitzers, or Nightingales. But many of us can live more rewarding lives by recognizing that we, too, may be called to a special mission in our lives' work. That's what being an engaged professional is all about.

• • •

When you hear the phrase "civil engineer," what comes to mind? A blue-suited professional in a glass-walled office examining blueprints for a new airport terminal? A man in a hard hat conferring with contractors as concrete is poured for a hydroelectric dam? A government bureaucrat drawing up plans for renovating a crumbling suspension bridge in an aging northeastern city?

These are accurate pictures of what civil engineers do. But spend a day with Chris Swan, and you'll discover that a civil engineer can also be a young man interviewing villagers in Ecuador about the causes of *la gripa,* an infectious disease that fells up to 50 percent of local residents with flulike symptoms every fall; a young woman installing a solar panel on the roof of a health clinic in rural Rwanda; or a college senior teaching kids in a bilingual third-grade class in Somerville, Massachusetts, about water conservation and the basics of a sustainable lifestyle.

All are part of Swan's vision of what he calls "citizen engineers," and they represent the leading edge of engineering education in the United States—part of a growing movement to transform the professions from merely technical fields into avenues for social, economic, and even political reform. At the same time, they are showing men and women from *every* occupation how work can provide not just a way to make a living but also an opportunity for creative engagement in some of the greatest challenges of our time—the environment, health care, and economic development.

Chris Swan grew up in Buda, a sleepy little town in central Texas. Chris's dad was a building contractor with an eighth-grade education, his mom a clerical worker at the local IRS office. One of ten kids in the family, Chris was part of Buda's small African American community, numbering (then as now) just about 2 percent of the population.

Most kids in Chris's shoes would have considered themselves lucky just to graduate from the local Hayes High School and then go to work with their father. But Chris had bigger ideas, and he had the smarts and the self-discipline to make them happen. In 1980, he graduated seventh in his class, having scored in the 99th percentile on the math portion of his Preliminary Scholastic Aptitude Test. Those credentials won him a spot at the nearby University of Texas (UT), where he majored in engineering. Four years later, Chris became the first member of his family to graduate from college.

He stayed in Austin long enough to earn a graduate degree at UT. Then he made the big move up north, settling in Boston, where he worked for three years as a staff engineer at a firm called GZA Geoenvironmental. Chris practiced "geoenvironmental engineering," a specialized field that focuses on environmental issues—water treatment, waste disposal, energy, green design, and so on. It originated as an unglamorous specialty called "sanitary engineering," then took off with the environmental movement in the late 1980s. Chris honed his practical skills in the job, working on things like foundation engineering and cleaning up hazardous wastes (and, not incidentally, met his future wife there). He left the firm to pursue a doctor of science degree at MIT, and then shifted into the career he'd actually dreamed about ever since he was a kid—teaching.

Chris is now an associate professor of civil engineering at Tufts University, where he has taught for fourteen years. He also served as the department chairman from 2002 through 2007. He can—and does—deploy technical knowledge with the best of them. He's an expert on what's called in the field "industrial ecology," and he has published research on topics like "reuse of fly ash from coal-burning facilities," "engineering properties of thermally remediated sediments," and "experimental and theoretical studies on the stress-strain-strength behavior of frozen media." But his real passion is for what he calls "citizen engineering." It's a unique approach to the way his profession relates to the larger society, and one that illustrates vividly how active citizens are making their mark in reshaping the world of work.

"I understand the traditional technical requirements for becoming an engineer," Chris explains, "and I support them 100 percent. When you design a building, it better stand up! But that's not all it takes to be an effective engineer. The citizen engineer must also understand the nontechnical issues that affect a design and determine what separates good building from the not so good. Why are we building a factory in that location? Why should we design it this way rather than that way? What social purpose will it serve? Who will be affected by it? How will it change the local environment? Would the community be better served if the factory were smaller—or broken up into three separate facilities—or located in some other town altogether?"

Chris continues, "The citizen engineer asks all these questions, and uses the answers to inform his engineering decisions. And this is the kind of engineer we are trying to train at Tufts—someone who is much more than just a technical expert."

An outsider to the world of engineering might think this is just another way of saying that Chris and his fellow Tufts professors are trying to train good engineers. After all, shouldn't any good engineer try to understand the purpose of the structures he designs, and build that purpose into his designs?

Maybe so. Maybe Chris is just making more explicit and clear an element of his profession that usually goes unspoken. The problem, as he sees it, is that these social aspects of engineering usually get taken for granted—and therefore neglected.

As Chris observes, many experienced engineers have actually been trained *not* to speak up about the social implications of their profession—not to question or challenge the assumptions on which their work is based. They've been trained to serve the client unthinkingly, whether that client is a corporation, a government agency, or a nonprofit organization. It's an ethos that needs to change, which makes Chris and his talk of "citizen engineering" slightly radical in professional circles.

In another sense, however, the ideal of socially engaged professionalism that Chris advocates can also be seen as a throwback to an earlier era.

"There is a traditional professional code of ethics for the engineer," Chris notes. "It lists a number of basic obligations, including honesty, sticking to one's knowledge base, and so on. These are all important requirements, and most engineers do a good job of living up to them. But the code also says, right at the beginning, that the engineer's chief responsibility is to the health, safety, and welfare of the public at large. This is an idea that, I think, has been neglected in recent years, as engineers have lost sight of their broader social mandate in their concentration on doing a piece of work according to a client's requirements. Yet it was once actively practiced by most engineers, especially during what I think of as the heyday of engineering, from around 1900 to the 1960s. During that period, engineers had greater status than they do today, and they were more involved in the whole process of designing and developing major projects."

Since then a lot has changed. The educational requirements for engineers have expanded and advanced greatly. This is a good thing, of course, except that it means that engineers today tend to be technical specialists with a high concentration of math and science skills rather than generalists with a broad understanding of society.

Furthermore, economic and political influences have been pushing the project development process so that engineers are being reduced to technicians rather than creative problem solvers. We're producing a lot of what Chris Swan calls "cookbook engineers"—people who are skilled at creating projects that are like mass-produced, fixed commodities. They can follow the directions in a specifications guide—cement so many inches thick, reinforced with metal rods of the following sizes—but they aren't always skilled at finding creative ways to design a project so that it fits a unique situation, including the all-important social and political context.

Part of the problem, of course, is that social, political, and environmental benefits of a project may be hard to quantify—while engineers live and work in a world where everyone, from the corporate financial officer to the contractor on the job site, loves and relies on numbers. "This challenge," Chris says, "makes reform of engineering education even more important. We need engineers who are comfortable thinking in more than just technical terms, moving little by little toward a more holistic perspective.

"What we're trying to do," he explains, "is to revive the old, broader ideal of what engineering is about by creating citizen engineers. This ideal states that the engineer should have a seat at the table when the big decisions are being made—not just about how and exactly where to build a dam or a highway or a prison, but about whether it's needed in the first place. No engineer should be in the position of having to be a lone whistle-blower when a project is badly off course. Making the engineer an integral part of the team makes the profession 'sustainable' in the sense that it fully uses and enhances the value of the engineer's knowledge."

Food for Thought, Seeds for Action

• Do you practice an occupation that has an ethical code or a recognized set of professional standards? If so, when was the last time you looked at it? Simply reexamining the code of conduct you are supposed to be following may be an eye-opening exercise that suggests new approaches to your daily work.

• For many corporate employees, a company mission statement or code of values can serve a similar purpose as an occupational code. Do you and your fellow employees take your own company's mission statement to heart? If you're not familiar with it, read the famous story of how Johnson & Johnson handled the 1982 Tylenol poisoning scare (one version of the tale is available at http://iml.jou.ufl.edu/projects/Fall02/Susi/tylenol.htm). Employees of J&J protected and reassured the public, salvaged the Tylenol brand, and saved the company billions because they knew and practiced the J&J Credo.

• If your line of work doesn't already have a recognized code of conduct or ethical standards, consider writing one. It should embody your own ethical values and encapsulate how those values are expressed in the work you do. Share your effort with a couple of like-minded colleagues. It may stimulate some lively discussion about what you can do to incorporate social benefits into your daily work.

Most important, the ideal of citizen engineer is not just about being a kindly do-gooder (not that there's anything wrong with that!). It's about being *a better engineer.*

Interestingly enough, the profession has been moving toward a holistic perspective for some time, in response to client demand. For example, environmentally friendly design has become increasingly popular. To respond to this demand, today's engineers need to know a lot more about the environment than they once did, as well as the social and political systems that affect how we deal with environmental issues. Chris Swan likes to summarize this trend by referring to "The New KISS Principle"—not "Keep It Simple, Stupid," but "Knowledge +Innovation =Sustainable Systems."

"When educators start thinking this way, they realize how important it is *not* to squelch their students' creativity," Swan observes. "Unfortunately, this is something we used to do in engineering education. Engineers can help design the great next-generation solutions for our society's environmental problems—provided we encourage them to think along these lines."

This approach to training engineers is not yet universally accepted or practiced. Some say that these broader elements of the profession are things to be learned in practice, not in school. But Swan and those who share his perspective assert that if engineering educators *don't* discuss these considerations in school—and teach students through practical experience how to integrate them into their work—they will just be creating technocratic cubicle dwellers.

Thankfully, there are signs that the engineering profession is changing and beginning to catch up to Tufts in this regard. In November 2007, Bill Marcuson stepped down as president of the American Society of Civil Engineers. In his farewell address, he did something unusual. Rather than focusing on the high points of his year in office or recent triumphs for the organization, he focused on some notable failures:

In a period of just two years, there have been three catastrophic engineering failures: the breaches of the levees in
New Orleans, the ceiling collapse in one of Boston's Big
Dig tunnels, and most recently the catastrophic failure of
the I-35W bridge in Minneapolis. Collectively, these
tragic incidents threaten to undermine the public's trust
in civil engineers and perhaps even our standing as a profession.

Marcuson went on to say:

If we are to earn the public's trust, civil engineers are
going to have to pay attention to detail, focus on public
safety and welfare, and take ownership of the public's infrastructure and environment. Clearly, upholding our professional obligation to protect health, safety, and welfare
requires more than technical expertise. Do civil engineers
possess the knowledge, skills, and attitudes needed to
practice as professionals in today's world? Are we prepared
to lead the public to make the right decisions, and to understand the consequences of failing to do so? Are we willing to assume the personal and professional risk needed to
exert our professional judgment? This will not be "business as usual" but it must be done.

This is very much the vision to which Chris Swan and his colleagues are dedicated. And one very visible symbol of how they are
translating that vision into reality is the work of Tufts's chapter of
the national organization Engineers Without Borders (EWB).

Engineers Without Borders is a nonprofit organization created
in 2001 by Dr. Bernard Amadei, a professor of civil engineering at
the University of Colorado in Boulder. It has a two-way purpose:
to provide engineering help to developing countries, and to help

engineers from the developed world learn more about the needs, problems, challenges, and opportunities of working in the developing world.

The latter mission is especially important for today's students, as so much of the economic growth—and the building—of the next few decades will be taking place in the developing world. Learning how to deal with the conditions that engineers face in regions like South Asia, Latin America, sub-Saharan Africa, and the Middle East will be crucially important for the next generation of engineers.

EWB projects are designed to be "sustainable" in at least two senses of the word: environmentally sustainable in that they do not damage local environments or deplete natural resources, and socially sustainable in that they empower developing communities by enhancing local skills, involve host community contributions, and will be owned and operated without external assistance.

Above all, EWB is not about first-world experts parachuting in to a poor community, constructing a massive project like a reservoir or power plant, and then disappearing. It's about working with local people to identify their needs and create lasting solutions to problems together. Amadei calls it "engineering with soul."

Today there are more than 230 college chapters of EWB in the United States. The Tufts chapter was founded in 2005. Its first project, in Tibet, was headed by Doug Matson from the mechanical engineering department. Student participants were selected through a rather ruthless peer selection process: If you wanted to be involved, you had to be able to show *exactly* what skills you would bring to the project. (Just being a nice person who wanted to contribute was not enough.)

The problems the students had to tackle were many and diverse, beginning with logistics—it takes six months to get a visa to travel to Tibet! As a result, they developed valuable leadership and project-management skills of a kind no classroom exercise can teach. Much more work—and more challenging work—is involved than you'll experience in the usual "study abroad" program.

A typical EWB project is the one Tufts students worked on beginning in 2005 near the town of Tabacundo in Ecuador. The mission: to convert a large hacienda owned by a local agricultural organization known as the Fundacion Brethren y Unidas (FBU) into an environmentally friendly structure. The goal was to provide a green building that could be used as a model for other builders in Ecuador and as a tool for teaching resource-efficient construction practices to the environmental and community groups FBU regularly serves.

On its surface, this might sound like a fairly straightforward project. Green building techniques and equipment are widely known in the United States, and it might be possible to take standard, off-the-shelf products—solar panels, recycling containers, and the like—and simply install them at Hacienda Picalqui. But that's not what sustainable building is really about, and that's definitely not how EWB Tufts operates.

Instead, the Tufts team, including thirty undergraduate engineering students and adviser Chris Swan, worked closely with local people to design and implement the project. A smaller group of five, including students with several different major fields of study, made several visits to Ecuador, gradually building the knowledge and the local relationships needed to ensure that the project actually fit the needs, interests, resources, and desires of the community. They conducted surveys of the local people to learn about health issues, educational opportunities, and economic conditions. They tested water supplies for bacteria, made notes about the local diet, and analyzed various income sources, from paid labor to the sale of homegrown produce.

Why is it important for an engineering team to learn in such detail about local conditions? As Chris Swan explains, there are many reasons. "When one of my students designs a structure to be built in a third world country, I don't want them applying American standards and assumptions. If they say, 'This part of the recycling unit will be made from a sheet of PVC plastic,' I'm going to challenge them. Where will you get the plastic down in Ecuador? And if they say, 'Well, we can bring it down on the plane when we travel to the country,' I'm going to say, 'And what happens three years from now when the plastic breaks, and the local people have no way to replace it?'

"The whole point," Chris continues, "is for an engineer to understand what is and isn't sustainable in real-world terms. Eventually, my student is going to realize that he has to spend time talking with the people and figuring out what kinds of materials are available and affordable there. Maybe the PVC plastic will end up being replaced with tightly woven palm fronds, or layers of cloth, or corrugated tin. And then the Ecuadorans will have a unit that has a chance to last thirty years, not just three."

The Tufts EWB team made plans for several environmental enhancements to Hacienda Picalqui. These included a rainwater collection and filtration system (important because, as their surveys revealed, endemic diseases caused by parasites in contaminated water supplies posed a major recurring health risk); a passive solar water heating unit; a retrofitting of the structure to take advantage of natural lighting; and, perhaps most ambitious, the design and construction of a biogas unit.

Biogas is an especially interesting and useful energy technology, though one that's little known in the developed world. It uses decaying animal waste as the source of two useful products—methane gas, which can be used for cooking, and a liquid, nitrogen-rich fertilizer sometimes called biol. Since biogas technology can use wastes from almost any domesticated animals—cows, horses, pigs, goats, chickens—it can be implemented in most rural agricultural settings. Since such areas are usually off the national utility grid in most developing-world countries, biogas is particularly useful. And, of course, it is completely renewable and, when carefully implemented, nonpolluting.

All in all, it's a perfect example of the kinds of site-appropriate, sustainable development that EWB strives to create—a far cry from the massive, capital-intensive projects that development agencies used to emphasize (giant dams, river diversions, and the like) and that all too often fell into disrepair and disuse after just a few years, having provided few of the expected benefits to the local people.

Most important for Chris Swan the educator, the Ecuador biogas project provided a wonderful learning experience for his budding citizen engineers. Over the weeks they spent meeting with the people of Tabacundo and wrestling to turn their simple dream into a reality, they absorbed a whole series of lessons about what happens when engineering blueprints get tested against real-world conditions.

Chris's students learned that, in the developing world, building supplies usually can't be ordered from a glossy catalog. Instead, they may have to be scavenged from whatever local sources happen to be available. For lining the pit in which the wastes from the hacienda's pig stalls were collected, they supplemented a small purchased supply of concrete blocks with a batch of adobe blocks salvaged from a demolished latrine. To seal the connections between tubes used to funnel the methane gas, they fashioned rubber strips from discarded auto inner tubes obtained from a nearby gas station.

They learned how complicated it can be to organize the details of any complex project—especially in the developing world—and how crucial it is to communicate effectively with everyone involved, especially including the client (in this case, their Ecuadorian host, FBU). E-mail links between the United States and Latin America proved to be sporadic, and just a week before the students were due to arrive in Tabacundo, FBU concluded the project had been canceled and no one was coming. Panic ensued on both sides, and though the trip went on as planned, the students learned never to take for granted even so simple and obvious a thing as making sure your client knows how and where to reach you.

The students also learned how to cooperate with people of widely varying backgrounds. The five-person travel team included students majoring in civil, environmental, and mechanical engineering, as well as a physics major and a community health major. It took time for them to learn to speak one another's "languages," to say nothing of communicating with their Ecuadorian hosts.

Similarly unpredictable real-world lessons have been gleaned by Tufts EWB members from other international projects. While working on a project to improve water supplies in a gold-mining region of Ghana and thereby reduce the incidence of schistosomiasis (caused by parasitic flatworms), the Tufts team discovered that the local people regard bloody urine in boys—a sign of disease—as a positive sign of maturity, and had to develop on-the-spot educational programs to overcome this misunderstanding. While working to build three projects in Tibet (a solar cooker, a water treatment project, and a composting latrine), another Tufts team came down with altitude sickness, ran out of cash (because no one anticipated that credit cards would be unusable), and accidentally discovered the cross-cultural potential of Frisbee tossing as a way of making new friends.

On this same project, interdisciplinary cooperation nearly broke down over failures of communication between engineers and nonengineers. The engineers had handled pretrip technical planning on their own, leaving the nonengineers (who had focused on cultural and social issues) feeling trivialized and ignored when design decisions were discussed in-country. Lesson for the future: Involve *all* team members throughout the planning process, and develop clear definitions for individual roles so that the importance of everyone's contribution can be recognized.

Recently, Tufts launched Engineers *Within* Borders, a group that engages in service projects for communities located near the university. Pam Zelaya and Sofia Hart, teachers at the Forestdale School in Malden, Massachusetts, are eager to describe how Engineers Within Borders has helped them spark interest in science, math, and problem-solving skills among the third, fourth, and fifth graders in the dual-language classes they teach.

Over the past three years, Sarah Freeman, Nathan Ladd, Julia Keller, and other engineering students from Tufts have become part of Pam's and Sofia's classrooms. Projects they've conducted with the students include an experimental study of water filtration, using a simple system like one the EWB program built in El Salvador. Nathan taught Pam's students how to test various kinds of sand, soil, and clay as possible water filtration media—and in the process not only helped them understand how scientists develop hypotheses and conduct experiments to test them, but also educated them on how devastating the lack of a simple resource like clean drinking water can be for the health and economic status of poor people in the developing world. (Later, the students swapped letters with a class of their peers from El Salvador, a pen pal program that Nathan arranged.)

Another time, Nathan taught the students about wind power by having them fashion sailboats using various materials—Styrofoam trays, aluminum foil, wax paper, and more. Then they set up a virtual "ocean" with the boats suspended on strings and a big electric fan providing energy. With much excitement and hilarity, the students raced their creations to determine which boat used the fewest materials to travel farthest and fastest.

Pam still marvels at the impact these simple projects had on her fourth and fifth graders. "The engineers showed our kids that inventions come about because of human needs, and that the things they use every day—cars, TVs, even houses—are designed and built by real people, not just produced by some magical process in a factory somewhere. It's so different from having them read a science textbook or answer questions from a standardized test. These are experiences our kids will never forget."

Perhaps not coincidentally, after two years of working on a range of projects with a team of eight Tufts students, the students at Forestdale earned the highest scores on math and reading exams of any school in the Boston area—after having previously lagged in the same subjects. And if, one day, a few of Pam Zelaya's students end up pursuing careers in science or technology, they may recall their days with Nathan, Sarah, and their other mentors from Tufts as having been the first step in that journey.

In time, Engineers Within Borders plans to focus on more ambitious projects focused on Somerville, Massachusetts—another community close to the Tufts campus that has suffered economically as the northeastern industrial belt has gradually lost business and jobs. Left in the wake of these changes have been large-scale unemployment, aging infrastructure, and legacy pollution from now-shuttered mills and factories. Engineers Within Borders will work with local people to study the problems and begin mapping solutions. Of course, they will use engineering talent and techniques. But they will also enlist help from experts in public health, economics, education, social work, and many other fields.

The work being done by the young engineers from Tufts is impressive. And there is every indication that they will bring the same ideals of public engagement, civic responsibility, and social concern into their careers after graduation. The implications for society of having a large pool of civically active engineering talent speaking out on issues of the day from infrastructure and the environment to housing and economic development are potentially huge.

Chris Swan remarks:

Think about what happened when Hurricane Katrina devastated the Gulf Coast in 2005 and destroyed large portions of the city of New Orleans. A meteorologist can explain why the hurricane developed the way it did and why it made landfall when and where it did. A social scientist can analyze the effects of poverty on the people of New Orleans and explain why some people were more harmed by the disaster than others. A politician can explain why the government response was inadequate. And an engineer can explain how and why the levees were breached by the rising floodwaters. But the only way all these perspectives can come together to identify, analyze, and ultimately solve the problem is when each of these specialties is socially engaged, expressing its concerns vocally, and working closely with the others through active citizenship.

Civil engineers are civil servants. We're hired to build things for civil society—bridges, roads, tunnels, schools, airports. But we mustn't be subservient any longer, merely accepting the assignments we are given and carrying them out without questioning the underlying assumptions. We must take an ownership role in regard to the social infrastructure we help to create. And we must assume a peer-to-peer advisory role when projects are being planned and designed.

Of course, engineers aren't the only professionals who are redefining their work in the mold of citizen activism. The same spirit is spreading through many other occupational fields, generating waves of change that are beginning to transform those professions. Here are a few examples.

The famous organization Doctors Without Borders (Médecins Sans Frontières, or MSF)—the first of the "without borders" groups—delivers emergency aid to people affected by armed conflict, epidemics, natural or man-made disasters, or exclusion from health care in nearly sixty countries. Staffers at MSF include not only physicians but also nurses; experts in logistics, water, and sanitation; and many other kinds of nonmedical professionals.

Founded in 1971, MSF prides itself on both providing emergency medical assistance and bearing public witness to the plight of the people it assists. The organization's people testify before governments, the United Nations, other international bodies, the general public, and the media, speaking out against violations of international humanitarian law from Chechnya to Sudan and using their respected status as dedicated healers to call for help for the suffering. Through its Campaign for Access to Essential Medicines, MSF advocates for lower prices for drugs for diseases such as HIV/AIDS and malaria, stimulates research and development of new treatments, and works to overcome trade and other barriers to accessing treatments.

Thus, MSF isn't focused solely on alleviating present suffering, important as that mission is. It is also actively promoting social, economic, and political change in an effort to prevent needless suffering from occurring in the future.

But the heart of MSF's mission—and the source of its unique credibility in speaking on behalf of many of the world's most deprived peoples—is its humanitarian relief work. When disasters strike, MSF is often among the first organizations on the ground. For example, in the aftermath of 2008's Hurricane Ike and other devastating storms that ravaged Haiti—the poorest country in the Caribbean, already reeling from a global spike in food prices—MSF quickly established a mission in Port-au-Prince and launched a nationwide survey to assess the damages and define the needs.

MSF workers had to travel by donkey or on foot into remote

mountainous regions inaccessible by highway. They discovered that 45 to 50 percent of the population—including an estimated three hundred thousand children—were suffering from malnutrition, in most cases not because of a lack of calories but because of protein deficiencies. Within days, MSF began airlifting those in gravest danger to a makeshift clinic in Martissant, the nearest town. Some were too far gone to help, but others responded to a diet of enriched milk. "When we found them," recalled Belgian Max Cosci of MSF, "they were nearly ready to die. Now they are doing much better."

In the aftermath of the 2010 earthquake, the MSF clinic in Haiti is now providing emergency care as needed. In partnership with UNICEF, the UN World Food Program, and the U.S. Agency for International Development, MSF continues to survey the country so that plans for effective long-term aid, focused on restoring the productivity of local farmers, can be developed. And the Haiti mission is just a single example of the scores of similar programs being conducted by MSF at any given time around the world.

Modeled on MSF, MBAs Without Borders was founded in 2004 as an international nonprofit organization dedicated to applying business expertise to the challenges faced by developing countries. The group matches experienced business volunteers with local businesses and NGOs to create projects aimed at alleviating poverty, reducing hunger, building homes, preventing disease, and promoting economic empowerment. The first-world business experts provide training to management and staff in finance, accounting, strategy, marketing, human resources, and business development; assist in the creation and implementation of business plans; help develop fund-raising strategies; and manage projects in the field.

Today, the business experts serving MBAs Without Borders are drawn from more than four hundred MBA communities from around the world, including Australia, Canada, Europe, India, Mexico, South Africa, and the United States, and they partner on projects in countries ranging from Cambodia, Colombia, and Ghana, to India, Poland, and Vietnam.

The business experts at MBAs Without Borders are especially adept at developing sustainable solutions to problems of poverty, hunger, disease, and environmental degradation. Rather than soliciting charitable gifts of food or medicines, or orchestrating corporate donations of services (important as these may be in emergency situations), the organization and its partners strive to create self-supporting systems that enable poor people to lift themselves and their communities out of poverty. For example, in India, an MBAs partner organization works to enlarge the domestic market for handloom and handicraft products so home-based workers can better support their families; in Tanzania, another partner organizes an international travel fair that is working to expand tourism in southeast Africa; in Ecuador, still another partner is helping to develop the global market for organically grown dried fruits and herbs grown in the fertile foothills of the Andes.

One of the more ambitious programs supported by MBAs Without Borders is Solar Aid, an African-based company that provides clean, renewable energy to poor communities that are rarely connected to the national energy grid. Access to solar-generated electricity offers people in these remote villages enormous environmental and health benefits. (Simply eliminating the indoor pollution caused by smoke-producing kerosene lamps and cookstoves is expected to save thousands of lives every year.)

Solar power also makes it possible for poor Africans to participate more effectively and profitably in their local and regional economies. One volunteer working for Solar Aid in Zambia recently wrote in his blog:

Yesterday, in Chilimboyi, we attended the official inauguration of the new solar system—which involved plenty of speeches, a play with a solar power theme, and a bit of dancing. . . . The day culminated with the lights being turned on—which is what this is all about. The community of Chilimboyi now have clean renewable light. They also have the opportunity to generate an income by using the system to charge mobile phones and other devices. They've even started selling "pay as you go" phone credit, which means people no longer have to travel into the main town just to communicate.

Small-scale programs like these may appear less impressive, at first glance, than the massive infrastructure projects—hydroelectric dams, airports, highway systems—traditionally favored by international development funds. Yet those giant projects often fall prey to government and business corruption, lack of funds for maintenance, and failure to ensure that the benefits reach those in greatest need. By contrast, Solar Aid and the other programs supported by MBAs Without Borders bring hope, income, and economic improvement to one family, one village, one district at a time—often with more lasting results.

Nurses, too, are joining the movement toward professional civic engagement. There's no single umbrella organization like "Nurses Without Borders," but rather dozens of projects run by individual nurses or groups of nurses who are dedicated to tackling particular health-care issues.

For example, registered nurse Sally Mata is president of the Greater San Jose Chapter of the National Association of Hispanic Nurses (NAHN) and senior staff nurse and consultant at the Gardner Family Health Network, which serves low-income families and undocumented immigrants in San Jose. Inspired by the philosophy of legendary labor leader Cesar Chavez, Mata has dedicated her career to bringing health-care opportunities to poor Hispanic families. She has helped set up diabetes education programs for low-income families and undocumented migrant workers, has worked in village clinics in Mexico, has helped neighborhood residents organize to save hospital services in low-income neighborhoods, and has helped create scholarship programs and educational support for Latino nurses.

As director of student health services for Children's Hospital/Austin Independent School District, nurse Judy Frederick became concerned about the low immunization rates in Texas, among the country's worst. Supported by administrators at Children's Hospital, she organized a community collaboration of all who had an interest in childhood immunizations—public and private health-care providers, firefighters, school officials, state health department officials, and EMS personnel. She became the group's facilitator.

When she discovered that immunization services in the area were fractured and uncoordinated, Frederick and her team began looking at ways to make immunization more accessible. Firefighters and emergency service workers started offering clinics. The Children's Hospital pediatric van, which travels from school to school, now offers immunization. Immunization rates in the district are now 95 percent, and many areas have 100 percent compliance, Frederick says.

Teachers, too, are getting into the act. As we mentioned in Chapter 1, Teach for America recruits some of the nation's brightest college graduates to teach challenging students in inner-city, rural, and other disadvantaged schools. As a program of short-term national service for young people, Teach for America is comparable to the Peace Corps, Americorps, and other similar organizations. But there is evidence that it is also creating the nucleus of a large group of teaching professionals committed to social activism in the long term.

There are currently over twelve thousand Teach for America alumni, with thousands more joining their ranks every year. Large percentages of these alumni remain involved in education, and most are active supporters of Teach for America's broader mission to reform the nation's schools and improve educational quality and equity for all. Thousands are still teaching, and many have won national, state, and district Teacher of the Year awards and other honors. More impressive, 250 alumni are working as principals in low-income schools, and others have founded and led education reform organizations such as KIPP, which is building a network of high-performing schools serving urban and rural areas, and The New Teacher Project, which is effecting systemic change in the way new teachers are brought into the profession.

The call to practice our occupations in a way that is socially beneficial isn't restricted to members of the traditional professions, like medicine or education. I believe it applies to everyone, in virtually every line of work. It's certainly an important reality for people like me who work in the travel-related industries.

By many measures, including annual revenues and employment base, travel and tourism is already the world's largest industry. We employ millions of people in both the developed and developing worlds, and our activities have an enormous impact, not only economically but also environmentally, socially, and even politically. The decisions we make today will affect the future of the world in countless ways. How cruise lines choose to operate will help determine the fate of fragile ecosystems like the Great Barrier Reef and the Galapagos Islands; tour company policies will impact the share of travel dollars that go to support local entrepreneurs in Africa and Asia as opposed to large U.S. or European companies; the design choices made by golf course operators, theme park companies, and resort developers in the American Southwest will affect the looming crises over water availability in that increasingly parched corner of the continent.

For this reason, it's gratifying to see that a growing number of people in our industry are looking for ways to embody their social and personal ideals in their work. Engaged professionals in travel and tourism are already beginning to make a positive difference in our industry and in the world. We try hard to practice these principles at Loews Hotel—for example, through our Good Neighbor Policy. The policy requires every Loews hotel to participate in local projects based on the needs and opportunities available in that specific community, from Tucson to New Orleans, Nashville to Washington, Philadelphia to Santa Monica (more about this later).

Of course, Loews is not the only hospitality company that operates in the spirit of enlightened citizenship. Here are a couple of sterling examples from other companies whose leaders can proudly claim the title of "citizen hotelier":

• Ho Kwon Ping, a Singaporean businessman who once worked as a journalist and was actually jailed for his politically controversial writings, has devoted his career as a hotelier to making the luxurious Banyan Tree resorts among the most environmentally and socially responsible in the world. A portion of company revenues is dedicated to the Green Imperative program, which restores coral reefs and other sensitive ecosystems, and Banyan Tree provides free schooling for the children of employees as well as free computer and language classes for local residents, even those who are not employed by the company.

• Sam Raphael, a former student activist, founded Jungle Bay Resort and Spa on the Caribbean island of Dominica. Like many hoteliers, he hires as many local people as possible to staff his resort (fifty-five of the company's fifty-nine employees, including most of the management, are from Dominica). More significantly, he and his employees donate significant time and money to local development through the Jungle Bay Community Fund, which, among other initiatives, provides loans of up to $12,000 to local businesspeople and farmers so they can become profit-making suppliers to the resort.

• Carla Beira, a Brazilian hospitality manager who has worked in sales for Accor, the French company that owns Sofitel, Novotel, and other hotel chains, has created a number of social programs by which Accor improves the lives of people in the communities where the company operates. For example, Beira launched a job-training program that prepares fifty underprivileged Brazilian teenagers every year for careers in the hotel business.

Each of these hospitality professionals—like many others—is demonstrating in concrete ways what it means to practice an occupation in ways that engage *the whole person*—not just the side that focuses on growth, efficiency, and profits, but also the side that cares about people, communities, and the environment.

Of course, taking up the challenge of becoming an engaged professional doesn't exempt you from the usual demands of business. Whether we're talking about engineering, medicine, teaching, hospitality, or any other occupation, there's still no substitute for world-class technical expertise and practical knowledge. The professionals of the future must be educated, tested, licensed, and monitored with greater rigor than ever before. But at the same time, they must also expand their focus beyond mere technical expertise.

And make no mistake—although the social benefits these professionals provide are part of their daily work, they are just as much a reflection of active citizenship as political organizing, charitable giving, or community activities. As Peter Levine puts it in his book *The Future of Democracy,* "Recognizing the civic potential of *paid* employment prevents us from equating civic engagement with volunteering, which narrows and even trivialized it. Civic engagement is 'public work' . . . a serious business that ought to occur in families, workplaces, professions, and firms, not only in voluntary associations."

To serve the enormous needs of our complex world, professionals in every field must learn to be engaged citizens, combining their specialized knowledge with a broad awareness of the social, economic, and political implications of their work. Educators like Chris Swan and his counterparts in many other fields are showing the way.

Food for Thought, Seeds for Action

• Does your occupation have an action organization comparable to Engineers Without Borders or Teach for America? Do some research to determine whether or not such a group already exists. If it does, contact the staff to find out how you can get involved in supporting their work. If not, check with the professional or business association that represents the industry in which you work. (Practically every industry has one or more such organizations.) Ask about social, philanthropic, and charitable programs they sponsor or support.

• If you work in a field that doesn't have an ongoing program for harnessing professional skills for social goals, consider how you might launch such a program. Think about the work and business talents you've developed in your career. Are there worthy causes that could benefit from the application of these talents? Are there charities, nongovernmental organizations (NGOs), or not-for-profit associations that could be strengthened by an infusion of energy and ideas from professional people like you? Think creatively about opportunities for service that you would find personally rewarding.

• Where are the young people who will be working in your field ten and twenty years from today currently being trained? Does their training include any discussion of or exposure to social and ethical concerns? Are they learning about how to apply their talents to socially worthwhile goals? If not, consider becoming involved in working with young people in your industry as a trainer, teacher, group leader, or mentor.

A City of Citizens

Mobilizing Eight Million
New Yorkers Around
Civic Engagement

When most Americans think about citizen engagement and people helping one another, my hometown of New York City is probably not the first place that comes to mind. For the average outsider or tourist, New York is a city of formidable size and complexity whose residents are famous for their tough-as-nails, no-time-to-waste, get-outta-my-way demeanor.

But as any *real* New Yorker will tell you, our hometown is really a city of neighborhoods—and of neighbors. As *New Yorker* writer E. B. White explained in his 1949 classic, *Here Is New York*:

> The oft-quoted thumbnail sketch of New York is, of course: "It's a wonderful place, but I'd hate to live there." I have an idea that people from villages and small towns, people accustomed to the convenience and the friendliness of neighborhood over-the-fence living, are unaware that life in New York follows the neighborhood pattern. The city is literally a composite of tens of thousands of tiny neighborhood units. . . . Each neighborhood is virtually self-sufficient. Usually it is no more than two or three

blocks long and a couple of blocks wide. Each area is a city within a city within a city. Thus, no matter where you live in New York, you will find within a block or two a grocery store, a barbershop, a newsstand and shoeshine shack, an ice-coal-and-wood cellar (where you write your order on a pad outside as you walk by), a dry cleaner, a laundry, a delicatessen. . . . Every block or two, in most residential sections of New York, is a little main street.

Sixty years later, White's loving portrait of a "small town" New York still rings true (well, except for the part about the "ice-coal-and-wood cellar").

As a city of neighbors who inhabit countless small towns-within-a-town, New York is really *not* the fabled hard-boiled Gotham of movies and TV shows, filled with wise guys eager to exploit the naive or the helpless. In fact, it's a city with a rich tradition of civic and social engagement. Many of the New Yorkers whose names resonate in local lore are best known for their contributions to the lives of their fellow citizens.

The list includes New York natives like Dorothy Day (the feisty Catholic labor leader, peace activist, and defender of the common man and woman), Elizabeth Ann Seton (the Manhattan-born nun who devoted her life to educating the children of the poor and became America's first native-born saint), Fiorello LaGuardia (the legendary reformer who led New York through the darkest days of the Depression and World War Two), Eleanor Roosevelt (the First Lady who won fame in her own right as a tireless advocate for racial equality, women's rights, and decent living conditions for all), and Jane Jacobs (the self-taught expert on city planning and urban renewal who faced down the powerful Robert Moses in her battles to defend traditional neighborhoods against the developer's bulldozer).

Countless ordinary New Yorkers exemplify the same spirit. As one small example, consider Partnerships for Parks. It's a program that engages over more than fifty thousand New Yorkers who work as volunteers to help maintain, protect, and beautify the city's neighborhood parks and make them accessible to all. When urban historians write about New York's world-famous Central Park as one of the magnificent achievements of civic development, they rightly credit its great designer, Frederick Law Olmstead, as well as the many mayors and city councils that have defended and supported it for more than a century. But without the thousands of engaged citizens who work to clear hiking trails, prune shrubbery, plant gardens, repair playground equipment, and paint park benches, the beauty and usefulness of Central Park, as well as that of hundreds of other urban oases that grace our city, would be only a shadow of themselves.

And much the same applies to the many other civic treasures that enrich the lives of millions of New Yorkers as well as countless visitors—our fabled museums, concert halls, libraries, cathedrals, historic sites and monuments, and other cultural attractions. Virtually all are dependent on the work of dedicated citizens who serve as maintenance staff, tour guides, and public information providers as well as in many other roles. In this sense, the "big New York" that the tourist admires is really just the "little New York" of caring, generous neighbors writ large. And when you add to the picture the countless other nonprofit institutions of New York that most tourists never see—the hospitals and clinics; the schools, colleges, and universities; the community centers, adult-education programs, employment offices, legal aid providers, social work centers, and on and on—the amount of unpaid effort inspired simply by devotion to service becomes truly mind-boggling.

So keeping a city like ours running and caring for all its people requires a vast amount of volunteer effort. According to a recent survey, over half of New Yorkers aged fifteen or older participated in formal volunteerism sometime during the past year, donating an average of thirty-five hours of their time per person. What's more, 74 percent of those reported maintaining or increasing their volunteer time this year as compared with past years. Thousands devote their time to helping people in need beyond the city limits. Volunteers with New York City Says Thank You, a foundation launched by Jeff Parness to commemorate the support enjoyed by the city after 9/11, have traveled the country helping victims of floods, fires, and tornados from New Orleans to California.

Today New York enjoys the leadership example of Michael Bloomberg, who made community service a hallmark of Bloomberg L.P., the media and financial services corporation he founded; who serves as the mayor of New York for a salary of one dollar a year; and who is a major philanthropist in his own right—the seventh-largest individual donor to charitable causes in the United States (according to the *Chronicle of Philanthropy*).

Mayor Bloomberg has always sought ways to expand the role of active citizenship in the life of New York. The election of Barack Obama as president on a platform emphasizing active citizenship provided Bloomberg with an ideal opportunity to redouble his efforts. So in his January 2009 State of the City address, Mike Bloomberg announced his intention to try to make New York the first city to respond to President Obama's call for national service. He gave First Deputy Mayor Patricia E. Harris the responsibility for developing a plan to make this happen. (The remarkable Patti Harris deserves a much fuller profile than I have space to offer here. The former director of philanthropy for Bloomberg L.P. and Mayor Bloomberg's closest, most trusted adviser, she is famous among New Yorkers for her tenacity, intelligence, attention to detail, and fierce devotion both to the city and its mayor. Assigning this project to Patti Harris was Mike Bloomberg's way of sending a message to everyone in city hall: "This project is our top priority. It *will* get done—and done well.")

The result was NYC Service, an unprecedented initiative officially launched in April 2009, designed to make service an integral part of life for all the citizens of New York. It's a challenging goal, especially in a time of economic turmoil and personal hardship for many.

It's also a first in our nation's history. Although the states and especially the federal government have long promoted service programs, from Roosevelt's Civilian Conservation Corps and Kennedy's Peace Corps to Clinton's AmeriCorps, no city has taken the lead in adopting citizen service as a driving theme of governance or a central focus of civic life—until now.

The shaping of NYC Service began with an unprecedented series of meetings involving hundreds of New York's most important nonprofit organizations. Held under the auspices of Mayor Bloomberg's city hall, these meetings included arts and cultural organizations, environmental groups, legal services organizations, senior citizens groups, job training providers, youth and family organizations, and many other kinds of nongovernmental organizations (NGOs), as well as representatives from public schools whose students were involved in service efforts. The conferences were supplemented by focus groups, interviews, and surveys.

In the end, advice, information, and ideas were provided by an amazing array of organizations, from the American Red Cross in Greater New York and the Metropolitan Museum of Art to Harlem Children's Zone and the New York City Food Bank; from the Fresh Air Fund and Teach for America to the Salvation Army and the Robin Hood Foundation; from the Jewish Community Center in Manhattan and the Arab-American Family Support Center to Esperanza Del Barrio and Episcopal Social Services. Never before had so diverse and extensive an array of representatives of New York's "third sector" (i.e., organizations that belong to neither the business nor government sectors) come together to share their ideas and their visions.

The leaders of these groups discussed their problems, challenges, obstacles, and opportunities. They made up wish lists of the kind of projects they would tackle if they had the resources, and they identified a number of ways that city government could help them—as well as some ways it was hampering their efforts. City officials used all of this input in shaping a plan for mobilizing the city behind active citizenship.

The next step in the process involved enlisting the help of every agency of city government. This, too, was unprecedented. For the first time in history, the mayor's office let it be known that citizen service was to be treated as a valuable asset in pursuing the goals of city government—and that every agency was expected to develop creative ideas for mobilizing this asset and using it productively.

Jim Anderson, the communication director of the Bloomberg administration who helped develop the NYC Service program, explains the idea this way:

> There's so much important work that government seeks to do where the resources of government just don't reach far enough. Sometimes it's a matter of money, especially in these tough economic times. Sometimes it's a matter of simple practicality, where the delivery of on-the-ground services to individual New Yorkers is just too complex or detailed for a government agency to handle. In many cases, citizen service can make the difference, bridging the gap between what government can do and what needs to be done.

An example that Jim likes to cite is the Flu Fighters program. Spearheaded by New York's Department of Health and Mental Hygiene, Flu Fighters is an effort designed to encourage New

Yorkers to get the flu vaccine. The program particularly targets elderly people, who are most susceptible to serious complications
(like pneumonia) that can result from the flu. The city has access
to doses of vaccine. It also has a great public-relations capability
for educating New Yorkers about the benefits of the vaccine, the
realities behind the myths about vaccination, and the dangers of
flu. (In 2006, influenza and pneumonia combined were the third-
leading cause of death in New York City.)

But what city government *doesn't* have is the ability to reach New
Yorkers, especially seniors, on a one-to-one basis. That's where Flu
Fighters comes in. At the suggestion of the Department of Health,
Flu Fighters will recruit thousands of New Yorkers to bring the vaccine message to their friends and neighbors. Armed with information
kits, these "volunteer educators" will perform acts as simple, and
vital, as calling an elderly acquaintance to say, "Have you had your flu
shot yet? If not, come along with me to the clinic—I'm driving a
couple of your friends from the senior center and we'd love to have
you join us." Flu Fighters will also recruit thousands of health-care professionals to administer the shots, thereby completing the circle.

It's a simple but vivid example of how the power of city government, strategically targeted, can leverage and expand the effectiveness of caring citizens and have a measurable impact on a
major civic problem—in this case, the danger of a devastating flu
epidemic. NYC Service will be an umbrella program to help create
and support dozens of citizen-power initiatives like Flu Fighters,
each of which is designed to multiply the helping power of government far beyond what government alone could do.

New York is the first major city in the United States to have an
official dedicated to improving the effectiveness of service initiatives. She is Diahann Billings-Burford, New York City's chief service officer and the de facto CEO of NYC Service.

Billings-Burford came to city government from City Year, one
of the country's most effective and innovative private-sector service

programs. Founded by Alan Khazei, City Year recruits diverse teams of young people for a year of full-time service in communities around the nation, where they tutor and mentor students, improve public spaces, and organize after-school programs and vacation camps for kids.

Unsurprisingly, one of the key components of NYC Service—Civic Corps—is modeled in part on City Year. Like City Year, Civic Corps channels citizen energies into organizations—from non-profits to public agencies—that have specific needs these people can help meet. And like City Year, it supports their efforts with training and material assistance in the form of a stipend. But make no mistake, the members of NYC Civic Corps are driven by the urge to serve, not the desire for a cushy sinecure. As a *Daily News* story put it, "The demands are high and the pay is low. Participants will receive a $1,129 monthly stipend as well as MetroCards to help them travel around the city."

These modest rewards haven't discouraged people from wanting to participate. The inaugural Civic Corps class (2008–2009) includes 193 members who are working in some fifty-seven different civic organizations and government agencies.

NYC Civic Corps differs from City Year in two important ways. One is the diversity of the volunteers. City Year is a youth program that involves young people between seventeen and twenty-four years of age. By contrast, the first class of Civic Corps recruits includes people from twenty-one to seventy years old. Almost 90 percent of the volunteers were born in the United States, but the rest hail from eighteen countries, including China, Colombia, India, Italy, Myanmar, Poland, Togo, and Ukraine. Twenty-four American states outside of New York are also represented. The Big Apple's traditional allure to people from around the country and the world is clearly still operative, with the appeal of civic service now added to the city's other well-known attractions.

The other difference is the diversity of the social challenges

Civic Corps is tackling. City Year is focused almost entirely on ed-ucation. Civic Corps, by contrast, is sending its citizen activists into organizations of many kinds, including Catholic Charities, the New York Food Bank, Girls Incorporated, the NYC Department for the Aging, Planned Parenthood, the United Way, the YWCA, and many more.

It's one thing to infuse the energy of new, full-time support staff into civic organizations; it's another to make sure that energy is used effectively. All too often, agencies that are unprepared to manage volunteers end up wasting their talents on busywork. To make sure this doesn't happen with the Civic Corps members, NYC Service uses experts from the Gap Foundation to provide leadership training to all of the participating organizations. These sessions will take place quarterly for the first year of Civic Corps and are designed to ensure that the time, energy, and abilities of the recruits will be used intelligently.

By the way, the Gap Foundation—created in 1977 by Gap, In-corporated, the international apparel company—is offering this service to the city and its nonprofit community on a completely pro bono basis—one of many examples of business organizations that are willingly stepping to the plate in response to Mayor Bloomberg's call for citywide support for his service program.

But Civic Corps is only one piece of the NYC Service story. Several other components are equally important. Each is designed to have a multiplier effect in promoting civic engagement by New Yorkers as well as concrete benefits to all the city's people.

One thread of NYC Service is about removing barriers to service—obstacles that the hundreds of NGOs surveyed by Deputy Mayor Patti Harris's team cited as making it more difficult for New Yorkers to help one another. Some of these barriers are relatively simple, but others are more complicated, requiring a so-phisticated response by government.

Consider, for example, the problem of screening would-be

volunteers. As you can imagine, many organizations, especially those that serve young people, have stringent policies in place to prevent inappropriate or risky individuals from becoming part of their staff—persons convicted of sexual misconduct, for example. These procedures are not only required for obvious public-relations reasons but also for reasons related to legal liability and insurance coverage.

But the screening procedures are time-consuming and expensive. They involve background checks, searches of police records, an FBI review of federal databases, and other complex processes. And since the nonprofit world is highly decentralized and fragmented—a source of its dynamism and creativity, but also a cause of inefficiency—there is no single standard or system in place to simplify the process and minimize the drain on resources. Thus, the civic-minded individual who applies to work, say, for Big Brothers in January and then for Meals on Wheels in May will need to be screened both times, probably by different security companies (since various NGOs hire various contractors to supply these services) and probably at a cost of $100 or $125 a pop. It's a waste of money, time, and energy, which discourages both nonprofits from making the fullest possible use of such services and citizens themselves from stepping forward to offer their time.

NYC Service is working to reform this dysfunctional system. Working with nonprofits that have struggled to manage the problem, the city is developing a system that will provide one-size-fits-all screenings for every NGO. An individual who goes through the system once will be automatically tracked for future changes in his or her status, with standardized data available to any nonprofit group that needs it. Big Brothers will be able to buy screenings at a reduced bulk rate, and when the same person applies to work for a second or a third organization, the cost will be minimal, since an accurate, up-to-date file already exists.

It will take time for NYC Service to work out all the details for this program. The goal is to have a more efficient, cost-effective system in place sometime during 2010. Once it is up and running, its potential impact could be nationwide, especially if legislation supporting a national volunteer screening system now being proposed by New York's senator Charles Schumer is passed.

Other ways in which the city is hoping to make civic engagement easier and more cost-effective include creating a new website (www.nyc.gov/service) that enables citizens to find service opportunities that match their interests in their own neighborhoods; making information about volunteering available via the city's 311 hotline; and partnering with local colleges and universities to expand and support existing service programs that are already helping to mobilize the city's six hundred thousand higher-education students in response to vital social needs.

As we've seen, New York is already one of the nation's most civic-minded cities. With these initiatives, NYC Service is simply putting the power of city government to work to make it even easier and more attractive for citizens to do what they already like doing—offering their time and talent to help one another.

•   •   •

However, NYC Service is also getting involved on a more granular level, supporting specific service initiatives aimed at helping the city and its people achieve important civic goals within six targeted areas of need.

The Flu Fighters program we described before is an example of one initiative within the health arena. Others include:

• Shape Up—a program developed jointly by the Health Department and the Parks Department that will use volunteers to expand the number and variety of fitness classes and activities available in city parks, community centers, and other venues.

• Walking School Bus—a program originally proposed by the city's Health Department and now being developed as a pilot program in conjunction with the Department of Education, in which school kids accompanied by parent volunteers will walk to school rather than taking the bus. The goal: to combat childhood obesity, one of the most rapidly growing health problems in the United States and around the world. The program is part of a full-fledged movement, complete with "International Walk to School Day," celebrated most recently on October 7, 2009. Schools around the United States and as far afield as Canada, Italy, and Australia have already launched Walking School Bus initiatives. Now New York will join the list.

• Blood Drive—a cooperative venture with the New York Blood Center to attract and use volunteers to increase the amount of blood that is donated for use in hospitals and clinics, thereby saving hundreds or even thousands of lives in the years to come.

Beyond health, the other five areas of "urgent need" being targeted by the NYC Service team include:

• *Strengthening Neighborhoods,* which includes initiatives like Block Beautification (which will help twelve local groups mount programs to transform public spaces in their communities); It's My Park Day (an annual event at which thousands of volunteers spruce up local parks, plant greenery, and host fun park-centered events for the community); and Show and Tell (through which the city's Department of Cultural Affairs will arrange to have volunteers escort young people and families to shows and concerts they otherwise couldn't attend).

• *Education,* including a Middle School Mentors initiative (created by the Education Department in partnership with Big Brothers Big Sisters of New York, Mentoring USA, and other established mentorship organizations), and Serve Our Schools (which will work with an array of nonprofits to increase the number of volunteers helping to improve city schools, with a special focus on attracting multilingual volunteers to help English students hone their language skills).

- *Environment,* including MillionTreesNYC (which aims to plant a million new trees in the streets and parks of New York by 2017, and by mid-2009 had already surpassed the 175,000 mark); the Rooftop Cooling Program (under which Mayor Bloomberg himself has already painted his roof white, a simple "green" strategy that can reduce energy costs by as much as 10 percent); and the Carbon Footprint Reduction Online Toolkit (which will help New Yorkers understand the steps they can take to support the city's goal of reducing greenhouse gas emissions by 30 percent by 2030).

- *Emergency Preparedness,* including the Ready Schools Campaign (which will organize information kits and school assemblies to educate young New Yorkers about what they and their families can do to be prepared in case of a citywide emergency), and an initiative to expand CPR Training. (In 2008, the New York Fire Department trained around seven thousand people to be CPR instructors; in 2009, NYC Service hopes to work with the Fire Department to help them increase that number to at least twelve thousand, with the cascading effect of producing at least forty-five thousand citizens newly trained in lifesaving CPR techniques.)

Perhaps the most interesting area of activity being targeted by NYC Service is Helping Neighbors in Need, launched during the deep recession of 2009. Millions of families are suffering economic distress, which in turn leads to hardship in every area of life. The initiatives being supported under the Neighbors in Need rubric include some of the most important and creative ones of the entire program.

For example, Language Services is an initiative that aims to provide assistance especially to New York's vast and varied immigrant community. Run out of the Mayor's Office of Operations, the goal is to provide training and certification to people who are willing to serve as translators for fellow New Yorkers dealing with a business, a government agency, or a school official.

Language barriers post a little-noticed but daunting life challenge for many city residents. Fully 36 percent of New York's population is foreign-born, and in some of our most vibrant and interesting neighborhoods, like Flushing, Sunset Park, and Corona, native-born Americans are a distinct minority. New York boasts more Asian Indians than any other U.S. city, more Bangladeshis than any other city in North America, and more Chinese than any city outside Asia. Four of the city's five boroughs are ranked among the twenty most ethnically diverse counties in the United States, with Queens coming in at number one.

Many of these newcomers to New York are still working on learning English; some may have pretty good English skills but lack the special vocabulary and sophisticated syntax needed to deal with, for example, a consultation with a doctor in a clinic, a complicated application form at a city office, or a discussion with a school principal about a child's test results.

Like the Flu Fighters dilemma, it's a classic problem of resources: There's no way a city administration can afford to provide skilled, knowledgeable translators for all of the tongues spoken by New Yorkers—170 different languages, according to a 2005 study. So in many cases, people lacking English skills go without the services they are entitled to, or must rely on children or friends to provide unskilled, perhaps inaccurate translation help. Yet the citizenry itself contains thousands of individuals who have the necessary skills, including the dual-language capabilities and the cultural sensitivity required. Many are from the city's immigrant communities themselves and would be happy to give of their time and talent to help their fellow immigrants. It's actually a great opportunity for service, and a vivid example of how people who may think they have "nothing special" to offer other citizens actually possess a vital skill that many New Yorkers badly need.

Unfortunately, thousands of people who could provide translation help simply lack the opportunity, the training, and the certification needed. The Language Services initiative is working with a number of city agencies on developing programs to bridge this gap and make the city a more friendly place for many of its newest residents.

The Financial Empowerment initiative is another program that enables ordinary citizens to provide powerful assistance to their fellow New Yorkers. The city's Department of Consumer Affairs has long been offering financial workshops for members of the general public who need to know more about the everyday challenges of managing their money. The topics covered run the gamut from balancing your checkbook and creating a family budget to dealing with creditors and responding appropriately to a threat of foreclosure on your home mortgage.

In tough economic times like today, workshops like these are more important than ever. Under the NYC Service program, Consumer Affairs will be getting help in recruiting, training, and deploying more volunteers to conduct these workshops and provide one-on-one counseling in neighborhoods all around the city. As a result, thousands of New Yorkers will become smarter shoppers, savers, spenders, and investors of their money—and some may even save their homes, salvage their retirements, or restore broken credit ratings in the process.

Telephone Reassurance targets a different population—elderly New Yorkers—through a simple program. Several groups already use volunteers as contact points for seniors who may feel isolated and vulnerable living alone in houses or apartments around the city. These volunteers make check-in calls to ensure that seniors hear a friendly voice at least once a week and to identify people who may be suffering health or other problems. NYC Service will be working to expand the pool of volunteers in this program and thereby the number of seniors who benefit from it.

Finally, Time Banking helps older New Yorkers in a different way—by providing them with a system for supporting themselves and one another. The NYC Department for the Aging plans to create a network of local community Time Banks that will let seniors swap services based on hours contributed. Thus, an elderly person who is spry and mobile might offer to donate hours going grocery shopping, doing laundry, or providing other physical services; another who is more limited might spend time reading aloud to someone with impaired vision; and a third who has special skills to offer might volunteer to provide music lessons or to help a fellow senior fill out her tax returns.

Do forty initiatives in six targeted areas of need add up to an especially ambitious program for the city? It depends on the lens through which you view it. With a little imagination, it would be easy to conjure up literally hundreds of worthwhile initiatives to improve life in New York that would be deserving of city support. But such an all-embracing approach would lead to scattershot efforts, diffuse attention, and likely minimal results. By focusing on six specific areas and forty carefully chosen initiatives, Billings-Burford and her team hope to demonstrate that significant impact can be created when the city puts its muscle behind citizen activists and the NGOs that recruit and organize them. If the forty initiatives active today work well, and if resources are available, perhaps the list will be expanded to sixty or more in the months and years to come. It seems safe to say that there will surely be no shortage of needs.

The role of city hall in supporting these service initiatives is quite varied. Rather than the kind of one-size-fits-all approach that too often gives "government bureaucracy" a bad name, NYC Service is thoughtfully tailoring its involvement based on the nature of the challenges, the state of play on the ground, and the resources and preferences of local communities.

The Middle School Mentors program is a good example of this. The middle-school grades have long been recognized by educators as crucial to the long-term success of students. Youngsters who successfully navigate these intermediary years end up with a good chance of graduating from high school and perhaps pursuing higher education, while those who become alienated and disengaged during middle school are likely to join the ranks of dropouts and, often, the unemployed. To tackle this challenge, New York Schools chancellor Joel Klein has identified the fifty "highest-need" middle schools in the city—those with the largest percentage of at-risk kids who could benefit from mentorship.

Now the principals of those fifty schools are each being asked to design a mentoring program tailored to local needs. Some are planning to continue and expand an existing mentor program. For example, they may choose to sign on with You Got Game, an organization that sends former college and pro athletes to work with middle-school kids who love sports, helping them to understand the importance of a college education for those who want to pursue athletic careers. Others may pair up with Mentor in the USA, another organization with a proven program.

Still other schools will create their own programs, targeting the kinds of students they perceive as most in need with the kinds of services they believe will be helpful. In one school, it may be sixth graders who need help in making the adjustment from elementary school to middle school; in the next, it may be eighth graders who need mentoring as they prepare for the leap to high school; in another, it may be a relatively small number of students who are struggling academically and need encouragement and inspiration to help them pass their courses; and in yet another, it may be exceptionally talented students who are bored with the normal curriculum and tempted to disengage from classes they don't feel challenged by. Each school will make the call as to where to place the focus.

Undoubtedly the results will vary from school to school. Some programs will prove to be extremely effective in reducing the dropout rate and promoting student success, other less so. That's part of the point. The entire process being driven by NYC Service is largely about experimentation and learning. Continual monitoring of progress, adjustments of plans, and sharing of lessons learned will be crucial to the program. Over time, Diahann and her team expect the cream to rise to the top. "Best practices" for service initiatives, not just in school mentoring but in health-care outreach, legal services, environmental improvement, and every other area, will gradually emerge. And the insights gained will enable the next generation of service initiatives, a year or two down the road, to be even more powerful.

In other cases, NYC Service is supporting programs that are already working very well and merely need specific kinds of help to expand their reach. For example, the CPR training kits used by the Fire Department are costly; under NYC Service, funding to help pay for them will be provided.

As you can probably tell, a major part of the mandate for Diahann Billings-Burford and her team will be evaluating and measuring the success of the city's service initiatives. That's not surprising, given the business background of the mayor who is behind NYC Service. "I work for Michael Bloomberg," Billings-Burford observes with a smile. And she continues:

> That means there's no such thing as not having data, counting and processing results, and then using that information to guide future efforts. In fact, that's one of the main reasons we have a chief service officer in this city. Volunteerism is a good thing, but this is about much more than just encouraging volunteerism. It's about impact. And we're not going to be satisfied until we can show that we're having a real impact on some of the city's most difficult

and important problems. I can't imagine that we would continue supporting any organization that we don't find, objectively, to be effective.

The evaluation process will take place on several fronts. The TCC Group, a respected consulting firm with nearly thirty years of experience in working with nonprofit organizations to improve their efficiency, strategic focus, and results orientation, has been engaged to evaluate Civic Corps and its impact on New York's nonprofit world. At the same time, the Mayor's Office of Operations is working to establish its own measurement system, including detailed metrics for each service initiative, and will publish reports twice a year presenting and explaining the results. Thus, an initiative like Flu Fighters will be evaluated according to three objective metrics: the number of volunteer educators recruited; the number of volunteer inoculators recruited; and the number of seniors receiving flu shots.

Six staff members at city hall will work to monitor and oversee the work of the Civic Corps volunteers, while three "portfolio managers" will track the forty service initiatives focused on the city's urgent needs. Their job is clear: not to create a new layer of bureaucracy or to set up arbitrary hoops for NGOs to jump through, but rather to ensure accountability, high standards, and measurable impact in return for the taxpayers' investment in citizen service.

The civic activism movement will thrive and spread only as long as it earns the respect and support of the citizenry through meaningful results. Under the guidance of a businessman-politician who believes in the power of a disciplined, fact-based system of measurement to improve any organization's performance, NYC Service is striving to make sure that New York's service community produces those kinds of results every time.

•   •   •

Although NYC Service is still in its infancy, communities around the country are already looking to New York as an example of what can be done on the citizen service front. They are coming to our city to learn from our program as well as sharing their own innovative ideas with New Yorkers and with one another.

On September 10, 2009, one day before the annual remembrance of the terror attacks of 2001, mayors of sixteen other cities visited New York to join in the announcement of a new nationwide program called Cities of Service. Leaders from some of America's biggest cities—Los Angeles, Chicago, Atlanta—joined forces with a number of smaller but equally civic-minded communities—Jacksonville, Florida; Vicksburg, Mississippi; Newark, New Jersey; and Dublin, Ohio—to pledge their commitment to mobilizing citizen volunteers, supporting local NGOs in their community service, and reducing the barriers that discourage participation.

At the same ceremony, officials of the Rockefeller Foundation and Bloomberg Philanthropies announced plans to offer grants to ten of the cities to create their own chief service officer positions parallel to the one held by Diahann Billings-Burford. And the seventeen mayors—representing both political parties and various ideological persuasions—pledged to work together to ensure that the voices of cities are heard in Washington, D.C., when legislation is written and budgets are drawn up to support the civic engagement movement. The leaders of America's cities have no intention of being ignored in the continuing debates over our nation's most urgent needs.

Of course, seventeen cities is only a small fraction of the thousands of municipalities around the country. Will the Cities of Service coalition grow beyond its modest origins? Don't bet against it. Another civic coalition that Mike Bloomberg helped to start, Mayors Against Illegal Guns, has grown from fifteen members in April 2006 to more than 450 today.

Businesses are also asking about how they can participate in the volunteerism movement, both in New York City and around the nation. Corporate Volunteers of New York, for example, has invited the leaders of NYC Service to meet with them to explore ways that corporate employees who want to volunteer can offer their support to the civic initiatives. Out in Hollywood, a leading corporate charity, the Entertainment Industry Foundation, has announced plans for I Participate, a multiyear campaign to encourage citizen service. By the time you read these words, you may have noticed some of their efforts, including public service announcements featuring top stars, as well as TV scripts and story lines featuring (and subtly promoting) volunteerism on ABC, CBS, NBC, Fox, and cable networks.

And many individual companies have jumped into the action. For example, Southwest Airlines has a tradition of providing community service in cities it serves. In the summer of 2008, soon after Southwest began flying out of New York's LaGuardia Airport, the airline called Billings-Burford to ask for a role in NYC Service. As of this writing, the company is in the process of being matched up with one of the city's fifty high-needs middle schools, so that Southwest employees can provide all the mentoring help needed by students at that school.

Those of us who have tracked the development of the "corporate social responsibility" movement in the United States from the 1990s until today had been wondering what would happen when the next big recession hit. Would companies maintain their commitment to serving the needs of the community at a time when sales and profits were down? Now we know the answer. Many companies are doing as much as ever, and in some cases more, as we'll discuss in more detail in a later chapter.

Coincidentally—or not so coincidentally, if you believe in the power of the zeitgeist—in April 2009, right around the time that NYC Service was being launched, the U.S. Congress passed and President Barack Obama signed into law the Edward M. Kennedy

Serve America Act. With Senator Kennedy's death less than five months later, it became an important part of his legacy, as well as a tribute to his brother John, whose creation of the Peace Corps forty-eight years earlier had inspired earlier generations of Americans with the power of service.

For many of us who admired Ted Kennedy and will miss him in the years to come, committing ourselves to civic service is perhaps the most fitting memorial we can offer to "the lion of the Senate." As President Obama said in the moving eulogy he delivered during Kennedy's funeral service, when we seek to honor him, "we can strive at all costs to make a better world, so that someday, if we are blessed with the chance to look back on our time here, we know that we spent it well; that we made a difference; that our fleeting presence had a lasting impact on the lives of others." The words sum up, with Obama's typical eloquence, both the spirit of Ted Kennedy and the spirit of national service.

The Serve America Act does more to strengthen our nation's commitment to service than any other law in history. It triples the size of AmeriCorps and increases tuition benefits for those who participate. It creates a new Service America Fellowship program as well as an Encore Fellowship program for Americans fifty-five and older who want to explore second (or later) careers in public service. It creates Youth Engagement Zones to promote service learning in troubled neighborhoods, launches a Campus of Service program to recognize colleges where service is practiced, and promotes summers and semesters of service for students.

Finally—in an important symbolic gesture—it designated September 11 as an annual day of service for all Americans. What more fitting and powerful way to declare the victory of democratic values over terrorism than a day when Americans freely come together to serve, support, and help one another?

The Serve America Act was cosponsored and partially written by Ted Kennedy's close friend, the conservative Orrin Hatch

(R-Utah), and passed the House and the Senate with support from both sides of the aisle. In years to come, the benefits of the law will be felt by communities of every kind across this country, from small towns in the Deep South to college towns in Washington, Minnesota, and Massachusetts; from farming communities in the Midwest to mining towns in the Rockies; from inner-city neighborhoods in New York, Philadelphia, and D.C. to retirement villages in Florida and Arizona; from Native American reservations in New Mexico to suburban tracts in California and New Jersey.

That's the beauty of service. It's not a Republican idea or a Democratic idea. It's simply an *American* idea, around which people of every creed and background can rally. And while government can play an important role in multiplying the power of citizen service, that power originates with, and is controlled by, the citizens themselves. That's why people helping people remains the hallmark of American citizenship, and a proud model from which the whole world can learn.

Food for Thought, Seeds for Action

- Does the city or town where you live or work have a service program like NYC Service? If it does, have you checked out the initiatives it supports to see where you might want to contribute? If not, could you play a role in helping to launch such a program? There are many ways an individual citizen could get involved. You and a few friends—or the company you work for—could offer to sponsor or conduct a simple survey of nonprofit groups in your community to begin identifying ways the town government could enhance existing service efforts. If you have computer skills, you could offer to help create and maintain an online database or website of volunteering opportunities and programs that any citizen can tap. You could help launch a program for communitywide recognition and celebration of civic activism—for example, an annual service fair or a day of awards and prizes to honor "citizens of the year." Or you could become a mentor to a student group at the local middle school or high school that is focused on creative ways of serving the community. Any of these activities could be an important step toward helping to make your town or city a model of service, great or small, for the rest of America.

• If you are involved with one or more nonprofit, charitable, or service organizations in your community, you may be able to learn from some of the initiatives being developed under the NYC Service umbrella. For example, think about how NYC Civic Corps is providing a uniform system of support and training for volunteers, who are then deployed in specific organizations and agencies based on their interests, abilities, and community needs. Could the nonprofits you work for join forces with others in the community to create a similar program? Quite often, when relatively small organizations form a coalition and pool their resources, they can accomplish much more than they might while working individually. This can apply not only to volunteer recruitment and training but to such other areas of operation as fund-raising, publicity and promotion, financial management, and human resources management.

|| 6 ||

Digital Citizenship

How New Forms of Civic
Engagement Are Being
Created by Technology

One of the most widely read and influential books of recent years was *Bowling Alone: America's Declining Social Capital,* by political scientist Robert D. Putnam of Harvard's John F. Kennedy School of Government. In that provocative work, Putnam traced what he saw as an alarming breakdown in America's civic culture from the 1960s to the 1990s, with fewer citizens involved in social clubs, political organizations, charitable groups, and other interpersonal networks. In the metaphor that framed the book, Putnam pointed to the decline of community bowling leagues and lamented the fact that millions of Americans had taken to "bowling alone"—a symbol for the alienation and excessive individualism that he feared threatened our cohesion as a nation.

Although Putnam proposed a number of factors as possible causes of this disturbing trend (including demographic changes, urban sprawl, and two-career families), he suggested that a major problem was the influence of the dominant communications technology of the 1960–1990 period. In an article summarizing his findings, Putnam wrote:

The culprit is television.

First, the timing fits. The long civic generation [often referred to now as "The Greatest Generation" of the 1930s to 1950s] was the last cohort of Americans to grow up without television, for television flashed into American society like lightning in the 1950s. In 1950 barely 10 percent of American homes had television sets, but by 1959, 90 percent did, probably the fastest diffusion of a major technological innovation ever recorded. The reverberations from this lightning bolt continued for decades, as viewing hours grew by 17–20 percent during the 1960s and by an additional 7–8 percent during the 1970s. In the early years, TV watching was concentrated among the less educated sectors of the population, but during the 1970s the viewing time of the more educated sectors of the population began to converge upward. Television viewing increases with age, particularly upon retirement, but each generation since the introduction of television has begun its life cycle at a higher starting point. By 1995 viewing per TV household was more than 50 percent higher than it had been in the 1950s.

Most studies estimate that the average American now watches roughly four hours per day (excluding periods in which television is merely playing in the background). . . .

Controlling for education, income, age, race, place of residence, work status, and gender, TV viewing is strongly and negatively related to social trust and group membership, whereas the same correlations with newspaper reading are positive. Within every educational category, heavy readers are avid joiners, whereas heavy viewers are more likely to be loners. In fact, more detailed analysis suggests that heavy TV watching is one important reason why less educated people are less engaged in the life of their com-

munities. Controlling for differential TV exposure significantly reduces the correlation between education and engagement.

A lot has happened since Putnam published his observations in
1995. Many have noted a resurgence in civic engagement by millions of Americans—the theme we've been exploring in the pages of
this book. Indeed, Putnam himself has authored a follow-up study
(*Better Together: Restoring the American Community*, coauthored
with Lewis M. Feldstein and published in 2003), which examines
how many Americans are creating vibrant and innovative *new* kinds
of community organizations—not bowling leagues or even traditional groups like the Boy Scouts, the Kiwanis, or the League of
Women Voters, but civic, business, and charitable collaborations
that are revitalizing towns and neighborhoods across the country.
Some have even suggested that *Bowling Alone* itself played a role in
this heartening trend, as citizens around the United States decided
to reverse the decline in civic involvement that Putnam had decried.

Even more fascinating, however, has been a dramatic change
in the role of technology. Where Putnam and similar critics as-
sailed television as a "boob tube" whose major impact on viewers
was to foster passivity, isolation, and social dysfunction, the explosion of newer tools for electronic communication—especially via
the Internet—is having the unanticipated effect of promoting remarkable new forms of social engagement.

It's too soon to say whether these new digitally mediated forms
of civic involvement will effectively take the place of traditional
face-to-face social engagement. But there's little doubt that the Internet and the related technologies that have proliferated in the
last decade—from social networking sites like Facebook and My-
Space to shared spaces for creativity, messaging, and information
like Twitter and Wikipedia—are generating new ways for millions
of people to connect to one another. Even the much-maligned

television is becoming a vehicle for the sharing of ideas and information among citizens through sites for user-generated content like YouTube. In the process, the electronically empowered millions who have taken over these technologies are redefining active citizenship for a new era.

One of the most striking illustrations of the power of the new electronic "civic media"—was the shrewd use of social networking sites by Barack Obama's 2008 presidential campaign. (Indeed, this was probably the wake-up call for millions of Americans who had never before recognized the power of computer-based networks to do more than facilitate game playing and music sharing.)

The Obama campaign was the first nationally successful political campaign built largely on a new-technology platform. The goal was to speak the language of Millennials—young Americans between the ages of thirteen and twenty-nine who had grown up using the new technology and were eager to support a candidate who represented social and political change. (Howard Dean's 2004 presidential campaign was the most prominent precursor, but of course that effort fell short of electoral success.) Obama and his millions of volunteers also used online technologies to orchestrate thousands of local fund-raising events, canvassing efforts, and one-vote-at-a-time recruitment efforts.

The results were staggering: Obama enlisted eight million volunteers using social-networking sites, he attracted two million "friends" on Facebook, and he drew more than a hundred million viewers to his video presentations on YouTube. (McCain mounted me-too efforts in all these areas, but his results were dwarfed by Obama's.) The campaign raised unprecedented sums of money using the Internet. And on election day, the Obama team used text messages sent to millions of supporters to complement traditional get-out-the-vote activities—at an estimated cost of $1.56 per vote garnered, as compared with the $32 spent to produce the same vote via printed leaflets.

The Obama campaign didn't merely use young volunteers, as most campaigns do. It created an innovative campaign infrastructure specifically designed by and for today's tech-happy Millennial generation, using the communication tools young people rely on and trust. As a result, it helped to energize millions of young people who, polls show, are now more engaged in citizenship, involved in politics, and eager to maintain their active role in civic life than their counterparts from previous generations.

Since taking office President Obama has continued to use new media to mobilize his supporters. The thirteen million citizens whose e-mail addresses were collected by the Obama campaign receive periodic updates about the new administration's policies as well as exhortations to share their views with their members of Congress (and to donate to Organizing for America, the official name of Obama's postelection campaign arm). In March 2009, Obama conducted the first live Internet news conference from the White House. More than one hundred thousand questions were submitted by e-mail, and logged-in participants cast over three and a half million votes to choose the questions that the president would answer.

It's not the first time that a savvy politician has pioneered the use of new media to connect with voters. In 1896, William McKinley and his brilliant chief strategist, Mark Hanna, waged the first modern political campaign, spending an unprecedented $3.5 million, employing fourteen hundred workers, and flooding the nation with posters, flyers, pamphlets, and articles in the new nationally circulated newspapers and magazines.

In 1929, as governor of New York, Franklin D. Roosevelt remarked in a speech at Tammany Hall, "I think it is almost safe to say that in reaching their decisions as to which party they will support, what is heard over the radio decides as many people as what is printed in the newspapers." Four years later, as president, he began using his famous "fireside chats" to restore national confidence and win public support for his economic program during the Great Depression, reaching over the heads of Congress and local politicians to touch Americans directly via the radio.

And in 1960, thanks to the attractive persona and youthful eloquence he displayed in the first-ever televised presidential debate, John F. Kennedy won the race for the White House over the arguably better-qualified Richard M. Nixon, whose serious demeanor was better suited to what was then the "old medium" of radio.

In demonstrating how the Internet can be used as a tool for energizing the citizenry, Obama is just the latest in this line of innovators. And in truth, communications media of all kinds have always helped to create communities. In the 1770s, the newsletters and broadsides created and circulated by the so-called Committees of Correspondence in the various American colonies helped to create the patriotic communities that ultimately spearheaded the revolution. In the 1800s, as Cornell professor Benedict Anderson has written in his book *Imagined Communities,* the dissemination of ideas and even entire worldviews by means of newspapers helped to create the modern concept of national identity. In this sense, Anderson says, the *London Times* may have been the single greatest unifying force in the British Empire.

And, of course, the power of media to connect and engage people isn't merely about politics. Millions of Americans have experienced the power of television to unite the nation at times of trauma or triumph, as when President Kennedy was shot, when men first walked on the moon, or when the Twin Towers were toppled on 9/11.

It may well be that the use of media to help create communities out of vast collections of individual citizens is especially important in the United States today—a country that is

- highly mobile and geographically dispersed, so that people with shared interests and concerns may live hundreds or thousands of miles apart;

- ethnically, socially, economically, and religiously diverse, so that institutions like churches or synagogues, fraternal organizations, and military or veterans groups that might have served as unifying forces in communities of the past may no longer be able to play that role; and
- filled with people who are busy and stressed and have multiple demands on their attention, making a brief visit to a media source more practical than, for example, membership in a club or attendance at a community meeting.

As a result, it's no wonder that many creative people and organizations are now experimenting with ways to use media—especially the powerful new electronic media developed in the last two decades—to build communities. It's a trend that is gathering steam with the coming of age of the Millennials, who are both highly civic-minded and deeply connected to electronic media. Not only does this generation love to receive ideas and entertainment via electronic media, but millions of them are active participants in electronic networks as well as content creators.

According to a 2005 study funded by the Pew Charitable Trusts, more than half of American teens are "media creators"—they blog, host their own websites, remix online content, and share their activities and ideas with others online. And it's not just white suburban males (the "nerd" stereotype) who embrace the electronic media; the same study found that urban youth were somewhat *more* likely than suburban kids to be media creators, while girls aged fifteen to seventeen were more involved in blogging and other social networking online than their male counterparts.

Meanwhile, the appeal of more traditional forms of media—especially newspapers—has been steadily declining among young people. So organizations that are interested in engaging young Americans in civic activities really have no choice other than to use the electronic media. That's where they live, and, increasingly, it's where the voters, community activists, and socially concerned citizens of the nation will be found.

Furthermore, today's electronic media offer many advantages for community building that even the hallowed local newspaper of old could not. They are interactive, combine multiple forms of information (text, images, audio, video, databases), provide easy links to almost infinite additional sources of knowledge, easily connect people to one another, and are instantaneously updatable in real time. So electronic media lend themselves more naturally to civic engagement than the simpler, slower, smaller, one-way forms of communication on which we once relied.

Thus, the Internet and its many components and analogues elsewhere in the digital universe have the potential to serve not merely as a more powerful counterpart of the newspaper but also, in various ways, as the town hall meeting, the door-to-door canvasser, the direct-mail solicitation, the telephone call from a neighbor, the stump speech by a candidate, the lecture by the traveling scholar, the demonstration by the farm extension expert, the exhibit at the local art gallery, and the performance by the visiting troupe of musicians or actors. In decades past, activities like these served to create communities by providing neighbors with shared experiences and knowledge. Today, these and more are available to everyone on the Internet—and smart individuals and organizations that want to build communities are making the Internet their most important tool.

The number and range of community-building new-media tools that are proliferating around the nation and the world is quite astounding. Here are just a few examples.

SeeClickFix (online at www.seeclickfix.com) is a remarkable new social networking site focused on solving local problems, big or small, anywhere in the country or abroad. It was launched in 2008 by a group of civic activists in New Haven, Connecticut, and now is working on behalf of citizens in locations ranging from New Jersey, Massachusetts, and Texas to as far away as Joondalup, Australia.

Founder Ben Berkowitz got the idea while struggling to deal with the local bureaucracy over a typical small-bore civic problem—in this case, unsightly graffiti painted on a vacant neighboring house. It took Ben several hours and many phone calls even to identify the town official to whom the issue should be reported, let alone to get it fixed. While waiting on hold with city hall for the umpteenth time, it occurred to Ben—then working mainly as a freelance web designer—that the Internet offered a perfect alternative to traditional ways of reporting and tracking local problems. He and three friends who became his cofounders began experimenting with the concept, and within months SeeClickFix was born.

Log on to the site and you'll be presented with an interactive map of the entire United States, courtesy of Google. (Google created the mapping software and granted SeeClickFix permission to use it. It's a fascinating example of the cumulative and multiplicative power of the Internet: An online tool created by a commercial organization for its own use proves to be immediately adaptable for civic purposes by a different organization, thereby creating enormous additional social value.) The website allows anyone who has observed a nonemergency problem in his or her neighborhood—from a dangerous pothole or a missing stop sign to a noise pollution problem caused by thoughtless motorcyclists—to report the problem, locate it geographically by zooming in on the map of the person's hometown, and then track the problem over time until it is fixed.

Ben's original concept was that SeeClickFix would serve as a quick and easy way for citizens to notify local authorities about problems in their communities, and it's widely used for that purpose. In fact, some have compared SeeClickFix to the 311 service-and-information hotlines that are staffed by local governments in many cities—including New York, where Mayor Michael Bloomberg never loses an opportunity to promote what he calls his "favorite phone number." In a growing number of towns, municipal department employees regularly log on to SeeClickFix to identify and prioritize problems they need to tackle. For instance, the road maintenance department may use SeeClickFix as a way of keeping track of unsafe conditions on local streets as well as of informing residents as to the progress of repair work. Utility companies in charge of water mains, gas pipelines, electrical systems, and the like also find the site valuable.

But SeeClickFix differs from a 311 telephone line in two crucial ways. First, it requires no investment in software, website design, maintenance, or other infrastructure by local officials. The SeeClickFix website already exists and can be used by residents and officials of any town, instantly (since Google Maps already covers the entire world). Some towns, especially smaller ones, may end up using SeeClickFix as a ready-made substitute for a 311 system. In other cases, SeeClickFix is a supplement for an existing phone hotline (for instance, in Philadelphia, where e-mail alerts generated by SeeClickFix reports go directly to the municipal 311 center).

Second, whereas 311 is basically a one-way tool for informing government workers about problems, SeeClickFix invites the entire community to participate in identifying problems, monitoring them, and taking responsibility for solving them.

Citizens participate in SeeClickFix in a variety of ways. The majority use it to note and publicize the existence of a problem: "There's water running into the street on South Roselawn Avenue in Artesia, New Mexico." "There's broken glass strewn across the length and width of the sidewalk of the First Avenue Bridge in Moorhead, Minnesota." "There's no safe crossing for bicyclists or pedestrians at the intersection of Clairmont Road and I-85 in Atlanta, Georgia."

Others use the site to add information about a problem someone else has noted—for example, a photo of the flooding of South Roselawn Avenue, or an account of a near accident they witnessed at the Clairmont Road intersection.

Still others take responsibility for fixing the problem. SeeClick-Fix reports many instances of local individuals or groups taking it upon themselves to improve a condition they read about online—for instance, by clearing away a dead tree limb that was blocking a street, tidying up an unsightly vacant yard, or reattaching a street sign that had been knocked to the ground in a storm. When a group of volunteers learned about a boat that someone had dumped in a local park, they showed up with tools to dismantle it, cart the pieces away, and clean up the area. There are even reports of rebel street repair crews of ordinary citizens who patch potholes in their spare time!

Finally, individuals or groups can use the site to create Tracking Areas of a few blocks or a few square miles that they personally volunteer to monitor. Any problem reported within the Tracking Area triggers an e-mail to the responsible party, which can then investigate and take whatever steps it deems appropriate. For example, the lack of a safe place for cyclists to cross I-85 has been reported to the Atlanta Bicycle Coalition, which is working with local officials to plan an overpass. Similar watch groups have been created by neighborhood associations, church groups, and merchant organizations.

Although SeeClickFix is growing rapidly and has achieved a significant degree of sophistication, it's still a youthful venture, with around seventy-five hundred active users around the United States. It's run on a for-profit basis, with Ben and his three partners having gone full-time as employees of the organization in March 2009, after a year of frenzied weekend and evening work. They garner their so-far modest revenues from a variety of sources, including fees from paid memberships in SeeClickFix Pro, which offers upgraded services to municipalities and other organizations that want to use the site professionally. (The city of Houston, Texas, for example, has purchased several memberships.) They also won a $25,000 grant from the We Media Pitch Awards, a contest for media ideas that promise to make the world a better place, sponsored by the Ethics and Excellence in Journalism Foundation.

SeeClickFix is a fascinating illustration of the ability of electronic media to empower ordinary citizens to take charge of their environment in new and constructive ways. It's also a remarkable experiment in creating a new relationship between citizens and government. On his blog, Ben Berkowitz quotes a passage from tech writer Tim O'Reilly as a vivid explanation of how this experiment works:

> Can we imagine a new compact between government and the public, in which government puts in place mechanisms for services that are delivered not by government, but by private citizens? In other words, can government become a platform? . . . Too often, we think of government as a kind of vending machine. We put in our taxes, and get out services: roads, bridges, hospitals, fire brigades, police protection . . . And when the vending machine doesn't give us what we want, we protest. Our idea of citizen engagement has somehow been reducing to shaking the vending machine.

Ben goes on to say, "I think that if you want people to stop shaking the vending machine you have to provide the keys to the backside of the machine." Once citizens can get inside the machine and make it work properly for everyone's benefit, the us-against-them attitude too many of us have developed toward government will no longer be necessary. SeeClickFix may be a small but powerful step in that direction.

The Center for Future Civic Media based at MIT's famed

Media Lab is a remarkable illustration of how new-media applications dedicated to promoting active citizenship are proliferating. The center is an incubator and catalyst for such applications—the more, and the more diverse, the better. Created in 2007 by three MIT faculty members—Christopher Csikszentmihályi, Mitchel Resniks, and Henry Jenkins—with the help of a grant from the Knight Foundation, the center is supporting dozens of innovative projects that seek to apply cutting-edge technology tools to social problems. And every project is "open source," meaning that software and other tools developed at the center are never patented or kept secret but must always be made freely available to anyone who wants to adapt or employ them. In the words of the center's former research director Ellen Hume, "Everything we do is a gift to the world."

Projects now under development at the center include:

• Speakeasy—a community-based translation project that uses cell-phone technology to quickly and easily connect recent immigrants who need help in dealing with the English language to volunteer translators who know their language. The value of a system like Speakeasy is obvious, particularly in twenty-first-century U.S. cities where thousands of non-native speakers of English arrive every year. Using Speakeasy, an immigrant who is attempting to deal with (say) a school principal, a traffic cop, or an official at the department of motor vehicles can dial a single number and be promptly routed to a translator who can facilitate a conversation in English. Piloted in Boston's Chinatown neighborhood, Speakeasy is now being developed for use with other languages throughout the city and elsewhere.

• Hero Reports—a website that encourages citizens to report acts of civic courage . . . moments when people "stand up, not in fear, but in hope." Created in part as a corrective to the post-9/11 focus on safety, security, and the prevention of criminal attacks (as emphasized by publicity campaigns like the program in New York that uses the slogan, "If you see something, say something"), Hero Reports urges citizens who see something *positive* to share it with their neighbors. Suitable reports might range from small acts of kindness (like giving up a seat for an elderly person) or an act of true heroism (like leaping onto the subway tracks to rescue a train worker who'd fallen there due to illness). Prototypes of the Hero Reports program have been developed for New York, Boston, Philadelphia, Detroit, and St. Louis.

• Between the Bars—an online platform designed to enable prisoners (who currently number 1 American in every 142) to participate in blogging. Between the Bars includes software tools to make it easy to upload PDF scans of letters, crowd-sourced transcriptions of the scanned images, and full-featured blogging tools that facilitate comments, tagging, RSS feeds, and notifications for friends and family when new posts are available. Integrating inmates into the universe of electronic media is a small way of helping them create or maintain healthy ties to the outside world and thereby improve their chances of establishing a new, crime-free life after their prison terms are over.

At a glance, these four projects might seem to have very little in common. They serve different constituencies, offer very different services (ranging from the intensely practical to the "merely" feel-good), and are likely to vary greatly in their impact on the world. But all are examples of what founder Henry Jenkins (now a professor at the University of Southern California) calls *civic media*—"virtually any form of communication that engages people in local community building."

The Center for Future Civic Media focuses on using electronic media to foster *local* communities rather than virtual or worldwide communities. Can the Internet, cell phones, social networking media, and other new forms of person-to-person communication replace the role of newspapers as a glue that unites neighbors around social purposes? Can they provide tools that can inform and inspire citizen activists the way great newspapers once did? And can those tools be economically sustainable? These are crucial questions for a world in which informed, engaged citizens are more necessary than ever, and in which the challenges faced by communities and governments are growing ever more complex and potentially disastrous—and they are the central questions the center's projects are designed to explore.

What is clear is that the Internet has already helped to nurture numerous forms of "collective intelligence" in which individual citizens are collaborating to educate and inform one another, as well as hosting lively, often constructive debates about issues of civic importance.

One of the best-known examples is Wikipedia, the online encyclopedia that is created through the unpaid, voluntary contributions of thousands of individuals. Self-described as "a multilingual, Web-based, free-content encyclopedia project," Wikipedia was founded in 2001 by Jimmy Wales and Larry Sanger. It's operated by the San Francisco–based Wikimedia Foundation and has grown to embrace versions in more than 280 languages. The English-language edition, which is consistently one of the most frequently visited sites on the Internet, boasts more than three million articles on virtually every topic imaginable, from the sublime (an eleven-thousand-word explanation of Einstein's special theory of relativity) to the obscure (forty-six words describing the village of Zarszyn in eastern Poland) to the ridiculous (over ten thousand words about Britney Spears—including 211 footnotes).

Anyone inclined to do so is able to create an entry on Wikipedia, edit an already-existing entry, or add comments. It's a process you might assume would lead to massive problems with fraud and error—and indeed there have been some well-publicized cases of pranksters or people with an ax to grind inserting nonsense or distortions in the pages of Wikipedia. But these are usually quickly spotted and removed by other users. Experts who've analyzed Wikipedia's content have usually been impressed by its quality. For example, a 2005 study of science-related entries by the editors of the journal *Nature* found that Wikipedia's data were "not markedly less accurate" than those found in the *Encyclopedia Britannica.*

Despite this record of achievement, in August 2009, Wikipedia announced the first major departure from its freewheeling openbook tradition. Articles on sensitive topics—for example, biographies of living persons—will have to be approved by a network of trusted "editors," numbering in the thousands, before being posted online. Jimmy Wales describes the new system as "a test." "We will be interested to see all the questions raised," he has commented. "How long will it take for something to be approved? Will it take a couple of minutes, days, weeks?" But he views the new regime as an inevitable concomitant of Wikipedia's success. "We have really become part of the infrastructure of how people get information," he told the *New York Times.* "There is a serious responsibility we have."

The communal creation of Wikipedia by thousands of "citizen researchers" has been compared to the old-fashioned barn raisings in rural communities, where dozens of local citizens would gather to lend their combined efforts to erecting one structure . . . the difference being that Wikipedia is a barn raising on a global scale. There's an old saying that captures the power of community to get things done: "Many hands make light work." If that's true, then Wikipedia illustrates the fact that millions of hands, cleverly organized, can accomplish practically anything.

Wikipedia is a citizen-made media creation that has become one of the most frequently consulted sources of information in the world. But there are many less-famous forms of collective intelligence that are providing venues for the work of "citizen journalists," "citizen photographers," "citizen artists," and "citizen writers."

An intriguing example is Many Eyes, a site created by experimenters in the Visual Communication Lab at IBM Research. It's an open web center where graphics software is freely available to anyone who wants to use it to present data of any kind in compelling visual form. Created by Martin Wattenberg, an IBM staffer "whose life goal is to turn numbers into pictures," Many Eyes provides an easy way for anyone to create an enlightening presentation of numeric information.

Some of the graphics available on Many Eyes are of real civic importance. For example, on a recent typical day, a visitor might encounter a multicolored map of the United States illustrating the relative popularity, by state, of the 2009 "Cash for Clunkers" auto trade-in program; a graph that captured U.S. census data on the foreign ancestry of Americans in the form of various-sized bubbles (a very large bubble for the 50.8 million of German ancestry, a tiny one for the 2.5 million from sub-Saharan Africa); and a "word tree" chart depicting the most common terminology used in House Bill 3200, one of the controversial health-care reform proposals then being debated in Congress and around the country. All three were among the most popular "visualizations" featured on Many Eyes, and all were created by ordinary citizens using the website's tools. "We want to democratize visualization," say the founders of the site, "enabling anyone on the Internet to publish powerful interactive visualizations and start their own data conversations."

Another, very different example is Snopes.com, a website devoted to truth-testing today's most widespread ("viral") urban legends, chain e-mails, Internet legends, and unattributed rumors. Created as a hobby in 1995 by amateur folklorists Barbara Mikkelson and her husband, David, Snopes attracts more than six million visitors monthly. And although the Mikkelsons handle a lot of the heavy lifting involved in creating and maintaining the site— especially the background research required to verify or debunk the legends—Snopes relies on participation by its millions of fans, who supply the raw materials that the site is dedicated to analyzing.

Some of the stories examined on Snopes.com are weird, silly, or of purely psychological or cultural interest—like the widespread tales about large checks available from Microsoft just for forwarding an e-mail to your friends. (Sorry, the stories are not true.) But others are important. For example, Snopes has done a thorough job of separating truth from fiction in examining rumors about leaders from Barack Obama (Was he really born in Kenya?) to Sarah Palin (Was that really her Wasilla High School report card, with the dismal SAT scores, being circulated on the Web?). (The answers, by the way, are no and no.)

Wikipedia, Many Eyes, and Snopes.com are each, in very different ways, filling roles that were once occupied by professional journalists, researchers, editors, and publishers—and are now being supplied, more and more often, by ordinary citizens who are eager to share knowledge and information with others. The power of digital technology is what makes this change possible. As MIT's Henry Jenkins has written, "Collective intelligence is increasingly shaping how we respond to real-world problems." He provides an example drawn from one of the greatest real-life tragedies of the past decade:

> On August 29, 2005, Hurricane Katrina tore apart the levee that protected New Orleans from Lake Pontchartrain and the Mississippi River. Not only was the ability of ordinary citizens to share self-produced media and information pivotal in shaping the view of the situation for the outside world (thereby bringing in more relief funds), but it allowed for those affected by the disaster to effectively

assist one another. After Jonathan Mendez's parents evacuated from Louisiana to his home in Austin, Texas, he was eager to find out if the floods had destroyed their home in Louisiana. Unfortunately for him, media coverage of the event was focused exclusively on the most devastated parts of New Orleans, with little information about the neighborhood where his parents lived. With some help from his coworker, they were able, within a matter of hours, to modify the popular "Google maps" web service to allow users to overlay any information they had about the devastation directly onto a satellite map of New Orleans. Shortly after making their modification public, more than 14,000 submissions covered their map. This allowed victims scattered throughout the United States to find information about any specific location—including verifying that the Mendez[es]'s house was still intact.

Of course, powerful technology tools—digital devices, software, websites, and so on—are not enough, by themselves, to ensure that the goal of great civic engagement on the part of all citizens is fostered in the years to come. People and organizations seeking to encourage active citizenship also have to be smart about using digital tools to reach out to people, build connections, and strengthen community ties. And more and more of today's most creative social entrepreneurs are doing just that. The following are a few examples:

• All for Good (http://www.allforgood.org)—a searchable website for locating volunteering opportunities in your own community, created as a public-private partnership under the auspices of Craig Newmark, the founder of the popular Craigslist website. Enter the name of your town or even just your zip code, and the site generates anywhere from a handful to hundreds of organization listings, each with specific descriptions of available volunteering opportunities.

• Kiva (http://www.kiva.org)—an online organization that makes the power of microcredit available to anyone through one-on-one connections between lenders and borrowers. Through Kiva, you can pick your own borrower in a country like Peru, Togo, Lebanon—or even the United States—and lend him or her money through an established microfinance organization. Over six to twelve months, your loan is repaid, and you receive regular updates about how the money is being used to found or expand a small business and its real-world impact in helping to lift an individual or an entire family out of poverty.

• Donors Choose (http://www.donorschoose.org)—a site dedicated to helping schoolkids and their teachers get access to supplies and materials they need while allowing donors to choose the specific project they want to fund. When you visit the site, you can identify a particular region or town you'd like to target, or you can select a certain cause that is dear to your heart—for example, you might choose to buy paints and brushes for an art teacher in rural Mississippi, microscope slides for a science class in Harlem, or building blocks for a preschool classroom in New Mexico. Donors receive feedback on their giving, including photos of the project and an accounting of how every dollar was spent.

• Causes on Facebook (http://apps.facebook.com/causes/about)—an application available on the world's most popular social-networking site that allows any member to "create a cause," recruit friends to support it, circulate information about the cause, and raise money for a registered charity that addresses the causes. When we recently visited the site, the most popular causes (with three to six million members each) were devoted to curing cancer, ending animal abuse, and fixing global warming—but there are hundreds of thousands of other causes covering everything from helping to educate girls in Africa (with over 360,000 members) to dedicating a U.S. postage stamp to Michael Jackson (14,961 members).

Thanks to these and other tools that facilitate digital citizenship, getting involved in civic activism is now easier than ever. As Micah Sifry of Personal Democracy Forum puts it, "Anybody can now commit an act of civic engagement." And Sifry adds, "The new digital environment means that we professional do-gooders now have a lot more competition. Or, if we choose to see it this way, we have a lot of new collaborators. It all depends on how we look at it."

Of course, one characteristic of this new digital age is that it's almost impossible to impose top-down controls on what people do with the new electronic tools. The same qualities that make digital communications so powerful—their interactivity, their speed, their ubiquity, their ease of use—also mean that the "experts" can no longer control either the medium or the message. To return to the world of political activism for a moment, consider these statistics: In the 2008 election, there were close to 150 million online views of videos created by either the Obama or McCain campaigns. But during the same time period, there were *1.5 billion* views of citizen-made videos that mentioned either Obama or McCain— ten times as many.

In 2008, the voice of the politicians was certainly amplified by the Internet—but the voice of the average citizen was amplified even more. And the same is true in the worlds of philanthropy, civic organizing, and social engagement. Leaders with official titles and impressive credentials still have enormous influence. But so, potentially, does any teenager, homemaker, small-business person, or retiree with a computer and a passion. For those who were comfortable with the old, top-down structure of traditional media, it may be an unsettling, even a frightening change. But I find it heartening to see how many millions of ordinary citizens are eager to have an impact on the great issues of our time. Our democratic system can't help but benefit from their involvement.

And in countries around the world where democracy is threatened or nonexistent, electronic tools are playing a growing role in fomenting change from the bottom up. Jared Cohen, a twenty-seven-year-old official with the U.S. State Department, has been charged with exploring the potential of social-networking media to encourage global civic engagement. In October 2009, he represented the United States at the Mexico City summit of a new organization devoted to this trend. In an NPR interview, Cohen commented:

> . . . the main idea behind the Alliance of Youth Movements is to recognize that civil society has fundamentally changed. You still have your traditional NGOs and organizations that are out there doing great grassroots work. But you also have a new cadre of civil society actors, and these are the young people who, you know, they have a URL or a website instead of an office, they have followers and members instead of a paid staff, and they use open-source platforms instead of having a robust budget.

This isn't idle talk. Four months earlier, Iran was in the midst of nationwide turmoil in the wake of a contested presidential election. Hundreds of thousands of protesters, including many young people, courageously took to the streets to denounce what they considered electoral fraud. Naturally, the repressive Iranian regime cracked down on the traditional media—newspapers, radio, television. But they were unable to control the new communications tools of the Internet, cell-phone text messaging, and Twitter. Opponents of the government used these tools to share information about the timing and location of rallies, to report police crackdowns, and to make contacts with the outside world. CNN received countless Twitter messages like the one from IranNewsNow that read, "Don't listen to what iran gov says u can or can't do! You can report the pics/vids coming from Twitter!" Videos of police beating peaceful protesters were viewed by millions on YouTube. And many mainstream reporters began gathering details for their stories from the Facebook pages, photo links, and text messages of Iranian protesters.

So important were these new electronic tools to the nascent Iranian democracy movement that, on June 15, 2009, when Twitter was scheduled to undergo routine maintenance of its global website, Jared Cohen e-mailed Twitter's cofounder Jack Dorsey to request, on behalf of the State Department, that the company consider postponing the temporary shutdown. Dorsey was responsive—after all, in April he and other high-tech executives had accompanied Cohen on a visit to Baghdad to learn about the vital role that social networking and other electronic communications tools were playing in the rebuilding of Iraq. Twitter decided to delay its maintenance by several hours. That way, it would occur in the afternoon, U.S. time—and in the middle of the night in Iran, so that important political messages could get through during the Middle Eastern daytime.

There's reason to hope that, in the future where television, radio, and newspapers are unable to report the truth, young people armed with computers and cell phones will be able to fill the gap.

•   •   •

As you've seen, digital citizenship represents a burgeoning area of change and explosive growth. But this movement is still in its infancy. What will it take to allow digital activism to fulfill its potential in the years to come?

• *General access to the technology.* In this area, change is rapid. Cities around the country, including Philadelphia, Boston, Cambridge, and Tempe, Arizona, are moving to make wireless Internet access available everywhere, usually at little or no cost. The popularity of the "netbook" computer, priced as low as $200 or less, as well as "smart phones" with built-in Internet browsers, is rapidly closing the digital divide that once separated rich from poor. Even in the developing world, new, low-cost devices like these are making the power of digital technologies available to hundreds of millions of people who can leverage it to improve their lives and the future of their communities.

• *Widespread digital literacy.* This is a set of complex skills not yet being taught in schools. It includes not merely the ability to turn on a computer and log on to the Internet, but also the critical skills required to participate effectively in online communities. Just as students need to learn how to read and critically evaluate printed sources, they need to learn how to recognize online scam artists, would-be manipulators, and unreliable or biased sources of information. They also need to learn how to understand and respect the diverse "languages" of online communities and to safely, profitably navigate the many "worlds" that are available through the Internet. Some schools are beginning to address these twenty-first-century skills; in time, they all should.

• *Cultivation of the digital commons.* This is an array of noncommercial spaces where civic-centered activities are privileged, government controls are minimal, and for-profit pressures are attenuated. In her book *The Internet Playground,* scholar Ellen Seiter notes, "The Internet is more like a mall than a library; it resembles a gigantic public relations collection more than it does an archive of scholars." It's inevitable and healthy for businesses to use the Internet to promote their interests, but it's important for non-profit groups, citizens' organizations, and ordinary individuals to continue to have free and unfettered access to the Web and its resources as well, and we need to make sure that the rules and common practices governing the Internet ensure such access.

But most important, of course, is a continued sense of engagement on the part of media creators and users. As long as people continue to care about the society in which they live, and continue to consider digital media as "their place" for self-expression, education, human interaction, and social organization, then the new civic media will continue to grow and flourish, producing benefits for everyone. The new "digital citizenship" is one of the most hopeful developments of recent years, and it's exciting to imagine some of the amazing breakthroughs we're sure to see in the future.

Food for Thought, Seeds for Action

- *Become a digital citizen:* You probably use a computer and an Internet connection for work or other purposes. But maybe you haven't yet begun to explore the range of civically oriented websites and activities that are flourishing on the World Wide Web. Start by visiting some of the sites mentioned in this chapter. You may find yourself wanting to participate in a digital forum about one of the public issues that you care about, donating electronically to support a charity you believe in, or sharing information about a topic you're an expert on for the benefit of thousands of other citizens like yourself.

- *Help the causes you care about develop a digital presence:* Many nonprofit organizations, citizens' networks, and community groups are already using the Internet to leverage their knowledge, connections, and power—but many are not. Take a look at the groups and causes you support, and evaluate how effective their digital presence is. If they don't have one, or if you can see ways in which their digital activities could be made more appealing, engaging, and impactful, why not volunteer to research and develop those improvements? You don't need to be an expert in programming or web design—volunteers or paid professionals with those skills can be recruited later. As long as you have imagination and a passion for the cause you're serving, you can contribute something meaningful to the project.

‖ 7 ‖

Doing Well by Doing Good

Citizen Businesspeople—
How Companies Are
Combining Profit with Service

As a businessperson, I've spent my life with a foot in two worlds—the world of for-profit enterprise and the world of social and civic activism. And over the years, I've found those two worlds overlapping more and more, sometimes to the point where it seems there's no real division between them.

This merging means that I'm not simply a businessman one day and an engaged or active citizen the next, pursuing different and perhaps incompatible goals through totally different means. Instead, I'm a *citizen businessman* every day of my life, trying to make the world a better place even as I try to live up to my business responsibilities on behalf of everyone involved in our organization. Do these two sets of responsibilities ever clash? Occasionally, and when they do, I work hard to reconcile them. But more often than not, I find they coexist harmoniously.

After all, as a businessperson, do I want to operate in a society that is dysfunctional, racked by ignorance, disease, and crime? Do I want to live on a planet that is seriously polluted and being transformed unpredictably by global warming? Do I want to try to sell my company's goods and services to a small fraction of affluent individuals while the vast bulk of society languishes in poverty and despair? Would either I or my business benefit from tolerating these and other terrible social problems? Obviously not. In general, what benefits society—spreading material abundance, social harmony, global peace and prosperity—will also benefit me and the companies I work with.

So for me, there's no disconnect between my responsibilities as a citizen and my responsibilities as a businessperson. And from what I can see, more and more of my fellow business leaders are taking the same attitude.

How do you define socially responsible business? The definitions vary, just as businesses and businesspeople do.

One definition is simply to avoid doing harm to people, society, and the environment. By this definition, the responsibilities of business are mainly negative ones. A company should *not* violate labor laws, safety regulations, or pollution rules; it should *not* sell products that are defective, engage in price-fixing, or exploit its customers (even when it would be easy to do so undetected). Of course, I believe in this definition and try to practice it, as do the vast majority of the businesspeople I know. But I would also go further.

Another, more challenging, definition is one that creates positive responsibilities on the shoulders of businesspeople. By this definition, a business should behave as a responsible, caring member of society, in much the same way that individual men and women should. This implies that companies should look for ways to support the communities in which they live and operate; to make the social fabric stronger; to help those in need; to improve the natural and human-made environment for all those who share it; and, in general, to do what they can to help make the world a better place.

Although this may sound unobjectionable, there are some businesspeople and economic thinkers who actually disagree with the notion that companies should strive to be good citizens of the communities in which they operate. Some extreme advocates of free-market principles say that the *only* responsibility of a business is to earn a profit, and that, as long as a company does so through legal means, it is fulfilling its obligations to the community by doing so.

It's certainly true that the ordinary work of business should be viewed as beneficial to society. After all, providing good-quality products and services at a fair price that people enjoy purchasing and using is certainly a positive, helpful activity. Creating jobs, stimulating economic activity, and paying taxes are also positive acts that every company engages in just by being in business. But are these the sum total of what corporate citizenship is about? Not necessarily.

Just as society can't truly flourish without the active engagement of individual citizens in all kinds of civic activities—from voting and participating in thoughtful debate about current issues to supporting worthwhile charities and helping to educate young people—so society relies on businesses to contribute to the well-being of our communities. And there's a rough justice in this. In the American legal system, a corporation is treated as the equivalent of a person, with many of the rights and privileges that go with personhood (for example, freedom of speech). If businesses are "people" when it comes to their rights, why shouldn't they behave like people when it comes to their responsibilities as well?

Companies also benefit from the physical and social infrastructure that society as a whole, including government, helps to build and maintain. If not for the public schools, businesses would be hard-pressed to find educated employees; if not for public systems of transportation and communication, we'd have no way of reaching customers or attracting them to our stores; if not for public programs for law enforcement and national defense, we wouldn't even have an orderly, peaceful society in which to do business. The

list could be multiplied, but you get the point. We in business benefit from and rely on the good things that society gives us. In return, it's only fair that we should play our part to help maintain the
fabric of society and, when possible, to make it even stronger for
future generations.

Of course, beyond the issue of responsibility, there are sound
business reasons for wanting to behave as a good corporate citizen.
Customers increasingly care about the social policies and behav-
iors of the companies they patronize. Bad publicity about corporate malfeasance—use of overseas child labor, abusive treatment
of employees, despoiling the natural environment, defrauding
customers—has been known to drive customers away by the millions. Some companies with bad reputations even attract organized efforts, complete with websites and propaganda machines,
to discourage customers from patronizing them. More and more
often, when companies behave in mean and selfish ways, it isn't
just despicable—it's also bad business.

Furthermore, business leaders are finding that more and more
employees, especially younger ones, place a high value on corporate social responsibility. Companies known as good citizens attract
more job candidates, and more high-quality applicants, than their
less-respected rivals. Top-flight people *want* to be associated with
companies that serve the greater good. The result is that, again,
companies themselves benefit from doing what's appropriate.

For all these reasons, I'm convinced that the movement toward active corporate citizenship is here to stay. And at my own
company, Loews Hotels, we've tried hard to play our part in support of that movement.

At Loews Hotels, we practice good corporate citizenship in a
number of ways. Because we share our customers' concerns about
the environment, we practice a Green Policy that includes everything from recycling and the use of eco-friendly inks and papers on
menus, flyers, and other printed materials to auditing the use of

energy in our kitchens and the use of water in our laundries to reduce waste.

In February 2009, we enhanced our green approach by launching Adopt-a-Farmer, a chainwide policy of supporting partnerships
with local farmers, fishermen, and other independent food purvey-
ors. Now Loews Miami Beach Hotel is getting its Everglades
striped bass from Triar Seafood, Loews Philadelphia is buying organic produce from Blue Moon Acres Farm in Pennsylvania's
Bucks County, and the Loews Regency in New York is getting arti-
sanal sheep's milk cheese from Old Chatham Sheepherding Company, which raises its flock in the Hudson Valley without the use
of artificial hormones. Our patrons enjoy sampling the unique
local fare, which enhances the distinctive quality of our hotels,
and we like knowing that we are helping to support enterprises that
have special value to their regional economies and ecosystems.

Because we believe in the value of diversity and the importance
of strong local economies in the communities where we operate,
we created our Minority Business Enterprise Program, through
which we encourage small businesses owned by minority-group
members or women to submit bids to become suppliers of goods
and services to our hotels. Within a year of its launch, we tripled
expenditures to qualifying vendors. The program has been recognized as one of the best practices in the lodging industry by the
National Association for the Advancement of Colored People.

And because we want to nurture close ties with the people, organizations, and institutions in the neighborhoods where we operate, we enthusiastically support local charities and worthwhile
causes under the umbrella name of the Good Neighbor Policy.

Since the nineteen Loews Hotels are each as unique as the
cities they call home, each hotel creates a distinctive community
outreach program under the auspices of the Good Neighbor Policy.
In fact, at each property, Loews employees volunteer to join what
we call the Good Neighbor Council, which chooses appropriate

causes to support and develops creative, effective ways to help them. We could write many pages describing the numerous good works our associates have performed in recent years, but here are just a few examples that can stand in for the rest:

- In New Orleans, volunteers from the local Loews Hotel worked for three weekends in the spring of 2006 to help renovate the historic St. Gerard Building, part of the Blessed Seelos Catholic Church in the city's Upper Ninth Ward district, which was devastated by Hurricane Katrina. Volunteers worked on construction, electrical and plumbing work, carpentry, painting, and refurnishing to restore the building for use by the parish's six-hundred-person congregation.

- In Tucson, employees at Loews Ventana Canyon Resort have decided to focus on helping women and children in need. In pursuit of this goal, they've performed an array of activities, from donating linens and furnishings to New Beginnings (which provides shelter and transitional housing for homeless women and children) to forming teams to participate in the Komen Race for the Cure and the American Heart Association's Heart Walk.

- In Nashville, the Loews Vanderbilt Hotel has hosted the annual "Gingerbread World" holiday event every year since 1984 to benefit Centerstone, the nation's largest not-for-profit provider of community-based behavioral health care. Kids get to decorate their own gingerbread houses and local women enjoy the camaraderie of "Ginger's Night Out," in the process raising over $700,000 to help individuals and families suffering from mental illness and substance abuse problems.

- In San Diego, some $45,000 was raised for charity in June 2009, at the Fourth Annual Loews Coronado Bay Surf Dog Competition. The name of the contest is literal, not figurative: First-place prizes went to Buddy, a Jack Russell terrier, and Kalani, a golden retriever. (Yes, we believe in having fun at the same time we are doing good for others!)

- In Denver, employees of Loews Denver Hotel raised thousands more for charity by hosting "Vino, Verdi, and Vermicelli" at the hotel's Tuscany Restaurant in the fall of 2007. It was an evening of fine wines and a six-course dinner that included entertainment by professional opera singers between courses as well as a silent auction offering hotel stays, dining packages, and donated sports memorabilia. We kept costs low and donations high by providing food and wine at cost and receiving a partial donation of employees' labor.

When Loews Hotels formally announced its Good Neighbor Policy in 1990, it was the first such program for companywide community involvement in the travel industry. In the years since then we've been gratified by the accolades we've won, including the President's Service Award, the highest honor given by the president for community service. But even more meaningful has been the satisfaction we've gained from knowing that the efforts of our employees have made a real difference in the lives of countless people in the cities where Loews Hotels are located.

Of course, Loews Hotels isn't the only company that takes seriously its obligations as a corporate citizen. Hundreds of other firms around the United States and across the globe have been stepping up to the plate. There's even a kind of "race to the top" under way, with companies competing to demonstrate how much they can do to embody the virtues of corporate citizenship—in terms of environmental responsibility, fair labor practices, positive community relations, high ethical standards, and overall sustainability. It's great to see companies vying with one another to be the best in this arena, and it's a source of enormous pride to their employees as well.

An interesting example—one of many we could cite—of how companies are setting new standards for citizenship is FedEx, the global shipping company. In 2009, FedEx became the latest corporation to join the trend of publishing a report, comparable to the financial reports that all public companies are required to issue, detailing its efforts to operate in a sustainable and responsible manner. FedEx's Global Citizenship Report offers an intriguing snapshot of how one firm is reexamining all its business practices and looking for ways to align them with the interests of the communities it serves.

Some of the topics covered in the FedEx report are traditional measures of corporate citizenship that might apply to practically any company. For example, the report provides data on contributions to charity by the company, the number of hours of volunteer time donated by FedEx employees, and in-kind gifts provided to nonprofit organizations. Other parts of the report analyze areas that are widely applicable in business but of special concern to a company in the global shipping business—for instance, the company's efforts to minimize fuel consumption by its vast fleet of trucks and planes, and programs under way to reduce the amount of paper and cardboard used in packaging items for delivery.

However, the most noteworthy portions of the FedEx report focus on topics unique to the shipping industry. FedEx provides humanitarian assistance to organizations like the Red Cross, the Salvation Army, and Heart to Heart, delivering food, medical supplies, and rescue equipment to stricken regions in the wake of hurricanes, floods, earthquakes, and tsunamis.

Furthermore, the company leaders have also stepped back from the details of daily operations and asked, *What is FedEx really about? What is the nature of the benefit we aim to supply to humankind?* And the answer they came up with is summarized in a single word: *access.* FedEx is about providing people and companies with access: access to friends and family; access to customers, suppliers, and markets; even access to information and ideas.

So a sizable section of FedEx's citizenship report deals with the company's efforts to provide access, in a sustainable, affordable fashion, to as many people around the world as possible. It's important and valuable for FedEx to provide shipping services to big corporations in the United States and Europe—but what can FedEx do for entrepreneurs in villages across the developing world to enable them to gain access to markets and thereby work their way up from poverty? It's great that FedEx makes it easy for a computer firm in Silicon Valley to deliver a replacement part to a customer in Florida overnight—but how can FedEx use its global resources to help connect people in the Horn of Africa or southern India with relatives, friends, or business opportunities in Canada or Kuwait or Tokyo?

To its credit, the company takes these challenges seriously, and it details the results in its citizenship report. We read, for example, how the support of FedEx for Path to Peace, a program that enables weavers of traditional Rwandan baskets to gain access to global markets through a "trade not aid" philosophy, has enabled twenty-five hundred African families to earn almost double the national average income. The report also describes how poverty rates in China have fallen since the implementation of new trade rules (such as updated, uniform customs protocols) that improve access to world trade, and it projects the impact that a new FedEx hub in Guangzhou is expected to have on the GDP and employment rate in the nine provinces of South China.

FedEx has also commissioned SRI International, the respected business research firm, to define and study the drivers and benefits of access in 109 countries around the globe. The idea is to measure the relationship between access and economic development as well as helping policymakers and businesspeople make smarter decisions concerning infrastructure and other key factors that impact access.

The FedEx Global Citizenship Report offers more than just a scorecard on the company's efforts to "do the right thing" in regard to the environment, charitable giving, and volunteering. It also shows how FedEx, and the global shipping industry as a whole, can play a positive role in improving the world economy for the benefit of all humankind. Those who read the report, including FedEx's own employees, come away with an understanding of how the driver of a delivery truck or a sorter of packages can be, not just a shipping worker, but a "citizen shipper."

As we discussed briefly in an earlier chapter of this book, today's difficult business climate is putting new pressure on the desire of companies to operate in a socially responsible fashion. When profits and revenues are shrinking and shareholders are growing increasingly restive, will companies continue to honor their commitments to their communities—or will corporate citizenship become another casualty of the Great Recession?

My observations suggest that most companies that were serious about civic engagement in the first place have maintained their involvements even during today's economic crunch. Many have even stepped up their activities in recognition of the greater needs in so many of our communities. However, in some cases, the *kinds* of civic activities that companies are engaging in have shifted as a result of the financial pressures we're all feeling.

For example, many of today's cash-strapped companies have had to cut back on monetary donations to charity. (According to a study by Giving USA and the Center of Philanthropy at Indiana University, corporate giving in 2008 fell by 8 percent, adjusted for inflation.) Instead, many firms are now placing a greater emphasis on employee volunteering and pro bono services to nonprofit and charity organizations. This doesn't mean that companies have stopped contributing their resources for social causes; in most cases, they are subsidizing the volunteer efforts of their staffers by giving them fully paid days or weeks away from the office to perform their charitable work. And many law firms, consulting firms, and other providers of professional services are taking on large projects on behalf of NGO clients at a fraction of the ordinary charge, and sometimes completely free. This may be the equivalent of a donation in the hundreds of thousands or even millions of dollars.

In hard economic times, some businesses are finding that pro bono work can also benefit them. Small businesses that have taken on unpaid work for charities and NGOs in the wake of the current business slowdown say that the projects keep employees occupied, maintain a keen edge on the company's skills, and serve as a form of indirect marketing. *Forbes* magazine calls the trend "enlightened opportunism," and there are plenty of examples of how it works.

One restaurateur in Boston was so impressed by the marketing impact of pro bono work that he actually decided to shift $20,000 of the restaurant's annual advertising budget to providing free services, such as catering for charity events. For many companies, unpaid work has led directly to paying contracts. An architectural firm donated the time to create design plans for several charitable organizations—for example, a playground for severely handicapped children. When some of the projects later received outside funding, the architect was tapped to complete the jobs on a paid basis.

Small businesses aren't the only ones devoting resources to pro bono work. Some large corporations are using the same strategy, often supplementing donations from company budgets with volunteer work by employees. For example, Target, the trendy discount retailer, has begun expanding its long-established program of making book donations to school libraries by having its store-building division provide labor and materials to renovate the libraries themselves. Target says its experience with building and outfitting retail spaces quickly and efficiently makes the library jobs relatively inexpensive, and up to three hundred company employees have been known to donate their time to help complete one of the projects. After Target refurbished the library at the Maxfield Magnet Elementary School in St. Paul, Minnesota, in April 2008, book borrowing by the mostly African American students reportedly increased tenfold. The impact on Target's reputation in the community can't be quantified, but it's clearly substantial.

Another strategic use of pro bono work by companies takes the form of deferred job offers. In the current recession, many newly graduated attorneys around the country have been informed by the law firms that hired them that there's no longer enough work to justify their six-figure starting salaries. However, rather than simply toss the young lawyers back into the job market—and risk losing the brightest among them to more aggressive competitors—many of the leading firms are offering to pay reduced wages (averaging up to $75,000) while the grads hone their skills with pro bono work. When the market for legal services recovers, their regular jobs will kick in. According to the Pro Bono Institute in Washington, D.C., around a thousand young lawyers are currently serving the non-profit community in this way.

Examples like these illustrate some of the ways that smart businesspeople are making efforts at good corporate citizenship part of the strategic toolkit at their companies. Contributing to the well-being of our communities shouldn't be a zero-sum game. With wise and creative planning, everybody can emerge a winner, which makes community engagement a more sustainable long-term approach.

●   ●   ●

But good business citizenship isn't only about the efforts of traditional companies to behave in ethical, responsible ways. Another of the positive social movements of recent decades has been the multiplication of attempts to *combine* the dynamism and self-sufficiency of business with the pursuit of worthy social goals that is normally associated with nonprofits or charities.

This is happening in several ways, which can be boiled down, in essence, to two phenomena: nonprofits learning from and adapting the expertise of businesspeople, and businesspeople devoting part of their resources to making the world a better place. The resulting convergences are producing some fascinating new civic, social, and economic phenomena—as well as providing tangible benefits to millions of people around the world.

Let's start by considering the ways that people from the nonprofit world are adapting the methods of business in their pursuit of social goals. One way this is happening, as we saw in our chapters about social entrepreneurship and NYC Service, is with the use of more and more metrics from business to measure the efficiency and impact of nonprofit programs. This is a long-overdue step. Today's philanthropists, foundations, and charitable givers are no longer satisfied with the feel-good benefits that they derive from their generosity. They also want to know that their donations are helping to produce *real solutions* to the social problems they care about. Today's biggest donors—people like Microsoft's Bill Gates, Berkshire Hathaway's Warren Buffett, and eBay's Pierre Omidyar—are also some of the world's shrewdest businesspeople. No wonder they want the charities they sponsor to be as well-run as the corporations they helped to build.

Another way in which the business and charitable worlds are melding is through the creation of nonprofit organizations that sell socially beneficial products and services. These nonprofit businesses participate in the marketplace, buying and selling goods and services, and thereby benefiting from the competitive market forces that generally bring out the best in workers and managers. At the same time, these organizations are doing good work that provides real benefits to the poor or to those who are otherwise disadvantaged in society.

One distinction seems important here. As you know, many nonprofit organizations have operations that sell goods or services and, in some cases, turn a profit. Museums operate gift shops and restaurants, publish books, and rent out their facilities for parties and receptions. Charities raise funds by selling tote bags, coffee cups, and calendars bearing their logos. Even Scout troops earn money by conducting bake sales and car washes. In each of these cases, a business venture that is basically identical to one that might be run by any profit-maximizing company is being conducted simply in order to generate revenues for a nonprofit organization. In this chapter, we're not talking about "nonprofit businesses" of this kind. Instead, we're focusing on businesses operated by not-for-profit organizations whose business plan has an inherent social benefit built into it.

For example, consider Rubicon Programs, Inc., a nonprofit organization based in Richmond, California. It was founded in 1973 by a group of community members who were concerned about the closure of state psychiatric hospitals. Thousands of mentally disabled people were being discharged into the streets of California, with their needs for social services and decent living conditions going unmet.

In response, the Rubicon founders decided to launch an organization to provide counseling, housing, and legal services to these needy people. In addition, they created a collection of what they called "social purpose businesses"—companies that would help take care of the mentally ill as well as other chronically poor people while selling goods and services in the competitive free marketplace.

Companies now being operated under the Rubicon Programs umbrella include Rubicon Bakery, which sells cakes, cookies, and breads to local shops, markets, restaurants, and other merchants, and Rubicon Landscape Services, which provides lawn and garden maintenance services to corporations, colleges, hospitals, and other institutional clients. In both cases, the Rubicon company hires and trains the mentally disabled, people just off welfare, and others who are normally considered "unemployable." Thus, these businesses do not simply produce revenues for Rubicon's other programs; they also provide direct benefits to the poor and disadvantaged in the form of education, job opportunities and experience, and income. Since 1973 more than forty thousand people have used Rubicon's programs to become economically self-sufficient.

Pioneer Human Services is a somewhat similar organization located in Seattle, Washington. Founded in 1963, Pioneer exists to help some of American society's most in-need groups: ex-prisoners, victims of drug and alcohol addiction, and the mentally ill. The organization runs a large array of counseling and treatment services, offering both outpatient and residential help to more than fifteen thousand clients each year. What is unusual is the way in which Pioneer funds these programs—through an array of businesses that include retail cafés, institutional food services, sheet-metal fabrication, aerospace product machining, wholesale food distribution, and contract packaging and fulfillment.

Pioneer Industries, for example, is a precision sheet-metal manufacturer with more than a hundred thousand square feet of factory space in two facilities, offering such high-tech services as laser and water jet cutting, CNC punching, shearing, forming, welding, hardware insertion, assembly, wet paint and powder coat finishing, and silk-screening. Pioneer Food Services operates a chain of four Mezza Cafés, which sell snacks, sandwiches, and complete meals, and also provides corporate catering services for parties and other affairs. These and other Pioneer companies train and employ workers from their target client populations—newly released prisoners, for example—even as they generate profits that go to support the broader Pioneer mission. Pioneer reports that its business revenues (some $64 million in 2008) cover 99 percent of the organization's needs.

A very different kind of nonprofit organization that has created and marketed a product with a social benefit in mind is One Laptop per Child (OLPC). This is a U.S.-based group created by faculty members of the MIT Media Lab and funded by a consortium of high-tech companies, including eBay, Google, and Nortel Networks. The goal: to design, manufacture, and market affordable, kid-friendly laptop computers for use in schools by poor children in the developing world.

OLPC originated in 2005 as a response by some of America's leading technology firms to the widespread concern that a "digital divide" between the rich and the poor will increasingly consign those without access to technology to lives of poverty they may never be able to escape. But as you can imagine, producing a real computer (not a toy simulation) for such a low price required some serious technological breakthroughs.

One such breakthrough came when Mary Lou Jepsen, the project's chief technologist, developed a new design for laptop screens that cut the manufacturing cost from around $100 to just $40 and reduced their energy consumption by over 80 percent—all while producing a screen image clearly visible in sunlight. Power- and cost-intensive components such as a hard drive, a CD drive, and an internal fan have all been omitted from the XO-1 laptop, whose design has been developed to obviate the need for such features. The computer runs the open-source Linux operating system rather than the industry standard Windows, thereby saving additional money. (In May 2008, however, Microsoft made its Windows XP software available to OLPC for $10 per unit as an optional alternative to Linux.) An ultrarugged yet cool-looking, multicolored design has been created to help the XO-1 both attract the attention of developing-world children and stand up to the rigors of use in remote villages of Africa, Asia, and Latin America.

When OLPC was launched, it announced a target price of $100 per computer. Although this price hasn't yet been reached—the most recent price has been in the neighborhood of $135—plans are in the works for a second-generation XO-2 with the projected price, in 2011, of just $75.

Some observers have criticized the project, saying that laptops are an inappropriate expense for school systems in poor countries, where books, sturdy classroom facilities, and teacher salaries should be higher priorities. Others have expressed worries about the environmental impact of millions of laptop computers flooding the marketplace, containing plastics and metals that will ultimately need to be recycled. And still others—especially some rival makers of computer hardware and software—scoff at the simple design and basic features of the XO-1, calling it a mere "gadget" rather than a "grown-up" computer.

Despite the controversies, almost a million and a half XO-1s have been delivered since the first units were produced in October 2007. (These figures are as of mid-2009.) In general, governments purchase the computers and hand them out to schoolchildren, who become lifelong owners of the devices. The largest deployments so far have been in Uruguay (over 300,000 computers), Peru (260,000), Colombia (175,000), and Rwanda (100,000). An order for 250,000 computers (not yet fulfilled) was received from India in early 2009. And even some U.S. school systems have bought XO-1s for their students—for example, 15,000 machines were purchased by school officials in Birmingham, Alabama.

OLPC has garnered more than its share of headlines in the mainstream press over the past few years. But perhaps the most interesting current example of a nonprofit organization that is harnessing the power of the market for social purposes is KickStart, a Kenya-based operation that develops and sells new technologies to benefit poor farmers in Africa.

KickStart was founded in 1991 by Nick Moon and Martin Fisher, two young veterans of the global antipoverty movement who had become disillusioned with the shortcomings of the traditional economic development model. Recognizing that 70 percent of the world's poorest people are subsistence-level farmers, they decided to focus their efforts on improving agricultural technologies. Even more important, they decided to use practical economic incentives to make their innovations attractive to those who needed them most:

> We decided to use a market-based model in which we would sell our new technologies directly to local entrepreneurs. We would identify profitable business models that thousands of people could start; design the tools and equipment needed to make these businesses possible; and most importantly, establish a private-sector supply chain to manufacture, distribute, and sell the new tools and equipment to the entrepreneurs. We would create awareness of the new business models and equipment with a mass-marketing campaign and sell them to poor entrepreneurs, who would use them to start thousands of profitable new businesses. Finally we would leave in place a fully profitable and sustainable supply chain that would continue to deliver the tools and equipment even after we left town.

The most popular technology that KickStart has developed is a new type of small, light-weight irrigation pump that can be operated by a single person using a StairMaster-like treadle device. The pump generates enough power to pull water from a pond, stream, or a hand-dug well as deep as twenty-five feet, and spray it via hose or sprinkler to irrigate up to two acres of land. The pump retails in Kenya for the equivalent of US$95, which is not a small sum for an African farmer. But because it enables the farmer to grow multiple harvests of valuable cash crops, the average net farming income of those using the pump has grown tenfold, from US$110 per year to $1,100 per year. For many farming families, this is the difference between poverty and a middle-class existence. No wonder KickStart markets this pump under the appealing brand name of "The Super-MoneyMaker"!

KickStart has also created and marketed a series of other entrepreneurial technologies suitable for rural Africa: a hand-operated hay baler; an oilseed press used with sunflower and sesame seeds in East and Central Africa; a block press that creates strong bricks for housing construction from a mixture of soil and cement. Moon and Fisher currently estimate that sales of their products have enabled the poor of Africa to launch more than sixty-four thousand new businesses, generating some $79 million a year in new profits and wages.

Currently, KickStart relies on donor funds to finance its technology-development efforts. In time, however, it hopes to achieve a "tipping point" where sales of products will make the organization self-sustaining. "[O]nce a tipping point is reached in a given market," Martin Fisher says, "we will start to make a profit on every sale. We will then reinvest these profits (along with more donor funds) to develop new technologies and enter new markets so that we can further our mission of getting millions of people out of poverty."

The nonprofit organizations profiled in the last few pages are each trying, in their own way, to use business techniques and the power of the marketplace to make the world a better place. Rubicon and Pioneer are creating jobs, providing career training, and funding services for the poor and disadvantaged; OLPC is hoping to bring affordable computer technology to millions of poor schoolchildren in the developing world; and KickStart is providing low-cost, practical tools for entrepreneurship to farmers in sub-Saharan Africa. In each case, the company founders have developed a business model based on offering innovative products and services that answer a real need, while also creating tangible social benefits that go beyond the sale itself. These innovative social thinkers might well be designated "citizen businesspeople."

Another type of business with a social component is a division of a for-profit organization that is designed to serve a business purpose while also producing some social good. Corporations may create such a division for any number of reasons: to support the personal goals or values of a powerful or respected corporate leader; to earn favorable publicity for the company, or to deflect criticism over past ethical and business lapses; to attract customers who may prefer to do business with a company they perceive as "good guys"; to win the friendship and support of government regulators or legislators who are considering laws that might affect the company; to reduce opposition from community organizations or public-interest groups that might otherwise try to block company plans for expansion; or to gain a foothold in a new market that holds promise for the future but is currently unprofitable—while also earning points in the court of public opinion.

It can be difficult to tell, in a particular instance, what combination of motives drives a particular company decision. In some cases, even the company executives may not be able to accurately describe the precise blend of motives that impel them. But it is interesting to note that not all of the motivations listed above are purely philanthropic or charitable. It's certainly possible to pursue the goal of being a responsible corporate citizen while expanding and improving your business—and many of today's best-run companies are doing just that.

One of the most intriguing motivations is the one we listed last: "to gain a foothold in a new market that holds promise for the future but is currently unprofitable—while also earning points in the court of public opinion." It's particularly relevant to the social problem that is perhaps the most serious in the world today, the persistence of poverty among billions of people in the developing nations.

In these first years of the twenty-first century, every smart businessperson in the developed world has an eye on two giants of the developing world—China and India. These huge countries have economies that are growing rapidly. As a result, tens of millions of people are moving into middle-class status, developing incomes and tastes that make them a huge new market for Western-style goods, from packaged foods, soaps, and shampoos to stylish clothes, cars, and electronic gear. Global corporations are jockeying for positions in the race to serve these eager new customers as they get their first taste of prosperity and the accoutrements of the "good life" it makes possible.

At the same time, the most foresighted companies are also looking even further down the road, thinking about the *next* wave of countries that may benefit from globalization and modernization. Marketers are studying nations like Indonesia, Vietnam, Nigeria, Brazil, and Egypt, wondering how they can position their companies to grab the lion's share of these markets when they are ready to explode.

And here is where the concept of bottom-of-the-pyramid marketing comes in. Significant businesses are already being built among the four billion people living on less than two dollars per day, who may be very poor individually but who collectively represent enormous untapped buying power. Companies that figure out how to sell goods and services to the poor may reap huge rewards in the decades to come—when and if these poor people make the successful leap out of poverty. After all, isn't it likely that the newly middle-class consumer in Peru, Cambodia, or Tanzania will stick with the familiar brand names she learned to love when she was poor?

C. K. Prahalad is a noted business consultant who, along with Professor Stuart Hart, has studied opportunities at the bottom of the pyramid. Prahalad explains how companies that focus on marketing to the poor can create new business models which in turn create economic opportunities. As examples, he mentions such companies as Casas Bahia, a Brazilian retailer to the poor with sales of over $1.2 billion and more than twenty thousand employees; Annapurna Salt, a Unilever subsidiary that has captured a significant share of the market in Africa with small, low-priced packages of iodized salt; Hindustan Lever Ltd., the largest soap producer in India; and CEMEX, the Mexican-based cement company that provides building materials at affordable prices to the poor.

All of these companies are earning significant profits by selling to the poor today. To achieve this, they have had to develop innovative business plans along with unique products and services designed to meet the special needs and constraints of poor people. In these instances, social benefits that derive from making useful goods available to the poor can be realized along with profitability for company shareholders—a win/win situation that is not always possible.

In other cases, where there appears to be no practical way of selling to the poor while achieving rates of profitability that meet shareholder demands, finding a win/win solution is much more difficult. Here we see other corporations trying to position themselves for *future* bottom-of-the-pyramid profits by creating experimental businesses with low or no profitability expectations in the short term. In some cases, these businesses are hard to distinguish from purely philanthropic or "social responsibility" efforts. They are satisfying several objectives at once—generating profits for the corporations that launch them, improving the lot of the poor, and giving employees and managers the psychological and spiritual pleasure that comes from knowing they are acting as responsible "citizen businesspeople."

An interesting example of the short-term challenges companies face as they seek favorable positions in the race for bottom-of-the-pyramid profits is the Pur water purification system.

Pur is a product of the giant multinational consumer-goods

corporation Procter and Gamble (P&G). Specifically designed to be economical and easy to use by extremely poor people in the developing world, Pur powder comes in "sachets" that are used to purify water in the kitchen or family home just before the water is used. A single Pur sachet is mixed into ten liters of water, where it combines with pathogens and other impurities and settles to the bottom. After twenty minutes, the water is filtered through cloth, which removes the impurities and yields clean, safe drinking water. Total cost: the equivalent of about ten U.S. cents.

P&G launched Pur on the international market in 2000. But sales were modest. The product worked well, achieving water-purity rates that meet standards established by the World Health Organization for potable water and hold the potential to dramatically reduce water-borne infectious diseases among the poor. But convincing poor people to invest some of their all-too-scarce money in a new technology and to change their household habits of water use was not so easy.

Within three years, it became clear to P&G that it would take a massive public health education program to convince developing-world consumers to make purchasing and using Pur a regular part of their family routine. Unfortunately, developing and implementing such a program, which would have to be tailored to many different cultures and languages around the world, would be complicated, expensive, and beyond the capabilities of the managers at P&G.

Convinced they had a valuable product on their hands, the leaders of P&G were loath to abandon Pur. Instead, they shifted their business model—at least for the short term—into a not-for-profit mode. Teaming up with a global NGO known as Population Services International (PSI), P&G made Pur available at cost to people in developing nations around the world. PSI uses its connections in more than sixty developing nations, as well as its knowledge of local cultures and conditions, to develop programs for educating poor people about the importance of clean drinking water and the simplicity of using Pur to treat their water. During emergencies, such as the devastating Asian tsunami of 2004, PSI helped make Pur available to millions of people who would otherwise have had no source of safe drinking water.

By the end of 2006, fifty million sachets of Pur had been distributed around the world through PSI's not-for-profit program, as compared with just three million sold by P&G under the for-profit business model. But the ultimate corporate goal—profit from sales of Pur to bottom-of-the-pyramid customers—has so far remained elusive.

The story of Pur illustrates some of the challenges that for-profit companies face in creating businesses that address serious social needs. Pur is an important technological breakthrough with the potential of improving the lives of hundreds of millions of people in the developing world, perhaps saving millions of children from deaths through diarrhea and infectious diseases that are spread by unsafe drinking water. But P&G has struggled to find a way of getting Pur into the hands of the people who need it most while earning a profit in the process. P&G's partnership with PSI represents one way to solve this dilemma—a way of balancing corporate citizenship with the financial demands every business faces.

Another approach is a concept developed by the World Business Council for Sustainable Development (WBCSD), a coalition of 170 international companies interested in corporate social responsibility, ecological balance, and economic progress for all. The WBCSD idea is known as "patient capital," and it refers to the idea of turning to unconventional sources of funding for businesses designed with a social benefit.

The leaders of WBCSD are successful businesspeople whose primary goal is to maximize profits for their shareholders. At the same time, they want to use their business expertise and resources to help alleviate serious global problems. In an effort to combine both goals, a number of WBCSD member companies have developed what they call "sustainable livelihood businesses," which the organization defines as "business models that benefit the poor and benefit the company." One example is Águas do Amazonas, a subsidiary of a South American utility company called the Suez Group, which has agreed to provide water and sanitation services to poor neighborhoods in Manaus, Brazil. Another is Shell Solar Lanka Limited, a subsidiary of Shell that is bringing solar power to some two million households in Sri Lanka that are not connected to the electrical grid.

The problem with these businesses is that they are unlikely to earn their corporate owners a significant profit, at least not for a number of years. This means it is difficult or impossible to support them through conventional financial systems, where market rates of return are required. Under the WBCSD's "patient capital" model, funds for such projects are raised through other, nonprofit sources, including multilateral financial institutions, development agencies, private foundations, and social venture funds.

Thus, Águas do Amazonas is financed through loans from the International Finance Corporation and BNDES, a Brazilian development bank, while Shell Solar Lanka relies on grants from the World Bank and the Global Environment Facility as well as loans to customers from local banks and microfinance institutions. As WBCSD notes, organizations like these are willing to undertake investments "characterized by a long-term horizon and particularly motivated by positive social and environmental impacts"—hence the term, patient capital.

The groups that provide patient capital in the WBCSD's model are also focused on social benefits. Thus, they are willing to accept little or no financial gain on the funds they provide. The patient capital gives the businesses they support a leg up during their early days of founding and start-up; in a short time, they will be expected to generate market rates of profit, which do *not* have to be reinvested in social services to the community but can instead be channeled to the same profit pool as all of the other income enjoyed by the parent company. In the end, these profits will be paid out to investors in the form of dividends, or perhaps be invested in other profit-maximizing ventures.

Finally, there's a relatively new way of combining business methods with social objectives. It's an idea originated by Muhammad Yunus of Bangladesh, whom I've mentioned several times in this book. Yunus calls it "social business," and it's the latest frontier in the search for creative new ways to make corporate citizenship even more powerful.

The concept of social business grew out of Yunus's experiences in creating and building Grameen Bank. As you may know, Grameen Bank provides "microloans" in amounts ranging from the equivalent of $50 to a few hundred dollars to poor people, mostly women, in the villages of Bangladesh. (And when we refer to poor people in Bangladesh, itself one of the world's poorest countries, we are talking about *serious* poverty; as Yunus explains, a rural Bangladeshi is considered too affluent to qualify for a loan from Grameen Bank if she owns even a single piece of furniture.) These tiny loans are used to start or expand small businesses—to buy a dairy cow, to open a little tea shop, or to buy equipment for weaving baskets or making garments to sell.

Yunus began lending to people in the village near Chittagong University where he was an economics professor, simply as an experiment. To the surprise of many, the poor people repaid their loans, with interest, on time. Eventually, Yunus launched a full-fledged bank—Grameen Bank—which now has over seven million borrowers throughout Bangladesh and a 98 percent repayment rate. The bank is financially self-sufficient, takes interest-bearing deposits, and offers a full range of services, including student loans, home mortgages, and insurance policies.

Most interestingly, Grameen Bank is actually *owned* by its borrowers and depositors. The board of directors consists of a dozen village women, elected by their peers, who set policy for the bank. And every borrower receives an annual dividend check representing her portion of the bank's surplus.

This is Yunus's definition of a social business: a company run on businesslike terms, financially self-sufficient, that is dedicated not to profit but to social benefit—in the case of Grameen Bank, to help lift poor Bangladeshi families out of poverty. And based on the success of the bank, which has inspired a global microcredit movement, Yunus has decided to create other social businesses to provide other kinds of social benefits.

The first such project launched by Yunus is Grameen Danone, a joint venture between Grameen and the big French company that is best known for its Dannon yogurt and its Evian bottled water. In one sense, this new venture is a traditional business expansion for Danone: The company is already active in many Asian countries, including India and Indonesia, so it is natural for them to consider operating in Bangladesh.

But unlike virtually every traditional business, the company has been designed deliberately *not* to maximize profits. Instead, Danone has agreed to take a maximum profit of just 2 percent on its investment, with any remaining surpluses going to support development and expansion of the company. The driving purpose: to improve the nutritional status of rural Bangladeshis, especially children, who suffer from terrible deficiencies of calories, protein, vitamins—almost every key nutrient that supports growth and development.

Grameen Danone designed its first product to address this problem. It's called Shoktidoi, a name that translates loosely as "power yogurt." It's a slightly sweet yogurt, flavored with molasses made from dates (a favorite local fruit) and fortified with vitamin

A, iron, protein, and other supplements. It's packaged in cute 50- or 80-gram cups bearing the Shoktidoi mascot, a cartoon lion showing off his muscles, and the Grameen Danone logo.

The yogurt is manufactured in a remarkable factory in the city of Bogra, northwest of the Bangladeshi capital of Dhaka. It's a tiny plant, just seven hundred square meters in size, that is equipped with state-of-the-art machinery and totally green, with solar panels, incoming and outgoing water treatment facilities, and a recycling system for used packages.

The rest of the Grameen Danone value chain is also highly unusual. Milk will be supplied by local dairy farmers, many of them Grameen Bank borrowers, who have been trained by the Grameen Agricultural Foundation in techniques for improving the quantity and quality of their milk production. The yogurt is being distributed both in retail shops and by the local "Grameen ladies"—women borrowers who will sell cups of Shoktidoi either door-to-door, among their neighbors, or over the counter in the small shops many of them run in the villages.

If the Bogra operation is successful, Grameen Danone will open more community-sized factories in other locations around Bangladesh. They figure it will take fifty such plants to serve the entire country. Eventually, other products may be added to the mix. If Grameen Danone achieves the long-term success that Yunus and his corporate partners are hoping for, the company could become a model for new kinds of organizations in a wide variety of industries, from food to health care to education to communication—social businesses designed to help the community while generating sufficient revenues to support self-sustaining growth.

Meanwhile, Muhammad Yunus has been traveling the world, speaking to CEOs, business school students, financial industry leaders, and policymakers about the potential benefits of social business. A number of major corporations have already indicated their readiness to experiment with the concept, several of them in collaboration with Yunus. New social business projects are currently in various stages of development with BASF (the giant German chemical concern), Veolia (a leading French purveyor of bottled water), Otto (a German textile trading firm), and Intel (the U.S.-based technology company).

Will social business become a widespread way of applying business methods to solving social problems? Time will tell. But its very existence—along with the broad popularity of concepts like corporate social responsibility and the convergence of for-profit with nonprofit organizational models—suggests how deep-rooted and powerful is the inner drive to contribute to society, even while conducting our daily business. Almost everyone *wants* to be an engaged citizen; the impulse grows from the basic human instinct to connect with our fellow beings. It's only natural to apply this impulse in our work lives just as in every other facet of our existence.

Food for Thought, Seeds for Action

- If you work in business, start thinking about corporate citizenship as it applies to your own company. How do *you* define the responsibilities of a corporate citizen? What special responsibilities and opportunities exist for your specific organization to play a positive role in the community (the way FedEx, for example, has taken on the challenge of expanding "access" for people around the world)? Is your company doing all it can to live up to its civic responsibilities? If not, how can you begin to promote change from within?

- Does your company provide pro bono services or in-kind donations to nonprofit organizations, charities, or other worthy groups in your community? If not, maybe you can develop a plan for offering such donations, either through a commitment of resources by the company or through volunteerism by individual employees. One suggestion: Look for opportunities to create benefits from resources that are currently being wasted or underused. Restaurants and supermarkets can donate food that would otherwise spoil; hotels and offices can donate used furniture and equipment; companies with space to spare can make it available for meetings by nonprofit groups, and so on.

• If you're in business, are there ways to make the goods and services your company produces available to underserved markets—for example, the poor, the handicapped or disadvantaged, or people in the developing world? Expanding your reach into such markets may take creativity and innovative thinking, as Procter & Gamble found with its Pur initiative. But bringing the benefits of free enterprise—including world-class products and services—to every sector of society can be a worthy goal for any aspiring "citizen businessperson."

‖ 8 ‖

Bridging to Act Two

*Changing Careers
in Search of a Deeper
Meaning for Life*

Though he was only forty-three years old, novelist F. Scott Fitzgerald was less than a year from death when he wrote those oft-quoted, fatalistic words, "There are no second acts in American life."

Fitzgerald had obviously never met a man like Dave Nelson. As Dave will happily explain to anyone who asks, he has successfully completed two acts of his life and has now fearlessly embarked on Act Three.

The first act: a thirty-three-year career as an executive at IBM, culminating in a fascinating stint selling information products and services in mainland China.

The second act: eight years as COO of the National Foundation for Teaching Entrepreneurship (NFTE), a fast-growing nonprofit devoted to teaching the ways of business to youngsters from inner-city schools—and enticing them to stay in school in the process.

And the third: Dave's new gig as a member of the board of AARP, the organization for older Americans that serves forty million people over the age of fifty and is in the thick of the national debates over retirement benefits, entitlement programs, and health-care reform.

In a world where millions of people are wondering about their own next acts—because of declining career prospects in today's tough economy, a newfound desire to create deeper meaning in their daily lives, or simple boredom with their workaday routine— Dave Nelson is a role model of sorts, having successfully navigated the transition from corporate "salaryman" to nonprofit social activist. There's a name for such people: *bridgers*. And it turns out that, in these early years of the twenty-first century, they're in demand as never before, with literally hundreds of thousands of high-level posts in the not-for-profit world crying out for the expertise, experience, and wisdom that bridgers from the business world can offer.

"No second acts"? It's a canard.

Actually, of course, Fitzgerald's dictum has always appeared somewhat shaky to astute observers of the American scene. As long ago as 1968, *Time* magazine was debunking it by pointing at middle-aged citizens who were "self-renewing" by joining then-new service organizations that embodied the hopeful spirit of the 1960s. They cited lawyer Richard Enslen, who left his firm in Kalamazoo to head a group of 150 Peace Corps volunteers in Costa Rica, and pediatrician Leon Kruger, who abandoned his prosperous medical practice in suburban Massachusetts to start a clinic for the families of poor black sharecroppers in the Mississippi Delta hamlet of Mound Bayou.

The difference today: Midlife bridgers are no longer just lone eagles like Enslen and Kruger. Now they're part of a national movement. For more and more men and women, second, third, and fourth acts are becoming the norm, often embodying dramatic plot twists and mind-bending self-reinventions they could never have predicted upon college graduation. And society at large is reaping the benefits.

•   •   •

Dave Nelson's life story began in classic American fashion. A member of the 1950s "Silent Generation," he grew up in the Mid-

west, played the tuba at Thornton Township High in Illinois (a setting he describes as indistinguishable from the happy-go-lucky
1950s high school in *Grease*), and after earning college grades just
a shade too low to qualify for medical school, attended the business program at Chicago's Northwestern University that is now
known as the Kellogg School of Management.

So far, so conventional. But even back then, Nelson sensed
there was something more in life for him than a gray-flannel business
career. "I roomed with a couple of other guys while I was at Northwestern," he recalls. "We used to talk about what we'd like to do if we
ever got to the point of having some choice in our lives. I thought I'd
like to be a teacher." So even before launching his business career,
Dave Nelson was thinking about what he might like to do afterward.

Armed with the business degree he earned from Northwestern's
Kellogg School in 1966, Nelson ended up interviewing for a job in
the Chicago office of IBM. The company was in the midst of its
amazing postwar rise to global dominance in the world of electronic
computing. "What a collection of people," Nelson remembers:

> I met one guy who'd been a jet fighter pilot before joining
> IBM. Another had been an apprentice to Frank Lloyd
> Wright. One woman had studied nuclear physics at the
> University of Chicago. And the man who would be my boss
> told me, "I came here after 25 years at Citibank. The people
> there were great—bright, capable, trustworthy, creative.
> And now that I've been here at IBM for three years I can't
> believe what I'm finding—it's a notch up." I came back
> home after the interview and told my roommates, "I don't
> know a thing about computers—but I know exactly where
> I want to work."

Nelson spent the 1960s, 1970s, and 1980s at the company,
rising from one level to the next through varied jobs in Chicago,

Philadelphia, and White Plains, New York. (Working at IBM—
nicknamed "I've Been Moved" by its widely traveled executives—
Nelson got accustomed to frequent changes of assignment.) He
married Patricia, a psychiatric social worker, and they raised three
kids together. Then, one day in 1995, he got a surprising phone
call from IBM's general manager in China.

"David," he said, "we're looking for a manager for our biggest
business unit here. It sells info systems and services to financial
institutions, not just in China but in Taiwan, Hong Kong, and
Macao—greater China, if you will. And frankly, your name is at
the top of my list."

Nelson took a deep breath. "Let me tell you about a conversation I had with my wife just two days ago," he replied.

It so happens that Dave and Pat had been taking their usual
Sunday morning stroll when Pat, out of the blue, had remarked,
"You know, maybe we should do something different with our lives."

"What sort of thing do you mean?" Dave wondered.

"I think we should move to China."

Recalling the incident today, Dave says, "I almost walked into a
tree. I asked her, 'Why China?' And Pat replied, 'Well, it would just
be so different. And maybe we need to shake up our lives a little.'"

And now, two days later, that very opportunity had landed in
Dave's lap.

The Nelson family—Dave, Pat, and teenage daughter Claire—
ended up spending three years in Beijing. Dave managed a team of
seven hundred IBM employees, all but a hundred of them native
Chinese, an experience he found eye-opening, stressful, and exhil-
arating, all at once:

> In China, I was known as *Laonee,* which literally trans-
> lates as "old Nelson." But the Chinese meaning is more
> like, "revered Nelson." For them, a senior manager is a
> trusted advisor on anything and everything. I remember

getting a call from one of my top managers at nine thirty on a Sunday night. "Nelson," she told me, "I just learned I'm pregnant, and I want your advice. Should I get an abortion?" I'd been a manager for a long time, and no one had ever hit me with a question like that.

I also had to do more teaching and training than I'd ever done back in the States. At an IBM facility in the U.S., I'd be working with people who had an average of twenty-two years' experience in business. In China, it was closer to twenty-two months. They were the best and the brightest in the country, since any ambitious young person would want to work for an IBM or a Motorola or a GE as opposed to one of the state-run enterprises. But I couldn't take anything for granted. I had to assume they knew nothing. It's one of the reasons I was working eighty-hour weeks throughout my time in Beijing.

And at the same time, I was juggling an incredible array of business deals. I'd get a call at night about an important negotiation the next morning, I'd go out to the airport to catch an eight a.m. flight to Shanghai, and the next thing I knew I'd be on television from the Great Hall of the People, helping to announce a huge new government project. What an experience.

For Dave Nelson, the China years were an amazing capper to a satisfying corporate career. But now in his late fifties, Nelson was looking ahead. His three kids were now grown up and off to college or beyond. After thirty-two years on the job, his IBM stock had skyrocketed in value, splitting four times in just the past decade, giving him and Patricia a comfortable nest egg and the power to choose their future path with relative freedom from financial worries. They were both young, active, and healthy, ready to take on new challenges. And so Nelson found himself revisiting his old dream of applying his personal talents to some work of social value, like teaching.

"Don't get me wrong," Nelson says. "It's not that my work at IBM wasn't socially valuable":

> IBM was a wonderful company to work for, and I'll always be proud of the way we treated our people. I'll give you an example. At one point in my career, I was an assistant to the president of IBM's U.S. operations. And one of my jobs was to handle what we called "open door investigations." If any IBM employee ever felt that he was being treated unfairly, he could—after trying to work through the usual chain of command—ask for a review of the situation by the local chief executive.
>
> Well, I vetted dozens of these investigations, dealing with all kinds of touchy situations and accusations of everything from expense account cheating to sexual harassment. Occasionally a top executive was charged with misbehavior. You can imagine that feelings ran high. But never—never once—did I ever feel personally compromised, nor did I ever witness the process being handled with less than the utmost integrity. At how many companies could I have said the same thing?
>
> That's one of the main reasons I stayed at IBM so long—because I felt so comfortable with the company's values, and because the company was religious about living up to them.

Nelson could also argue, with some justification, that the products and services IBM created had a social value of their own:

> Pat and I used to debate about this when we were first married. She was a caseworker for the Cook County De-

partment of Public Aid, helping poor people improve their lives. Meanwhile, I was selling IBM equipment to companies like the First National Bank of Chicago. You couldn't imagine any job that was more purely capitalist. So Pat would say to me, "You've got to quit IBM. Why spend your life making money for some greedy corporation? Let's start a school and be Montessori teachers together."

But I would push back. I'd say to Pat, "Remember those horror stories you tell me about the problems your clients have with the department—how a family will come in, desperately needing some kind of assistance, and you *know* they're eligible for it, but you can't give it to them because their file is missing or the paperwork is incomplete or you can't find the approval from your supervisor? Now imagine you had a great information system from IBM that could solve all those problems. Think how much more effective you could be."

Pat accepted my argument. But only up to a point. Deep down, she still believed that the non-profit world is the place to be if you really care about people. And that's how lots of people think.

In the end, the bottom line at IBM was the same as at most other corporations—the bottom line. And by age fifty-six, Nelson was ready to try shifting gears to some other kind of work, in which enriching the lives of other people would be more important than filling the coffers of a company.

An unexpected letter from a boyhood friend that appeared in Nelson's in-box during his final summer in Beijing intensified that focus. Ron Lewis had been a buddy of Nelson's when they were both in seventh grade, and he'd gone on to enjoy a successful career as an attorney in Washington, D.C. Now he wrote to Nelson, "Dear Nels: You may find this news amusing, but I just wanted to let you know." Attached was a press release announcing that Lewis had just been named the second-highest-ranking officer of the Pew Charitable Trust, one of the largest philanthropic foundations in the world. His assignment: to give away a quarter of a billion dollars every year for the benefit of humankind.

Nelson wrote back, "Ron, my reaction to your news is not amusement. Try envy."

So when Nelson returned to the United States in 1998 on the successful completion of his China tour, he visited his boss and announced that he was ready to schedule his retirement from IBM, and—more important—to begin planning a dramatically different scenario for his personal Act Two.

To Nelson's surprise, the process of relaunching himself on a new career path ended up taking almost two years.

Part of that process was defining what he really wanted to do in the nonprofit world, which was largely unfamiliar territory for him. He considered, and then quickly discarded, his old dream of becoming a teacher. Working in a high school or elementary school wasn't for him. He enjoyed speaking with students at the college and graduate-school levels, having found himself in demand as a lecturer at places like Kellogg, Yale, and Wharton since his return from China, but without a Ph.D. to his name, he was an unlikely candidate for a faculty position at the typical university.

Nelson thought about following his buddy Ron Lewis into the foundation world, but one of his first new mentors, a friend of a friend named Jim Forbes, scuttled that notion. "Jim looked over my résumé and said, 'Nelson, you'd go crazy working in a foundation. You're an *operating* guy. You've got to be *running* something.' And as soon as he said it, I realized he was right."

Having given advance notice to his boss at IBM and led his department through the transition, Nelson eventually devoted himself full-time to learning about the nonprofit world. He followed up every lead, wangled introductions with dozens of nonprofit executives and board members, and applied for every managerial job opening he heard about. Everyone he met was impressed by his track record at IBM. But the perfect fit proved elusive—especially since Nelson had *no* experience in the nonprofit world.

Finally, in December of 2000, through yet another indirect contact, he heard about an organization called the National Foundation for Teaching Entrepreneurship—NFTE, always pronounced "nifty." Having grown from a tiny nonprofit start-up in 1987 to a burgeoning group with national ambitions, NFTE had just developed a five-year growth plan with the help of the world's premier management consulting firm, McKinsey & Company. (McKinsey had charged NFTE around a hundred thousand dollars for the engagement, roughly one-twentieth its value on the open market.) Now NFTE's founder, Steve Mariotti, was looking for a chief operating officer (COO) to carry out that plan.

When Nelson walked into the New York offices of NFTE, he was met with extreme skepticism.

Like everyone else who looked at Nelson's résumé, Mariotti was impressed. But he was also worried. NFTE's mission was to teach entrepreneurship to inner-city kids—to infuse them with a sense of the excitement, creativity, and opportunity that exist in the (to them) unfamiliar world of business. How would a thirty-three-year veteran of the world's ultimate white-shirt corporation fit that mission? To put it bluntly, what did an IBM executive know about entrepreneurship?

What's more, NFTE was a relatively tiny outfit. "We're a ragtag operation," Mariotti told Nelson. "We've got thirty-eight people working here. The carpets are frayed, the walls need painting. Everybody has to make their own copies and pour their own coffee. Are you going to be comfortable in a place like this?"

These were realistic questions that Nelson himself took

seriously. But he didn't think of himself as a typical gray-suited IBM type (if such a thing exists). He'd always had an entrepreneurial streak, which he'd used to good effect in launching and building new product lines in one area after another. He'd just come back from three years of improvising and experimentation in China, where the very rules of capitalism were being reinvented in a wide-open environment. Unlike some Fortune 500 executives, Nelson didn't flinch from a hands-on challenge—he relished it.

"Old man Watson," Nelson said, referring to the legendary founder of IBM, "used to say that the ideal IBM employee was a wild duck capable of flying in formation. I think that's me. I was always looking for new and better ways of doing things—and then once I found them, leading a team to use them. If that's what you want, I'm your man."

What clinched the deal was Nelson's personal belief in the mission of NFTE:

> It's all about reaching kids who otherwise would drop out of school. Do you know what the national high school drop-out rate is today? It's 32 percent. And that's exactly what it was when I graduated from Thornton Township High forty years ago—that same 32 percent. That's just not good enough for the twenty-first century. At NFTE, the mission is to give kids something to learn and practice that's relevant to them and to the world they're growing up in—a world where business shapes everything they do.

NFTE founder Steve Mariotti swallowed his fears and made Dave Nelson his COO. What's more, he did it with no strings attached, making it clear that Dave was now the chief daily decision maker for the organization. "Steve's trust in me was complete. He handed me that five-year growth plan, gave me the keys to the car, and said, 'Get us there safely.' That defined our relationship for the next eight years."

Having landed the do-gooder job he'd long dreamed about, Dave Nelson now began his reeducation in earnest. The nonprofit world, he quickly learned, was a lot different from IBM.

One big difference was the kind of people Nelson was working with. In many ways they were just as smart and dedicated as anyone at IBM. Most were infused with a genuine sense of passion for NFTE's mission, and many were extremely creative, some brilliantly so. But few had any significant business experience. Those who'd held paying jobs before NFTE had been schoolteachers or done clerical work in insurance companies or brokerage firms—which meant that making organizational decisions, allocating resources, developing business plans, setting goals, and taking the necessary managerial steps to achieve them were all foreign concepts that Nelson had to begin slowly, painstakingly teaching them from day one on the job.

The funny thing is, they *loved* it. "The big thing I brought to the process was focus," Nelson recalls. "Everyone at NFTE had been working hard to try to realize this enormous promise they all felt they had. But without focus, they weren't getting anywhere. So when I brought them that focus, they weren't resentful at all— they were very grateful."

Nonetheless, helping his freewheeling, creatively minded young charges develop the disciplined mind-set that employees in for-profit businesses usually take for granted wasn't easy. Several years into the process, Nelson had to make an end-of-year presentation to the NFTE board of directors about the organization's finances. In preparation, he asked his staff members to provide him with estimates of their final expense figures. It was just five days before the books would close for the year. "In a nonprofit," Nelson explains, "revenues are hard to estimate":

They're mainly contributions from donors, grants from corporations and foundations, and so on, and you never know when an unexpected gift may come through or when a donor you've been counting on might have to pull back. So you have to cut some slack on revenue projections, which are always pretty unreliable.

But costs are another matter. Costs are things you spend money on—salaries, insurance, rent, utilities, supplies. You have control over costs, and you know, or should know, how much you are spending practically down to the dollar. So when my staff members handed me their cost estimates for the year, I felt pretty comfortable with them. But after my presentation to the board, when the actual year-end figures arrived, I was shocked to find that we'd miscalculated expenses by more than a million dollars—on a base of just twelve million! I wondered, *How could this happen?*

In retrospect, I can see how. Deep inside, most of the people at NFTE didn't care much about numbers. They cared about our mission. They cared about schools, students, and teachers. They worried about getting the curriculum right, making our programs effective, and creating powerful connections with young people who needed our help. But ask them to keep track of a bunch of numbers and they couldn't be more bored.

It was quite a lesson for me. I realized that this was China all over again—that I didn't dare take even the most basic business knowledge for granted. Later, I worked with our young staffers to understand why the numbers are so important, and they did much better.

Little by little, department by department, Nelson brought businesslike order into the relative chaos he'd discovered at

NFTE. He developed and implemented a performance appraisal system; a system for setting, achieving, and documenting individual and team goals; and a series of improvements in the organizational governance scheme, including strengthening of internal controls and a revision of the bylaws to apply the same rules for transparency and accuracy that for-profit companies follow under the Sarbanes-Oxley legislation.

Nelson also created programs for providing employees with training in business skills, management, and leadership. People in the nonprofit world value lifetime learning, but their organizations usually can't afford it. "In my time at IBM," Nelson remarks, "I never had less than two weeks a year of professional education. At NFTE, we were lucky if we could afford two days." Nelson plugged the gap by arranging pro bono training programs from friends at IBM and supporters at the Babson College school of business. His NFTE staffers were stunned to discover how much they didn't know—and thrilled to receive the training they'd never been offered before.

Nelson also gradually upgraded the skills level of NFTE staffers by reducing turnover, creating long-term career paths for the best employees, and adjusting salaries to enable the organization to attract and retain workers with advanced degrees. "When I arrived at NFTE," he says, "around 14 percent of our people had graduate degrees. When I left, it was 50 percent." Yes, NFTE's payroll is now higher. But the capabilities of its people are so much greater that its bang for the buck has grown even faster than the salaries.

Nelson spent eight years at NFTE, more than twice as long as any single post he'd held at IBM. He guided the organization through the most dynamic growth phase in its history, expanding its student base from seven thousand to over forty-four thousand, its domestic offices from six to twelve, its international operations from three countries to thirteen, and its net assets from $5.4 million to

$18.8 million. And before departing NFTE, Nelson orchestrated a succession process that brought in an effective successor (an experienced education reformer named Amy Rosen) who is now leading the organization to even greater heights of achievement.

Along the way, Nelson was honored by Civic Ventures, a San Francisco–based think tank devoted to studying the links among work, social purpose, and the baby boom generation that describes itself as "leading the call to engage millions of baby boomers as a vital workforce for change." Nelson was one of seventy Americans named a Purpose Prize Fellow by Civic Ventures in 2006, a title bestowed on those who work as social innovators in an "encore career."

As a role model for people who want to navigate the transition from the for-profit to the nonprofit worlds, Dave Nelson has a wealth of wisdom to share with other would-be bridgers.

One of his chief recommendations: Although your business background may enable you to bring enormous value to a nonprofit organization, don't expect your new colleagues to be impressed by it. Instead, remember that you are now working with a group of idealistic, probably young people who know little about business and care less. In fact, they probably identify "business" with the unscrupulous executives, fast-talking salespeople, and greedy stock traders they see caricatured in movies or on the nightly news. So avoid holding up your experiences in the for-profit world as a model of behavior for your new organization. Doing so will only breed resentment and alienation.

To prevent this, Nelson imposed on himself a simple rule when he first joined NFTE—that he would *never* mention IBM in a business meeting. Nelson describes this as a very deliberate personal communications strategy:

> They all knew where I'd worked. Why polarize people by talking about it? Mention IBM at a place like NFTE, and immediately everyone thinks about all the qualities IBM

has that NFTE doesn't—big, rich, bureaucratic, hierarchical. The image creates barriers rather than connections among people.

So instead of saying, "Here's how we did it at IBM," I just made suggestions: "How about trying it this way?" Over time, we all learned *together* about the best ways to run NFTE. It felt like a team effort, not the hot-shot business guy imposing his ways on everybody else.

Ironically, learning to see myself as other people see me was a skill I'd developed at IBM. By working hard to imagine the worst possible perceptions that my colleagues at NFTE might have about me, I was able to anticipate and disarm them.

After Nelson had been at NFTE two years, his colleague Mike Casland, a longtime manager at NFTE, leaned over to him during a meeting and remarked, "Dave, it'd be okay for you to mention IBM now." Dave grinned. Mike was handing him a small victory trophy—a sign that Nelson had been fully accepted in the nonprofit culture of NFTE, *despite* the "black mark" of his decades as a leader at one of the world's most successful corporations.

Today, having retired from NFTE, Dave Nelson is a member of the Board of the Directors of AARP, the national organization for Americans over fifty, as well as a member of the board's audit and finance committees. He's shifted from working on behalf of disadvantaged youth to serving primarily older Americans. And the job is no honorary position—a mere name on a letterhead. As Nelson describes it:

It's a non-compensated position that demands my full attention thirty-five to forty business days a year. The finance committee alone meets for two days at a time. We have a billion-dollar business to run. It's serious stuff, and becoming a board member is far from easy. I was one of just seven people selected out of four hundred applicants. The vetting process almost makes a CIA application pale by comparison.

Ironically, Nelson himself had resisted becoming a member of AARP despite receiving direct-mail solicitations for over fifteen years: "I perceived it as being about aging. I'm more interested in *living*. That's what my story is all about. And when I said that to the people at AARP, they said, 'That's exactly the direction we want to go.'" Now Nelson is helping AARP develop programs that will help millions of Americans launch their own rewarding second acts.

•   •   •

Moving successfully from the for-profit to the not-for-profit world isn't as easy as one might assume. As we've seen, it took Dave Nelson all of two years to make the transition from IBM to NFTE. It's a familiar story to David Simms of Bridgespan, an organization that specializes in helping nonprofit organizations find the leaders they need to help them achieve their missions. Despite the fact that huge numbers of businesspeople are actively searching for new opportunities to enjoy greater meaning and satisfaction in their careers, thousands of job openings they might find rewarding are going begging due to communications failures, mismatched skills, and false expectations. It's a serious social challenge that Bridgespan is working hard to meet.

Bridgespan is a nonprofit consulting organization that was incubated in the year 2000 at Bain & Company, the highly respected strategy consulting firm based in Boston. Its cofounder and chairman, Tom Tierney, had been CEO of Bain during the 1990s. Bridgespan's mission is to take the business strategy concepts developed by Bain and adapt them to the very different economic, social, and cultural context of the nonprofit world. The goal: to help organizations with a social mission achieve breakthrough results through brilliant deployment of strategy, capital, and talent. And one division of Bridgespan is devoted to talent—finding it, developing it, training it, and using it effectively to achieve great results.

Bridgespan has been conducting wide-ranging surveys into the leadership challenges facing America's nonprofit sector. Its findings have been sobering. The statistics alone tell a daunting tale:

- In a 2006 study, Bridgespan discovered that, because of rapid expansion, increased demand, the enormous growth in complexity of nonprofit work, and the impending retirement of many baby boomers, nonprofit organizations would need to recruit some 640,000 senior leaders—chief executive officers, chief operating officers, chief financial officers, and others at a comparable level—before the year 2017.
- In 2008 alone, Bridgespan found that nonprofit organizations had some 77,000 unfilled senior executive positions, confirming the magnitude of the number forecast in the 2006 study.
- Each year, there are approximately 1.3 million positions on nonprofit boards of directors that go unfilled.
- In December 2008 and January 2009, a Bridgespan survey to measure the impact of the recession on nonprofit talent demand found that organizations were already anticipating having to fill around 24,000 senior leadership positions during 2009. Since the vast majority of nonprofits do *not* have a succession plan for the top spots in place, this means thousands of leadership jobs that must be filled from outside, with all the cultural and psychological challenges that entails.

Yet, paradoxically, even as nonprofit organizations are struggling to fill thousands of crucial positions, thousands of experienced managers from the for-profit world are failing to find the opportunities they're seeking to make the transition into nonprofit management.

David Simms works at the intersection of these two separate worlds. He witnesses the frustrations on both ends. In fact, the founding of the talent division at Bridgespan in 2002 came about as a result of those frustrations. As Simms explains,

> . . . during the first couple of years of Bridgespan, because we were a consulting firm operating at the crossroads between the for-profit and non-profit worlds, we found we were getting hundreds of unsolicited résumés from friends and friends of friends who were looking for opportunities in the non-profit sector. So we could see the problems on either side of this chasm. The non-profit organizations couldn't find the talent they needed. The individuals who wanted to find work that was fulfilling and meaningful didn't know where to get plugged in. The obvious question was, could Bridgespan become some kind of matchmaker? And that was the impetus behind the launching of a division focused on talent.

David Simms himself has been a bridger, having worked not in two enterprise sectors but in three—the worlds of for-profit business, nonprofits, and government. He worked at Bain & Company as a business consultant, served in the State Department as a White House fellow, and worked for five years as CEO of the Red Cross's Blood Services program in Baltimore and Washington, D.C. Simms has also been a longtime board member of Opportunity International, a microenterprise organization that provides small loans to poor entrepreneurs through partners in twenty-eight countries around the world. With his varied background, Simms is perfectly positioned to help lead Bridgespan's effort to connect would-be bridgers with the nonprofit organizations that so desperately need their talents.

In working to conduct executive searches for nonprofit groups in the years since 2003, Simms has made a number of discoveries about the nature of the bridging phenomenon.

One is that shifting between the for-profit and nonprofit worlds is far more common than most people believe. "Some of the data from our last survey, in 2008, was frankly shocking to us," Simms says:

> We found that 42 percent of the non-profit CEOs we surveyed had significant management experience from the for-profit sector. More broadly, 53 percent of the organizations we spoke to had senior team members with significant private sector management experience. So the idea that there are non-profit and for-profit worlds that are isolated from one another is simply not true anymore, if it ever was.

Furthermore, leaders in the nonprofit world are strongly aware of the value that business experience can bring to their organizations. Particularly in difficult economic times, qualities like a tough-minded approach to strategy, a goal-oriented leadership style, and a no-nonsense bottom-line orientation are all deeply appreciated by nonprofit leaders.

But this recognition of the value of a business perspective doesn't necessarily translate into open doors for the would-be bridger. Simms has found that there are still big cultural and psychological gulfs that need to be crossed by the person who wants to shift into the nonprofit world:

> The great strength of the business world is that there are clear guidelines for judging the performance of a manager

and of an organization. There are quarterly earnings reports, market share statistics, customer satisfaction scores, and profit-and-loss forecasts. In a non-profit, those things may not exist, or if they do they may not carry the weight they do in a for-profit business. So if you're working for an environmental group, for example, and someone asks you, "Did you do a good job last month?" you can't just look at your monthly P&L and give a definitive answer. Instead, you find yourself wondering, "How *did* we do last month? Did global warming get better or worse? Are the oceans less polluted? Is the air quality cleaner?" And those kinds of questions aren't always easy to answer.

This isn't to say that money isn't important to us. Of course it is, because we need resources to carry out our work. But making money isn't our goal the way it is for a corporation. It's simply a means to an end. We're trying to improve the environment, or reduce poverty, or help educate young people, and the money matters only to the extent that it helps us make the world a better place.

As I like to put it, *Mission trumps money.* Understanding that, and making changes in leadership style to reflect it, is the single biggest adjustment that managers from the business world have to make when they try to cross the divide into non-profit management.

The "mission trumps money" challenge is the one Dave Nelson ran up against at NFTE when his staffers submitted woefully inaccurate spending estimates just a few days before the end of the budget year. It wasn't that his managers at NFTE weren't smart enough to keep accurate spending accounts; they just didn't see the importance of it as compared with their mission to improve the lives of kids. And Nelson had failed, to that point, in one of his personal leadership missions, which was to show his young followers the intimate connection between the two. It's a connection that busi-nesspeople take for granted, but that people in the nonprofit world need to learn.

Another cultural gap between the two worlds involves decision-making practices. In a for-profit business, the most junior staff member is likely to be respectful, even deferential around members of the management team. At a typical corporation, when two vice presidents are debating the best approach to a strategy problem dur-ing a meeting, you wouldn't expect a young assistant with three weeks on the job to pipe up with an opinion. But at a nonprofit, that wouldn't be unusual. "It's about commitment," Simms explains:

> Even the youngest person at a non-profit organization has made a commitment to the shared mission. They feel a personal passion about the work they are doing, and they've probably made some sacrifice to participate in it—for ex-ample, taking less pay than they could earn at a for-profit company. So when an issue arises that relates to the mission, they feel entitled to express their opinion. Their commit-ment is just as strong and meaningful as anyone else's, and to them, that means their voice is just as important.

As you can imagine, this takes some getting used to. The first time an executive with decades of experience at a place like GE, Citibank, or IBM finds himself being questioned or challenged in front of his nonprofit team by a twenty-two-year-old staffer fresh out of college, his instinct may be to slap the youngster down with a brusque or sarcastic remark. But in the nonhierarchical world of the nonprofit, that would be a disastrous mistake. As Simms ex-plains, "A good non-profit leader will know how to marshal that youthful energy and passion, allowing everyone to be heard but also guiding the decision-making process so that, in the end, the right choices get made."

Challenges like these mean that any businessperson who assumes that helping to run a nonprofit organization will be *easier* than succeeding in business is in for a rude surprise. In fact, that assumption may be a major reason why some would-be bridgers fail to make the transition. "We don't have hard evidence yet as to why some people fail to bridge successfully from the for-profit to non-profit worlds," Simms says:

> But anecdotal evidence suggests that the problem almost never lies with their technical skills—their financial knowledge or technology know-how or H.R. expertise. It's usually about culture—about accepting the need for collaboration, the different pace of decision-making, the demand for consensus.
>
> It's fascinating to note that, when the management guru Peter Drucker was once asked, "What's the best-run organization in America?" he replied, "The Girl Scouts." And when the questioner responded, "I didn't say, the best-run nonprofit," Drucker answered, "I understood the question, and I gave you the answer." Drucker believed that the Girl Scouts was the best-run organization in America, bar none—not *despite* being a non-profit, but in part *because* it was a non-profit.
>
> After all, think about it this way: A non-profit leader doesn't have all the leadership tools that a for-profit leader has. She doesn't have the kinds of compensation packages to offer, or the command-and-control systems, or the disciplinary techniques that a corporate executive typically has. Instead, she has to lead through persuasion, influence, and inspiration. It's not necessarily harder than what a for-profit leader does, but it's certainly different. And it's a challenge that's easy to underestimate when you enter this world from the outside.

Having tackled these challenges of bridging from both directions—as an adviser to would-be bridgers as well as a counselor to nonprofit organizations in their efforts to recruit and develop executives—David Simms may be better positioned than anyone in the world to offer insights to those who are interested in making the transition from the for-profit to the not-for-profit world. Their numbers are huge, and growing. Almost 10 percent of U.S. workers between the ages of forty-four and seventy have already moved into the "social sector" (which includes nonprofits, schools, and other civic institutions), and fully half of so-called trailing-edge baby boomers (currently between forty-four and fifty years old) say that they, too, would like to make the move.

For those millions of would-be bridgers, here are some of Simms's most important pieces of advice.

If you believe that someday you may want to work in the nonprofit sector, start today—as a volunteer. Simms has met all too many businesspeople who say they dream of working in a charitable, philanthropic, or service organization, yet have a résumé filled with nothing but for-profit employment. When questioned about this, they generally say, "Well, I've been working so hard as a manager at XYZ Corporation that I haven't had time to do outside volunteer work." That may be true. But it seriously damages your credibility as a candidate for work in the social sphere. After all, nonprofit work is all about the mission and the values it embodies. How believable is it that a person might suddenly develop those values at (say) the age of fifty-five after *never* exhibiting them previously? So if you plan on becoming a bridger some day, find the time *now* to do pro bono work, volunteer service, or part-time work for a nonprofit group.

Learn about the nonprofit world by serving on a board. One of the best ways to become immersed in the challenges and opportunities of nonprofit work is by offering to fill one of those 1.3 million board of director slots that go begging every year. Even young people with modest skills and experience can usually find board positions that are appropriate for them. "At age twenty-five, you're not going to be recruited to join the national board of the American Red Cross," Simms notes. "But there are plenty of local organizations that would be delighted to have your services."

Simms illustrates the point with the story of Lindsay Coleman, who is Bridgespan's associate director of marketing and communications:

> Lindsay was the second person I hired here back in 2003, and one of the first things I told her was, "I believe that people should serve on boards." And although Lindsay was just a couple of years out of Wake Forest at the time, she said, "Okay, let me go out and find one." She ended up becoming a board member for an organization called the Friday Night Supper Program, which feeds the homeless here in downtown Boston. She introduced Bridgespan to the group, and a number of us have done some hands-on work with them, helping to prepare and serve meals on Friday nights. And Lindsay has gone on to become one of their most effective fundraisers, as well as learning all kinds of leadership and management skills she could never have learned in her day job. She's been contributing to the community and growing as a person and a professional thanks to her board service.

Try your hand at development. "There are more jobs available in development—fund-raising—than anywhere else in the non-profit world," Simms observes. But for many people, this is an intimidating prospect. How many of us relish the notion of calling our friends and asking them to write us a check, even for the most worthy of causes? The natural salesperson may find this easy to do, but most others shy away from it.

David Simms suggests that a large part of the problem may be attitude:

> Raising support is very important for almost every non-profit. But instead of thinking about it as asking for money, why not think about it as sharing the insights and joy you've experienced as a supporter yourself?
>
> For many people, it's easier and more effective to start by inviting people to join you in non-monetary ways. Instead of asking someone to write you a check for five thousand dollars, invite them to come along the next time you take part in a mercy mission to Africa. "Come with me to Ghana," you might say. "Let me show you what poverty in the developing world looks like. And let me show you the transformative power of a small loan in the hands of a mother whose kids can now go to school for the first time, and who have access to health care for the first time—all because I cared enough to step outside of my personal comfort zone."
>
> Do you see the difference? Rather than asking for something, you're offering someone an amazing reward that you've already experienced yourself and that is very hard to get in the for-profit world.
>
> If you can introduce others to the joy you experience as a volunteer, then making the transition to a paid job in the non-profit sector doing some kind of development work is actually a short and easy bridge to cross, not a difficult one.

Be prepared to adjust your expectations concerning salary and working conditions. The typical nonprofit organization is less well funded than most for-profit companies. So if you are coming from a well-paid position in the for-profit world, you may need to accept a lower level of compensation in a similar job at a nonprofit.

In addition, working conditions may be less posh: As Dave Nelson learned when he joined NFTE, it helps if you are willing to fetch your own coffee and make your own photocopies (and even to offer to do the same for your colleagues once in a while).

Still, circumstances vary greatly among nonprofits just as they do among profit-making companies. Some large, well-established nonprofits offer pay and benefits that are extremely competitive with the best for-profit employers. One way to get an accurate sense of what to expect is to study the salary surveys periodically published by organizations such as GuideStar (dedicated to gathering and publicizing information about nonprofit organizations), the *Chronicle of Philanthropy,* the *Nonprofit Times,* and Abbott, Langer & Associates (which specializes in salary studies). You can also learn about the compensation structure at a specific nonprofit by downloading its 990 tax form from the GuideStar website (www .guidestar.org), which lists salary information for the top-paid employees of the organization.

Learn the lingo. Although many of the management and leadership challenges in the nonprofit world are similar to those in the business world, the language and some of the underlying assumptions may be different. When you first enter the nonprofit arena through job interviews or conversations, be sensitive about the language you use. Terms like *ROI* (return on investment), *EBITDA* (earnings before interest, tax, depreciation, and amortization), and *CAGR* (compound annual growth rate) aren't widely used in the nonprofit world. More important, if you drop them casually into your communication (as you may be accustomed to doing in a for-profit context), you may suggest to your listeners that the only measurement of success that you understand is a financial one, which may lead them to question your ability to be truly dedicated to a social mission.

More broadly, there are forms of self-expression that are considered appropriate in the business world that are likely to "turn people off" in the nonprofit world. If you have a type A personality—

aggressive, self-confident, assertive, ambitious, high energy—you may need to tone it down a notch or two when making a transition to the nonprofit arena. It's not that energy, ambition, and self-confidence are frowned upon; rather, the distinction is between an individual orientation and a group orientation. Nonprofits tend to operate in a collaborative fashion, with personal goals subsumed to the overarching mission. An interloper from the for-profit world who joins the team with the goal of "shaking things up," "making a mark," and "turning things around" is likely to be viewed as ham-fisted, insensitive, and egocentric.

If you've been working in the business world at any level and are interested in finding ways of making a personal contribution to the well-being of your community, your nation, or your world, the nonprofit world is eager to enlist your help. Like any transition, bridging to the nonprofit world offers some significant challenges. But hundreds of thousands of Americans are making the leap every year, with successful pioneers like Dave Nelson leading the way.

Food for Thought, Seeds for Action

- *Planning for your second act:* If you work in the business world—or if you are a government worker, a home-maker, or otherwise involved in work with no explicit social mission—you may want to begin planning a second career with a civic focus today. Today's extended life expectancies and healthier lifestyles mean that millions of people in their late fifties, sixties, and beyond are able and eager to contribute to society and enrich their own lives by working in a new field. And those who start thinking about the transition two to three years before they need to make it are most likely to achieve success and happiness in the process.

• *Reach out to nonprofit groups with missions that excite you:* The best way to prepare for a second act as a bridger is by establishing connections with nonprofit groups that share your values and ideals. Think about the causes that energize you. Are you motivated by concern for the natural environment? The well-being of kids? The needs of mothers and families? The problems of homelessness and hunger? The challenges confronting our health care or educational systems? A desire to spread happiness through the arts, recreation, or sports? Identify the organizations in your town, county, or state that are engaged in the most productive work in a field you believe in and offer to help out as a volunteer or board member. You may find yourself opening doors that will lead to a rewarding second career.

• *Match your skills and experience with the needs of nonprofit groups.* Job postings on Internet career sites as well as on sites dedicated to nonprofit careers, like the one maintained by Bridgespan, will offer clues as to the kinds of business skills nonprofit groups are looking for. In some cases, the connection to a skill you've used in a business career may be obvious: Both for-profit and nonprofit organizations need people with skills in finance, marketing, communications, technology, and operations, for example. But nonprofits often look for candidates who have experience working across disciplines, managing multiple stakeholders, and operating with limited resources. Look at your working background to identify experiences you've had that will lend themselves to a successful transition into the nonprofit arena.

‖ 9 ‖

Revitalizing Our Democracy

Restoring Idealism
to Public Service

As we've seen throughout this book, millions of people in America are enthusiastically taking part in today's movement toward active citizenship. Yet there's a curious, and unfortunate, gap in the perceptions of most people when it comes to civic engagement.

When successful businesspeople speak about their desire to "give something back" to their cities, states, or country; when young people talk about wanting to devote part of their lives to community service; and when activists describe their dreams of fostering creative, entrepreneurial innovations to address pressing social problems, they are usually thinking about work in the *private* sector. They generally have in mind participating in the activities of charities, nongovernmental agencies, foundations, nonprofit organizations, and sometimes for-profit businesses that have social or environmental goals. It's very rare that they think in terms of the public sector—that is, government work.

Why is this the case? Isn't government, at all levels—federal, state, and local—supposed to be the ultimate expression of the people's will, the most powerful force for social improvement, and the final safety net for those in need? Why shouldn't government be one of the first options that idealistic people consider when seeking an opportunity to serve their communities . . . rather than one of the last?

Actually, the reasons aren't mysterious. Government service has suffered a terrible image problem for at least the last generation. One of the most popular and charismatic political leaders of the last fifty years, Ronald Reagan, famously declared, "Government is not the solution—government is the problem," even as he was being sworn in to direct the very government whose value he seemed to disdain.

In Reagan's wake, dozens of lesser politicians have echoed his message. Government, they say, can't do anything right; it's inherently inefficient, wasteful, bureaucratic, and intrusive. They point to the collapse of the Soviet Union as evidence of the weakness of any society that is centered on and driven by government rather than private enterprise. And they love to repeat cynical lines like, "The scariest thing you can hear is, 'I'm from the government and I'm here to help.'" It's not surprising this theme continues to be echoed by candidates—quite a few elections have been won this way in recent years.

The cynicism about government is not entirely without justification. We all know about the spectacular failures of government, from the too-little, too-late response by FEMA to the devastation of Hurricane Katrina, to the failure to rein in the financial excesses that helped produce the economic collapse of 2008–9. We've seen plenty of evidence that government is too often manipulated for the benefit of well-connected special interests, campaign contributors, and corporations rather than serving the needs of all the people. And the spectacle of partisan gridlock, dishonest posturing, and hypocrisy that dominates the news from Washington (and too many state capitals as well) leads many citizens to turn away from government in disgust.

If we're going to accomplish anything worthwhile, it sometimes seems, we need to rely on citizen initiatives, entrepreneurial

with, transforming organizations intended to protect the public into private servants. When we impose invasive background checks and harsh, often partisan public scrutiny on those nominated for leadership positions in government, we lead many distinguished citizens with much to contribute to shy away from public service. And when we repeatedly cut the budgets of essential government agencies, forcing them to lay off their most experienced (and highest-paid) workers, we make it even harder for those agencies to provide the services we expect.

Today, we're reaping the results of three decades of indifference or hostility toward public service—not just in the spectacular failures of agencies like FEMA and the SEC but in steadily worsening, chronic crises affecting the environment, public education, the health-care system, and the national infrastructure. Government has to step up to tackle these problems. And that means restoring our recognition of the value of public service and our respect and support for those who choose to make it a career.

Among those who have been working to address this challenge is Max Stier, the youthful president and CEO of the Partnership for Public Service. The largest independent organization focusing on the quality of government, the Partnership believes good government starts with good people. It is active on many fronts, but its central goal is to make government work better for everyone—and to achieve this, in Stier's view, you must simultaneously inspire a new generation to enter public service and transform government itself.

For Stier, there should be no conflict between supporting private organizations focused on social good and acknowledging the value of government:

> One of the enormous strengths of our society is the incredible flowering of the non-profit sector that we've witnessed in recent years. But the sad thing is that, as a

result, government has been bled out of the concept of public service. When people talk about "public service" today, our research suggests that they don't even think about government as being part of it any more.

· And in fact the situation, until recently, was even worse than that. Most people actually saw government as being in opposition to them. So non-profits felt they had to work against government. Philanthropy didn't engage with government. The business community lobbied government on the policy side and ignored the operations side, with the result that government effectiveness suffered. And so government has become an insulated, isolated institution in our society, and that's a gigantic problem.

Stier and the Partnership have made it their mission to break down these barriers. To do so, they study the problems of government as a whole, focusing not on the work of any individual agency but rather on long-term challenges and issues that no single cabinet secretary or even presidential administration is really capable of addressing.

In this respect, government, for all its resources, is far worse off than most private institutions. In a corporation or not-for-profit organization, the CEO and the board of directors are charged with protecting the long-range health of the institution. No one in government can really fulfill this role.

A president serves a four-year term, spending much of it positioning himself (or someday herself) for a successful reelection bid. Inevitably he is focused on fulfilling his key campaign promises by launching one or a handful of major initiatives or programs rather than working to improve the overall functioning of the hundreds of separate agencies that make up the federal government.

In fact, our political system actually creates *disincentives* for a president to focus on strengthening the functioning of government. A president who improves the nuts-and-bolts operations of a particular departmental bureaucracy will probably get little or no credit for it—after all, it isn't a particularly sexy or even visible activity. All the political rewards will go to his *successor,* whose own pet initiatives will be implemented more swiftly and effectively by the strengthened organization. Why should a president knock himself out to bequeath a more powerful set of tools to his successor, who is likely to be from the opposite party?

Go down the organizational scale and similar structural problems crop up. The average political appointee—a cabinet secretary or undersecretary, for example—has a tenure of just eighteen to twenty-four months, which is far too short a time to bring to fruition any serious organizational reforms. No wonder most career managers in government find their work frustrating: far more than in private industry, their work is continually being sidetracked by shifting priorities as partisan appointees come and go, each bringing his or her own perspectives and goals.

Finally, the government has no equivalent of the board of directors that oversees the typical private-sector organization. The closest analogue is the Congress, whose 535 members are too numerous to serve in a strategic capacity, too divided by partisan agendas, and too focused on a host of distracting individual goals, chiefly getting reelected every two years.

So no one within government is positioned to take the long view—to ask questions like, "How does the talent base of government stack up against the major challenges we are likely to face in the next five, ten, or twenty years? What kinds of organizational and structural changes should we be making to ready ourselves for the problems and opportunities to come? What can we be learning from private industry about the use of modern information technology to improve services and increase efficiencies?"

Max Stier and the Partnership are trying to raise such questions from their outsider's perspective.

One of the big worries that keeps Stier up at night is an emerging crisis for the staffing of government:

By our estimates, the federal government's going to be losing about half a million people over the next five years, primarily through retirements. It's a function of the overall aging of the American work force, but it's much more pronounced in the public sector than in the private.

Why? One big reason is the well-intentioned effort to "reinvent government" that was led by Vice President Al Gore in the 1990s. Gore is a very smart man, and many of the changes he made to streamline government were necessary. But in the process, we downsized government by some four hundred thousand workers, and it wasn't done strategically. That is, no one was looking at the long-term needs of our agencies and figuring out what kind of talent would be required a decade or more down the road.

So what ended up happening is that we lost our government's bench strength—the mid-level managers who would normally have become the top leaders a few years later. With no new hiring, we ended up with a cohort of top-level leaders that just aged in place without any effective succession planning as to who would succeed them.

As a result, today we have government organizations that, in the best circumstances, are finally starting to hire some fresh talent. But they're shaped like dumbbells, and misshapen dumbbells at that—a heavy piece at one end, where the remaining older workers are, nothing in the middle, and then a little something growing on the other end. It's not a healthy pattern.

The problems in certain agencies are acute. In the in-

telligence community, for example, over half the employees have been on the job less than five years. They've just
seen a massive transformation due to a huge outflow of
talent, withered recruiting mechanisms, and a lost generation of expertise. No wonder government isn't as well run
as it should be.

Few Americans realize that the size of the federal workforce
today is about the same as it was in the 1960s, when the population of the country was fully 40 percent lower than today. This
means we're asking the same number of workers to serve the
needs of a much larger customer base.

This huge shortfall in talent has been filled, in part, through
the use of private contractors, on whom the federal government
spent some $532 billion in 2008. But this creates problems of accountability and quality. Many of the worst perceived scandals of
government mismanagement—things like the infamous $600 coffeepots purchased by the Defense Department—arise not from
malfeasance by government employees but from the difficulty of
monitoring and controlling outside contractors. Outsourcing government services doesn't solve the challenges of public service—it
just kicks them down the road, making them that much harder to
manage.

Downsizing government was arguably a necessary step. Few
Americans would want to address our pressing problems by simply
hiring hundreds of thousands of federal workers. But a relatively
smaller government workforce means that the talent we have must
be supported and used with the greatest possible efficiency.

The Partnership is working to help government tackle the talent crisis. Among other programs, it advises government agencies
on how to best manage their most important asset—their people;
sponsors campus speakers and a student ambassador program to
inform young people about the opportunities in public service; and

is working to create a federal scholarship program for graduate students in high-skill, high-need areas.

But one of the Partnership's chief tools for addressing the crisis is a somewhat surprising one—its biannual set of ratings of job satisfaction among employees of specific government agencies. This study is based on the government's own employee survey, which the Partnership proposed and in which nearly a quarter of a million government workers participate. Results of the fourth Partnership study were released in May 2009. Trumpeted in newspapers and magazines under the heading of "The Best Places to Work in the Federal Government," the Partnership's ratings are used by new graduates and others interested in government employment as a kind of job-hunting guide. Perhaps more important, though, the ratings are used by federal managers to benchmark their employee satisfaction and commitment scores, understand where they excel and what they need to address, and monitor their progress toward improvements.

The connection between employee satisfaction and agency effectiveness isn't obvious—after all, the central mission of a government agency isn't to make employees happy. Yet Max Stier points out that the connection is actually very real.

The Partnership's data actually track employees' opinions about the agencies where they work along ten different parameters, including strategic management, the match between employee skills and the agency's mission, effective leadership, and teamwork. Taken together, these ratings create a profile of *employee engagement*—that is, the degree to which workers are energized and empowered by the agencies where they work. As Stier says, "there's a straight-line connection" between engagement and organizational effectiveness.

Stier likes to tell a story that he originally heard from Jim Clifton, president of the Gallup polling organization. Gallup was approached by the Ritz-Carlton luxury hotel chain to develop a survey tool for measuring the satisfaction of hotel guests. No mea-surement system they'd previously used had produced meaningful, reliable results. But based on his decades of experience in tracking opinions for the corporate sector, Clifton refused the assignment. "Let me do an employee satisfaction survey instead," he said. "It's a lot easier—and the results will tell you everything you need to know about customer satisfaction."

The moral: Satisfied employees are engaged employees—and engaged employees make for satisfied customers. It's as true in government as it is in the private sector.

Furthermore, a *bad* agency rating on the Partnership's em-ployee satisfaction scale can serve as an early warning system for identifying troubled agencies. Anyone studying the 2003 survey results (based on data compiled in 2002) would have noticed that the unit ranked last in employee engagement was the Federal Emergency Management Agency—the very organization whose catastrophic performance in response to Hurricane Katrina just two years later would become an emblem of government failure.

Today, some of our government's most crucial agencies are dis-playing similar "blinking warning lights" (as Stier called them in an article he wrote for *Washington Monthly* with John D. Donohue of Harvard's Kennedy School of Government):

- The Centers for Medicare and Medicaid Services, part of the Department of Health and Human Services, ranked 186th out of 222 cabinet agencies in the latest set of Partnership rankings—a disturbingly low rating for an agency that will play a critical role in the cost-control efforts at the heart of President Obama's ambi-tious program for health-care reform.
- The Office of Thrift Supervision, whose ineffective over-sight efforts contributed to some of the major bank fail-ures of 2008–09, ranked 192nd in the Partnership list.

- The Federal Aviation Administration, charged with overseeing efforts to maintain and improve the safety record of America's vast fleet of commercial airliners, ranked 204th.
- The Defense Contract Management Agency, which monitors some eighteen thousand private companies providing goods and services to the Pentagon in a time of increasing cost overruns and spiraling budget deficits, ranked 206th.
- The Defense Nuclear Detection Office, which is our chief line of defense against efforts to smuggle "loose nukes" into the United States, ranked 208th.
- And FEMA itself, while modestly improved from the dead-last ranking it earned in 2003, still hovers near the bottom of the Partnership ratings, coming in 211th out of 222 agencies.

Which agencies rank highest on the Partnership's survey? In 2009, the top ratings among large agencies (with two thousand or more full-time, permanent employees) went to:

1. The Nuclear Regulatory Commission
2. The Government Accountability Office
3. The National Aeronautics and Space Administration (NASA)
4. The Intelligence Community
5. The Department of State

Among smaller agencies, the best performers were:

1. The Surface Transportation Board
2. The Overseas Private Investment Corporation

3. The Congressional Budget Office
4. The Office of Management and Budget
5. The National Science Foundation

Perhaps most significant, the overall performance of government agencies in the survey improved, modestly but significantly. Since the initial rankings were released in 2003, the overall index is up 4.6 percent, and, in the current ratings, 71 percent of agencies upped their scores.

The Best Places survey has been attracting increased interest over time, including, for example, a front-page story in the *Washington Post* highlighting the 2009 results. Thus, it can serve as a powerful tool for focusing public attention on the varying levels of effectiveness of different government services. "People love ratings," Stier observes, whether they're the annual "best college" rankings published by *U.S. News* or Zagat's customer-driven scorings of restaurants. The Partnership ratings aim to do something similar for government agencies, making service quality a top-of-the-agenda issue for policymakers and concerned citizens alike.

It has taken time for national leaders to buy in to the importance of the Partnership's ratings. Stier recalls that, after the first results were released in 2003, the head of one low-scoring agency called him to complain, demanding to know where the "ridiculous" figures had come from. Upon being informed that the source was opinions offered by two thousand of his own employees, he quickly backed down—and soon began working to address the management issues the survey had highlighted.

Today there are signs that key people in the federal government have come to recognize the value of the Partnership's ratings. Peter Orszag, director of the Office of Management and Budget under President Obama, has announced that he plans to require agencies that scored at or near the bottom of the ratings to develop specific plans for improvement—and that the quality of those plans will be taken into account in determining the size of next year's budgets. As Stier notes, one of the best ways to make people pay attention to something is to make their budgets dependent on it.

So rating government agencies on employee satisfaction helps to improve government services in two ways: It creates benchmarks for employee engagement for which agency managers can strive, and it produces positive buzz around well-run agencies, encouraging some of America's smartest and most ambitious workers to consider them as employers.

Another Partnership program designed to showcase the importance, and therefore enhance the effectiveness, of government service is the annual Service to America Medals. Nicknamed the Sammies, these awards honor federal workers whose dedication to public service has produced extraordinary benefits for the nation and its people. Each year's winners are announced in September at a gala dinner in Washington, D.C. Among the thirty finalists for 2009 Sammies:

- Clare Rowley, a twenty-five-year-old economic analyst with the Federal Deposit Insurance Corporation, who helped run a loan modification program after the 2008 failure of IndyMac Bank that enabled more than twelve thousand mortgage borrowers to remain in their homes. By the spring of 2009, Rowley was using her expertise to help senior Treasury Department officials design policies to stem the national mortgage foreclosure crisis.

- Fran Ligler, a scientist with more than twenty years' experience at the U.S. Naval Research Laboratory's Center for Biomolecular Science and Engineering, who has invented numerous sensor systems for detecting everything from biothreat agents and hazardous chemicals to infectious diseases and pathogens in food supplies. Ligler—who says that, when she joined the agency in 1986, she expected to stay in government for just a couple of years—has published hundreds of refereed papers and four books in the course of her work, and holds twenty-four patents (with nine more pending).

• Michael German, an employee of the Department of Housing and Urban Development and national team leader of the Interagency Council on Homelessness, which has worked with 850 state and local organizations to effect a 30 percent reduction in long-term homelessness in America. "The key," he says, "is not building more shelters, but more housing, even just small apartments or rooms, and hooking people up with available state and federal services such as Medicaid, Social Security, food stamps, veterans benefits or VA health care."

• Kristen Taddonio, the twenty-six-year-old director of Climate Choice, a unique industry-government alliance run out of the Environmental Protection Agency that is helping automakers adopt greener technologies. Taddonio has worked with General Motors and other companies to develop alternative refrigerant systems for air conditioners, and helped fifteen states update their laws to encourage more eco-friendly engineering solutions.

• Jeffrey Knox, an assistant U.S. attorney and chief of the Violent Crimes and Terrorism Division in the Eastern District of New York, who has helped lead groundbreaking investigations and prosecutions of violent organizations including al Qaeda, Hamas, and the Liberation Tigers of Tamil Eelam. For example, he supervised the eighteen-month-long coordinated effort among intelligence agencies, law enforcement agencies, the U.S. military and foreign governments that led to the arrest of four suspected conspirators charged in a plot to detonate fuel storage tanks at New York's JFK airport.

Anyone who has succumbed to the widespread, casual cynicism about government work that pervades American society will find it eye-opening to read the inspiring stories of the other 2009 finalists, chosen from among hundreds of other well-qualified nominees. They make it abundantly clear that government service can be not just productive and rewarding but noble, transformational, and even heroic.

. For Max Stier, the Service to America awards fill a gaping hole in public awareness. "There are some qualities about government that are just overwhelmingly positive," he says. "But these stories don't get told very well." It's the old story about the media: Bad news makes headlines, while good news gets taken for granted. One day a year, the Service to America medals shine a spotlight on some of the thousands of ways government service helps make life in the United States better.

One overriding goal of all the programs created by the Partnership: to help close the "knowledge gap" that prevents talented Americans from thinking of government service as one of their best work opportunities. "We want the smartest mathematicians in the country to realize that the National Security Agency offers some of the most fascinating work in their field," Stier says. "We want top engineers to realize that the Department of Defense employs more civilian engineers than anyone else in America."

The Partnership does more than publicize the value of government work. It also advocates for systemic changes designed to make public service more appealing to talented Americans.

For example, there's no apparent logic underlying the rules that determine which agency jobs require Senate confirmation. "Why should an assistant secretary for congressional affairs be Senate-confirmed?" Stier wonders. A similar irrationality plagues the issue of political appointees *versus* career civil servants: NASA, which happens to be one of our best-run agencies, has just four political appointees, while the Department of Homeland Security has well over a hundred. No one seems to be able to explain—or to justify—the difference.

Periodic efforts have been made to trim the list of positions requiring Senate approval, but they have always run afoul of the personal priorities of individual Senate members. All it takes is one senator to say, "Oh, you can't remove *that* position from the list—I really care about that one!" In this way, the list never gets any shorter, but instead continues to expand, year after year, tying up the valuable time of Senate committees and delaying the full staffing of any new administration by weeks or months. Thus it was that, in the spring of 2009, in the midst of the worst financial crisis since the 1930s, several key positions in the Obama administration's Treasury department remained unfilled for crucial months thanks in part to needless delays in the confirmation process.

What's more, the confirmation process has become an increasingly painful, intrusive process, with senators from both parties probing the private lives of nominees in search of details with which to embarrass the opposition. One might almost imagine that the system had been designed to discourage first-rate people from serving in government. Max Stier sums it up this way:

> When you help run a government agency, you can usually take responsibility for more things than you can in the private sector—you can actually *own* a particular service, which gives you the opportunity to make an extraordinary difference in the lives of many people. So there are all kinds of positives about public service. But to get in, you're going to have to go through an obstacle course that makes the Marine Corps's training camp seem like a piece of cake.

That's not all bad, Stier quickly points out: In a perverse way, the "obstacle course" job candidates are forced to run imposes its own kind of quality test. "You want people who have the persistence gene," as Stier says. But after a certain point, the screening process becomes dysfunctional—and we've drifted well past that point today.

It's a needless waste: Thousands of smart, caring men and women desperately *want* to serve their country and are willing to give their time and talent to do so, often at lower rates of pay than they could command in the private sector. Yet we've tolerated the creation of a system that actually *discourages* them from serving. That needs to change.

Max Stier says that both government agencies and prospective employees also need to change the way they think about how government work fits into the career stories of workers:

> There's always been an assumption that a government job is a career job—that you sign on with an agency in your twenties and work there for thirty years or more. That's a remnant of the old pattern most working people followed back in the 1950s and 60s, both in the public and private sectors. But few people live that way any more. Today, most people will work at six or seven employers in the course of their careers, and many will actually have two or three different careers. Government agencies need to adjust to this new reality. They need to actively recruit people at varying life stages for three- to seven-year stints. And they need to provide interesting challenges and growth opportunities in those shortened tenures, rather than assuming that anyone who's serious about the work will stick around for three or four decades.

If human resource managers in government take Stier's advice to heart, it may help alleviate the "misshapen dumbbell" problem we described earlier. Hiring smart, experienced professionals who are now in their forties and early fifties for second careers in public service can be a promising way of filling the depleted ranks of middle managers who play such an important role in making any organization run efficiently.

With all the gigantic challenges faced by our dysfunctional, unwieldy system of government, you might expect Max Stier to be pessimistic about the future. But when we spoke with him, he was surprisingly hopeful about the Partnership's mission. "We've always had to cope with tough political and economic realities," he told us:

> Sometimes we operate with a tailwind, sometimes a headwind. Today we think we're enjoying a tailwind. There are two main reasons. One, ever since 9/11, the American people have a renewed appreciation for the importance of government. That's picked up steam in the recent months, with the Katrina disaster and now the economic collapse. When people are fat and happy, it's easy to think they don't need government. When you have real problems as we do today, you see that government is a necessary tool. And two, we now have a leader in Barack Obama who is addressing these issues. One of his campaign pledges was to try to make government cool again. And we're trying to help him.

Unfortunately, even President Obama occasionally succumbs to the temptation to echo the prevailing cynicism about government service. In the midst of the national health-care debate in the summer of 2009, Obama was heard telling voters at a town hall meeting, "I don't want government bureaucrats meddling in your health care." The president's use of that negatively charged word *bureaucrats* drew a rebuke from none other than Max Stier in a *Washington Post* op-ed piece. Hopefully it was just an aberration, and Obama will return to his stated mission of encouraging

Americans to appreciate the work of public servants rather than reflexively denigrating it.

·   ·   ·

As the Partnership for Public Service reminds us, government can play an enormous role in the revitalization of civic engagement on the part of millions of Americans. And although direct government employment is a significant—indeed, a vital—aspect of this work, it's far from the only one. In fact, an even more important challenge for government may be its role in providing leverage to encourage, support, empower, and coordinate the work of hundreds of private organizations that are tackling social problems, rebuilding communities, and improving lives all around the nation.

For a variety of reasons—political, economic, social—government support for citizen activism, volunteerism, and service has expanded more slowly in recent years than the enormous needs of our society. Today that is changing. In fact, the United States now appears to be on the verge of a great new flowering of civic engagement in which partnerships among nonprofits, businesses, community groups, philanthropists, and government are poised to drive some amazing and powerful new initiatives for the betterment of our country.

The presidential administration that came to power in January 2009 is certainly an important factor in the new climate. As Americans learned during the 2008 election campaign, President Obama spent several formative years of his youth as a community organizer in the down-at-heels Altgeld Gardens neighborhood of Chicago, which was economically reeling after a series of steel mill closings. This was a path Obama chose despite the lucrative opportunities available to him as a star graduate of Columbia University—in fact, he left a job as a financial consultant and took a sizable pay cut when he moved to Chicago. During his five years as an organizer (1983–88), the young Obama worked on issues related to housing, employment, and environmental quality, including a controversial battle with city authorities over asbestos in a public housing project.

Not all of Obama's community organizing efforts were successful. But the job taught the future president about coalition building, the challenges of moving intractable bureaucracies, and the difficulties of overcoming ingrained cynicism and hopelessness among people who've long felt beaten down by lives in harsh circumstances. He left Chicago to attend Harvard Law School and ultimately to enter politics, determined to take the lessons he'd learned from his years of community service and apply them on a grander scale.

Obama's wife, Michelle, has even stronger credentials as a bona fide leader of the civic service movement. From 1993 to 1996, Mrs. Obama served as founding executive director of the Chicago branch of Public Allies, a national nonprofit organization whose goal is the development of the next generation of leaders through paid apprenticeships in community organizations and educational programs. (One of its founders was Vanessa Kirsch, whom we cited in our chapter about social entrepreneurship.) Mrs. Obama served on the board of Public Allies until 2001.

Public Allies is a sterling example of the kind of nonprofit group that smart political leaders of both parties have long sought to support. Since its founding in 1991 Public Allies has trained more than twenty-five hundred future leaders through its signature Ally Program, with over 80 percent pursuing continuing careers in nonprofit public service. The first President Bush named Public Allies as a model for national service (one of his famous "thousand points of light"), and his administration helped fund its initial pilot program. Federal support for the organization continued under presidents Bill Clinton and George W. Bush.

The national commitment to supporting innovative and effective nonprofit programs, then, has deep bipartisan roots. But the personal stories of Barack and Michelle Obama make it clear that they are invested in the concept of community service to a greater extent than any other first couple in recent history. Their continuing commitment to supporting community-based nonprofit organizations through government funding is one reason people who are eager to develop innovative ways of tackling social problems through private-public partnerships are so optimistic about the future.

Another hopeful sign is the existence of America Forward, a remarkable coalition of more than eighty nonprofit organizations that is working to create nationwide momentum behind the civic activism movement. Launched in 2007 by the indefatigable Vanessa Kirsch and directed by New Profit's Kelly Ward, the America Forward coalition includes most of the country's best-known and most-effective social entrepreneurship ventures, from Public Allies and Eric Schwarz's Citizen Schools to Teach for America and City Year. These organizations joined forces to advocate a series of steps that will enable well-managed nonprofits to share their expertise, create and strengthen their partnerships, increase and stabilize their sources of funding, and grow to scale.

That last step—growing to scale—is arguably the most important one, as well as the most difficult, and the one where government support is most vital.

Deborah Jospin is a former director of AmeriCorps, the "domestic Peace Corps" service agency created under President Clinton that has supported the volunteer efforts of more than five hundred thousand Americans since 1993. She also served as an adviser on national service policy to President Obama's transition team. Here's how Jospin makes the case for federal involvement in the expansion of effective nonprofit programs:

> Other than maybe the [Bill & Melinda] Gates Foundation, the federal government is the only organization with

the resources to bring a major social program to scale. So, for example, if you want to ensure that every kid in America with the ability to benefit from college gets to go to college—or if you want to cut dropout rates across the board, or to make sure that every pregnant woman has access to prenatal care—then at some point the government has to step in. There are wonderful nonprofits that are showing the way, with small-scale programs that have a proven track record of effectiveness. But they can only do so much on their own. A program like Eric Schwarz's Citizen Schools is doing incredible work. But they're only in a dozen cities—they should be in a hundred. And eventually that is going to take government support.

Money isn't the only resource that government can bring to effective nonprofits. The power and influence of government—especially at the federal level—has a way of getting the attention of all the relevant players who are needed to tackle the really big social issues. So, for example, when there's a need for a conference to explore best practices and shape solutions to problems like homelessness, hunger, or health care, the chances of attracting a wide range of participants (from nonprofit organizations, state and local government, business, and foundations) are markedly increased when the invitations go out from the White House. On an ongoing basis, the federal government could also serve as a clearinghouse for ideas and information about problem-solving tactics and strategies—"a commission for what works," in Deb Jospin's words—enabling nonprofits in disparate arenas to learn from one another rather than repeatedly reinventing the wheel, as they now must do.

The members of the America Forward coalition have been pressing to enlist the federal government's clout behind such efforts. With Obama in office, the momentum is now on their side.

During the first half of 2009, three crucial pieces of the coalition's agenda were rapidly enacted:

- Passage of the Edward M. Kennedy Serve America Act, which dramatically improves the federal funding of service opportunities both for young people and for citizens of other ages. Specifically, it authorizes an increase in the size of AmeriCorps from seventy-five thousand volunteers to two hundred fifty thousand by 2017, as well as creating education awards and other grants to encourage high school students, senior citizens, and working Americans to donate their time and energy to nonprofit and community service activities.

- Creation of the White House Office on Social Innovation and Civic Participation, the first government entity specifically charged with exploring and promoting partnerships among non-profits, business, philanthropies, and government to help solve social problems. In a July 2009 article on the Huffington Post website, Harvard business guru Clayton M. Christensen, author of the classic book about "disruptive technologies" that have transformed numerous industries, *The Innovator's Dilemma,* hailed this new office, noting, "Support for these types of disruptive innovations in the social sector could surface new, more effective, higher-impact solutions to our most stubborn social challenges."

- Establishment of a federal Social Innovation Fund with an initial budget of $50 million, which will provide seed money for experimental community programs and matching grants to support the expansion of programs whose effectiveness has already been demonstrated. The fund will be administered by the Corporation for National and Community Service, the independent federal agency that oversees the national commitment to service, running programs such as AmeriCorps and Senior Corps.

These three initiatives represent the first few steps in a new drive, now supported by the Obama administration, to transform the once-adversarial relationship among nonprofits, government, and business into a cooperative, mutually beneficial partnership. As Deb Jospin notes, the shift is as much psychological as it is organizational: "People are coming to realize that repeating old mantras—'Government is bad, nonprofits are wasteful, business is selfish'—isn't productive. Instead, we can learn from each other, support one another, and grow a better society together."

It's exciting to imagine the potential impact such a partnership can have. To quote Jospin yet again:

> We now have a great opportunity for the concept of truly effective public service to explode in the next few years— provided we get all the right people around the table, working together: CEOs, mayors, academics, nonprofit directors, philanthropists, and others. And the amazing thing is that today everyone *wants* to be at the table. It's a moment unlike any other we've seen . . . one we *must* take advantage of.

●   ●   ●

Alan Solomont, former chairman of the board of the Corporation for National and Community Service (and currently U.S. ambassador to Spain), is one of the most thoughtful and eloquent advocates of the service ideal and the important role government can play in supporting that ideal.

Solomont's devotion to national service grows out of his own experiences, beginning with the awakening of his social and political consciousness during his years at Tufts University. He attended college from 1966 to 1970, a tumultuous time in American history, and he recalls those years as "a time I felt I was a member of a community—my college community—where I felt I could make a difference. As a result, I learned how to be an active citizen."

For a young left-leaning American in the late 1960s, being a citizen often meant political activism. Solomont majored in urban studies, looking for insights into the economic and political forces that shape society. He attended the chaotic 1968 Democratic convention in Chicago, joined the anti–Vietnam War movement, participated in a campaign supporting the rights of minority workers on a Tufts campus building project, and even briefly helped occupy the university president's office during a demonstration. ("No, we didn't trash the place," he says. "In fact, we got a number of compliments from the administration about how civil we were.")

After college, Solomont moved into a $23-a-week tenement apartment in Lowell, Massachusetts, and spent several years working as a community organizer, helping to launch a neighborhood food cooperative, working on labor issues, and campaigning to promote rent control and better housing conditions. "It was a transformational experience for me," Solomont says. "Although I went on to have a business career, my years working as a community organizer have informed everything else I've done since."

Later, Solomont helped build an elder-care company and eventually began to apply his social fervor to fund-raising among business leaders on behalf of the Democratic Party. (He jokes, "I used to organize poor people. Now I organize rich ones.") The connections he made in these efforts, together with his continuing commitment to grass-roots community building, led to his being named to the board of the Corporation for National and Community Service by President Clinton. He was later reappointed by President Bush and served as the board's chairman under President Obama.

Solomont is excited about the long-term potential of today's citizen service movement. He sees the coming together of several strands of change—the advent of the Millennial Generation, the unprecedented array of social and economic challenges America faces, and the election of Barack Obama—as creating a unique national opportunity. "When the history of our time is written,"

Solomont predicts, "the emphasis isn't going to be on the financial crisis, the wars in Iraq and Afghanistan, or any other immediate issue. It's going to be on the way our civic values changed—the way we redefined patriotism with a new focus on citizen service."

Solomont points to several hopeful signs, some obvious, some less so. The passage of the Edward M. Kennedy Serve America Act is one of the most important, especially because of the broad support it earned in Congress from both sides of the aisle. (It passed in the House by a vote of 321–105 and in the Senate by 79–19.) "National service is one of the few areas in Washington where truly bipartisan work is going on," Solomont says. And he points to history to underscore the broad popularity of the service concept:

> AmeriCorps was started by Bill Clinton—a Democratic president whom many Republicans disliked. But the program survived and even received the support of his successor, Republican George W. Bush. Both McCain and Obama advocated increased funding for national service during the 2008 campaign. And now the program has been greatly strengthened and will be enormously expanded under President Obama thanks to the bipartisan Serve America Act. Its two chief Senate sponsors were Ted Kennedy—a Democrat who built on the legacy of President Kennedy, who founded the Peace Corps back in the sixties—and Orrin Hatch—a conservative Republican who was inspired by the service tradition that plays an important role in his own Mormon faith. National service isn't liberal or conservative, Democratic or Republican—it's American and universal.

Some service advocates, such as Alan Khazei, founder of City Year (and the husband of America Forward's Vanessa Kirsch), believe that some form of public service ought to be mandatory for all young Americans. They say that a year of work on behalf of one's country—whether in the military or in a civilian role—should be a shared rite of passage that all citizens experience. But Solomont sees it somewhat differently:

> Personally, I think every young person ought to experience civic service, as I did. But I don't think that making it a legal requirement is politically viable. Nor do I think it's necessary. I think we'll get very close to universal service without making it mandatory, just because the concept will become so deeply engrained in the national ethos. As Alan Khazei himself predicts, in time, when young people meet, it'll be just as common for them to ask, "What did you do for your year of service?" as it now is for them to ask, "What was your major?"

There's no doubt that the shared experience of community service can have a lasting positive impact on the people who participate. For many in the so-called Greatest Generation of the 1940s, military service offered such a life-changing experience. But civilian service can have an equally powerful personal and social impact, as Thomas Sander of Harvard's Kennedy School has observed:

> Banding together to provide community service builds Army-foxhole-like solidarity. Programs like City Year, in which ex–gang members may serve alongside college students who have deferred admission, prove that small corps can accomplish vital community service. They also implode stereotypes. We learn that what unites us—our musical tastes, the jokes we find funny and, more fundamentally, our belief in healing cities through grime and sweat—dwarfs our divisions. Why is this important?

Virtually all forms of social engagement have declined over the past generation, from the time spent visiting neighbors to the number of community projects and close friendships. And these social and civic connections actually lubricate society, helping connected Americans improve their health and happiness and find meaningful work. These connections also strengthen communities. Among the most critical yet hardest-to-build social ties are bonds that cross racial, ethnic and class cleavages, especially as our communities become increasingly diverse. Daily, many of us inadvertently reinforce racial barriers; national service can catalyze our moral obligation to dismantle them.

Even more important, it can make a real difference in the health and prosperity of our country. With community service becoming an almost universal expectation for young Americans, Solomont is hopeful that our nation will finally be able to get traction in tackling some of the most significant social problems we face, such as the endemic failures and inequalities of our public education system. "The biggest change we're now seeing in the public service arena," he notes, "is that it's no longer just about the person performing the service—about giving them an uplifting, transformational experience. It's about *impact*—producing real, lasting, measurable change."

The new spirit of partnership across sectors, uniting nonprofits, business, and government in support of millions of citizen volunteers and activists, promises to create such an impact on a scale never before imagined possible.

Food for Thought, Seeds for Action

• *Consider public service:* We live in an era when needs and resources are converging to create new opportunities for Americans to consider public service. As millions of baby boomers and Gen Xers pass through middle age and move toward the traditional retirement years, many are looking for second (or third) careers. (Owing to the current economic downturn, some have been forced into this search by economic necessity.) At the same time, as the Partnership for Public Service has highlighted, millions of government jobs requiring high-level skills, energy, and experience are expected to become vacant in the next decade. Perhaps a five- to seven-year stint serving your nation as a government employee is the opportunity for which you've been seeking.

• *Reach out in partnership:* As Deb Jospin has suggested, the old adversarial relationships among business, nonprofits, and government are finally falling by the wayside, being replaced by a new spirit of partnership. If you're currently serving as a leader in the private sector—for example, as a business professional, entrepreneur, or manager—now may be the perfect time to begin exploring the potential for alliances with community organizations and government agencies that are trying to address some of the same social issues you are concerned about. Today's nonprofit organizations are more results oriented, business-like, and entrepreneurial than ever before, and increasing numbers of government agencies are shedding their traditional bureaucratic ways to become flexible, creative, and innovative. As a result, cross-sector partnerships are flourishing. Why not pick up the phone and make an initial connection with one of your counterparts in a different sector of society? You can never tell what kind of exciting new initiative may ultimately result.

To Learn More

52 Ways You Can Join the Movement

There are thousands of ways you can become part of today's movement toward active citizenship. Some involve giving just a few minutes of your time and energy every day; others are so all-engrossing you may find yourself devoting a lifetime to them. On the next few pages, we offer fifty-two suggestions—one for each week of the year—to help you start your own exploration of this exciting new world. Good luck!

1. *Join millions of other Americans who are giving their time and talent in all fifty states* through ServiceNation at http://www .servicenation.org/.
2. *Help transform the educational opportunities enjoyed by kids in your community* as a "citizen teacher" with Citizen Schools—learn more by visiting their website at http://www.citizenschools.org/.
3. *Fund a young person's work to improve health care in one of the world's most needy regions* by supporting Global Health Corps at http://ghcorps.org/.
4. *Find out how you can invest in some of today's most creative social entrepreneurs* by visiting the site of the Acumen Fund at http://www.acumenfund.org/.
5. *Get involved in finding and growing the most powerful solutions*

to America's pressing social problems by learning about the work of America Forward at http://www.americaforward.org/.

6. *Learn how to serve your country by working for Uncle Sam* by exploring the Partnership for Public Service's list of Best Places to Work in the federal government at http://data.bestplacestowork.org/bptw/index.

7. *Encourage the young people in your life to get started with service early* by joining Youth Service America, devoted to kids five to twenty-five, at http://ysa.org/.

8. *Learn how to improve the management of any nonprofit organization or a socially minded for-profit company* from the world-class experts at Virtue Ventures—visit them at http://www.virtueventures.com/.

9. *Help bring affordable, renewable energy to people in the developing world* by supporting the work of Beyond Solar at http://www.beyondsolar.org/site/Home.html.

10. *Discover some of the amazing new forms of civic communications technology* being invented by the geniuses at MIT by visiting the Center for Future Civic Media at http://civic.mit.edu/.

11. *Explore creative approaches being developed to problems ranging from homelessness and human trafficking to global warming* by visiting the website of Change.org at http://www.change.org/info/about.

12. *Learn how local citizens' groups are using the power of dialogue and cooperation to create solutions to civic problems* from the leaders at Everyday Democracy at http://www.everyday-democracy.org/en/index.aspx.

13. *Give a year of your life to work in a small, dedicated group making life in America better*—or support City Year, the organization that helps thousands of young people from every background do just that, at http://www.cityyear.org/default_ektid13307.aspx.

14. *Discover an organization that trains inner-city kids to become active community leaders,* founded with the help of Barack and Michelle Obama, by visiting Public Allies at http://www .publicallies.org/site/c.liKUL3PNLvF/b.5106423/k.BD7E/ Home.htm.

15. *Help bring desperately needed drinking water to some of the hundreds of millions of people who lack it* by supporting Scott Harrison's charity: water at http://www.charitywater.org/.

16. *Be inspired by the ways in which national service is already benefiting our nation,* and learn what you can do to help the cause, at http://www.nationalservice.gov/.

17. *Learn about opportunities to use your talents by working at one of America's thousands of nonprofit organizations* at Jobs for Change at http://jobs.change.org/.

18. *Investigate the state of America's civic health—and what you can do to improve it—*from the National Conference on Citizenship at http://www.ncoc.net/.

19. *Find the perfect volunteering opportunity in your own community* by consulting the "Craigslist for service," All for Good, at http://www.allforgood.org/.

20. *Make a loan of $25 or more with the potential to change a life* through the online microlending program created by Kiva at http://www.kiva.org/.

21. *Become a more responsible business leader* by learning what companies like yours are doing to improve their communities at the website of the Business Civic Leadership Center at http://www.uschamber.com/bclc/default.

22. *Help preserve and protect our National Parks* by volunteering through the Nature Conservancy at http://www.nature.org/.

23. *Consider investing in an enterprise that is transforming the world* through the savvy portfolio managers at New Profit Inc.—learn more at http://newprofit.com/.

24. *Turn your Facebook membership into a way of getting involved*

by browsing the thousands of worthwhile initiatives represented at Causes on Facebook at http://apps.facebook.com/causes/about.

25. *Help improve the lives of some of society's most marginalized citizens* by supporting the work of Pioneer Human Services at http://www.pioneerhumanservices.org/.

26. *Check out the innovative, interactive site for neighborhood improvement* at SeeClickFix by visiting http://seeclickfix.com/citizens.

27. *Match your interests and abilities with student volunteer opportunities* by visiting Student Volunteer at http://studentvolunteer.com/.

28. *Experiment with new ways to communicate and interpret information of civic importance* at the "democratic visualization" site Many Eyes at http://manyeyes.alphaworks.ibm.com/manyeyes/.

29. *Ever dream of going abroad as a Peace Corps volunteer? It's never too late*—check out the options at http://www.peacecorps.gov/.

30. *Find out how to start a community garden* from the experts at the American Community Gardening Association at http://www.communitygarden.org.

31. *Explore possible jobs in the nonprofit sector* and learn how to prepare for the switch from the for-profit world by visiting Bridgespan at http://www.Bridgespan.org/.

32. *Help people around the world who are threatened by violence, neglect, or catastrophe* by donating funds or volunteering time to Doctors Without Borders at http://www.msf.org/.

33. *Get involved in the national movement to improve the way Americans eat* by learning about the work of Will Allen's Growing Power at http://www.growingpower.org/.

34. *Discover opportunities to hone your public service skills* by learning about the training and fellowship programs offered by the

Partnership for Public Service at http://www.ourpublicservice
.org/OPS/programs/ali/index.shtml.

35. *Support the amazing school that is revolutionizing inner-city education,* the Harlem Village Academies—learn more at http://
www.harlemvillageacademies.org/.

36. *Put your business skills to good use* by helping entrepreneurs
build businesses that can lift families and villages out of poverty
through MBAs Without Borders at http://mbaswithoutborders
.org/.

37. *Feed the world* by backing the work of World Hunger Year,
which supports community-based organizations around the
world at http://www.whyhunger.org.

38. *Learn about fledgling businesses with the potential to change the
world* by visiting Virgance, an incubator that specializes in discovering and supporting them, at http://www.virgance.com/
index.php.

39. *Donate your wisdom to the young* by becoming a mentor
through Experience Corps, which helps people fifty-five and
over help students in need at http://www.experiencecorps.org/
index.cfm.

40. *Check out the social enterprises that* Fast Company *magazine
calls today's best* by visiting their most recent annual list of honorees at http://www.fastcompany.com/magazine/131/eureka-
social-enterprises-of-the-year.html.

41. *Discover the unique investment fund Bill Clinton calls "insurer
to the poor"*—LeapFrog Investments, which specializes in financial services for low-income people in the developing
world, at http://www.leapfroginvest.com/.

42. *Offer your professional talents to organizations that need them* by
pro bono work through the nonprofit Taproot Foundation at
http://www.taprootfoundation.org/.

43. *Help make the greatest city in the world even greater* by becoming a New York City volunteer at http://www.nycservice.org/.

44. *Help bring the power of computing to children all around the world* through One Laptop per Child at http://laptop.org/en/.

45. *Be amazed at how a community nonprofit is making life better for practically every child in Harlem* by learning about the Harlem Children's Zone at http://www.hcz.org/.

46. *Make healing the currency of international diplomacy* through the voluntary services provided by Physicians for Peace at http://www.physiciansforpeace.org/.

47. *Discover the power of microenterprise to help poor people feed, clothe, house, and educate themselves* by visiting Trickle Up at http://www.trickleup.org/.

48. *Help provide technologies that can change the lives of millions* in Kenya and around the world by visiting KickStart at http://www.kickstart.org/.

49. *Give a break to a San Franciscan who really needs one* by supporting the innovative self-help efforts of Rubicon Programs at http://www.rubiconprograms.org/.

50. *Turn your next trip abroad into an opportunity to change the world* by learning about volunteering/travel programs at http://www.voluntourism.org/.

51. *Support the organization that helped make social entrepreneurship one of today's most hopeful trends* by learning about Ashoka at http://www.ashoka.org/.

52. *Extend a hand to families and communities recovering from disaster* by supporting the New York Says Thank You foundation at http://www.newyorksaysthankyou.org/.

Sources

Epigraph

Barack Obama quotation: speech, "A Call to Service," Cornell College, December 5, 2007.

John W. Gardner quotation: John W. Gardner, *Living, Leading, and the American Dream* (San Francisco: Jossey-Bass, 2003), p. 192.

Chapter 1 Social Mindstorms

Scott Harrison story: Interview with Scott Harrison by author, July 29, 2009. Also see charity: water website at http://www.charitywater.org/; and Nicholas D. Kristof, "Clean, Sexy Water," *New York Times,* July 12, 2009.

Grameen Bank story: Muhammad Yunus with Alan Jolis, *Banker to the Poor: Micro-Lending and the Battle Against World Poverty* (New York: Public Affairs, 1999); and Muhammad Yunus with Karl Weber, *Creating a World Without Poverty: Social Business and the Future of Capitalism* (New York: Public Affairs, 2007).

Story of the Clinton Foundation's UNITAID initiative: Bill Clinton, *Giving: How Each of Us Can Change the World* (New York: Knopf, 2007), p. 181.

Harlem Children's Zone story: Robin Shulman, "Harlem Program Singled Out as Model," *Washington Post,* August 2, 2009; and Harlem Children's Zone website at http://www.hcz.org/.

Will Allen story: Growing Power website at http://www.growingpower.org/; and Elizabeth Royte, "Street Farmer," *New York Times,* July 1, 2009.

Alex Green story: Dan Barry, "Volunteers Find Muck and Meaning in Service," *New York Times,* September 7, 2009, p. A7.

Paula Lopez Crespin story: Cecilia Capuzzi Simon, "So You Want to Be a Teacher for America?" *New York Times,* July 26, 2009, Education section, p. 8.

Chapter 2 A New Breed of Leader

Stories of Krista Morris, Stephanie Coplan, and Malek Al-Chalabi: Interviews by author, May 6, 2009.

Tisch College story: Interviews with Lawrence S. Bacow, Robert Sternberg, Lee Coffin, Robert M. Hollister, Nancy Wilson, Peter Levine, and Chris Swan by author during 2008 and 2009. Also see Tisch College website at http://activecitizen .tufts.edu/; and Robert M. Hollister, Molly Mead, and Nancy Wilson, "Infusing Active Citizenship Throughout a Research University," *Metropolitan Universities Journal* 17, no. 3 (October 2006): 38.

Larry Bacow quotation ("Citizenship is part of the DNA here"): Interview by author, October 4, 2008.

Research data on the Millennial Generation: Interview with Peter Levine by author, April 22, 2009. Also see *Millennials Talk Politics: A Study of College Student Political Engagement* (College Park, MD: CIRCLE, 2007); Morley Winograd and Michael D. Hais, *Millennial Makeover: MySpace, YouTube & the Future of American Politics* (New Brunswick, NJ: Rutgers University Press, 2008); Neil Howe and William Strauss, *Millennials Rising: The Next Great Generation* (New York: Vintage, 2000); and Eric Greenberg with Karl Weber, *Generation We: How Millennial Youth Are Taking Over America and Changing Our World Forever* (Emeryville, CA: Pachatusan, 2008).

Lee Coffin quotations: Interview with Lee Coffin by author, May 6, 2009.

Quotation beginning "Although values do not cause people to participate": Peter Levine, *The Future of Democracy: Developing the Next Generation of American Citizens* (Medford, MA: Tufts University Press, 2007), p. 73.

Chapter 3 Social Entrepreneurship

Information on Citizen Schools: Interview with Eric Schwarz by author, April 23, 2009; interview with Ann Bevins by author, May 11, 2009; and Citizen Schools website at http://www .citizenschools.org/. Also see Shirley Sagawa and Deborah Jospin, *The Charismatic Organization* (San Francisco: Jossey-Bass, 2008); and "Transforming Student Learning in the After Hours," *Edutopia.org*, online at http://www.edutopia.org/print/ 5816.

Background on social entrepreneurship concept: see David Bornstein, *How to Change the World: Social Entrepreneurs and the Power of New Ideas* (Oxford: Oxford University Press, 2004); and Steven Hamm, "Capitalism with a Human Face," *Business Week*, December 8, 2008, p. 49.

Information on Mercy Corps: "45 Social Entrepreneurs Who Are Changing the World," *Fast Company.com*, online at http://www .fastcompany.com/social/2008/profiles/; and Mercy Corps website at http://www.mercycorps.org/.

Information on Apopo: Steve Hamm, "Social Entrepreneurs Turn Business Sense to Good," *Business Week,* November 25, 2008; and Apopo website at http://www.apopo.org/newsite/content/ index.htm.

Information on the Sekem Group: Sherin Deghedy, "Egypt based SEKEM Group—Proving Profitable Social Development Model," November 3, 2008, online at http://www.dinarstandard .com/current/Sekem100108.htm; and Sekem website at http:// www.sekem.com.

Information on Witness: article, "45 Social Entrepreneurs Who Are Changing the World," *Fast Company.com*; and Witness website at http://www.witness.org/.

Information on D.light: Marci Alboher, "A Social Solution, Without Going the Nonprofit Route," *New York Times,* March 5, 2009, p. B5; article, Elsa Wenzel, "d.light rolls out affordable solar LED lamps," CNET News, online at http://news.cnet.com/8301-11128_3-9970627-54.html; and "Solar Energy in the Developing World: Orissa, India," online at www.beyondsolar.org/downloads/summary.pdf.

Information on Virtue Ventures and new funding for social enterprises: Interview with Kim Alter by author, April 27, 2009; and Virtue Ventures website at http://www.virtueventures.com.

Information on New Profit Inc.: Interview with Vanessa Kirsch by author, June 1, 2009. Also see New Profit Inc. Annual Report, Cambridge, MA, 2007–2008; New Profit website at http://newprofit.com/; and Cheryl Dahle, "Social Justice—Alan Khazei and Vanessa Kirsch," *Fast Company.com,* December 19, 2007, online at http://www.fastcompany.com/magazine/30/khazei.html.

Chapter 4 Engaged Professionals

Chris Swan story: Interviews with Chris Swan by author, January 15, 2008, and April 22, 2009. Also see "2007 Farewell Address" by W. F. Marcuson III, website of American Society of Civil Engineers, online at http://content.asce.org/President%20Page/FarewellAddress.html.

Engineers Within Borders: Interview with Pam Zelaya and Sofia Hart by author, November 12, 2008. Also see Engineers Without Borders website at http://www.ewb-usa.org/; and Bryan Walsh, "Blueprint Brigade," *Time,* November 29, 2007.

Doctors Without Borders: Website at http://www.doctorswithoutborders.org/.

MBAs Without Borders: Website at http://mbaswithoutborders.org/.

Socially engaged nurses: See Cathryn Domrose, "Nurse Activists Strive for Change," *NurseWeek News*, April 25, 2005.

Quotation on "the civic potential of *paid* employment": Peter Levine, *The Future of Democracy*, p. 6.

Chapter 5 A City of Citizens

Story of NYC Service: Interviews with Diahann Billings-Burford, James Anderson, Kristine Brown, Aaron C. Miner, Nicholas Gerry-Bullard, and Amanda M. Rey by author, August 20, 2009, and September 24, 2009. Also see *NYC Service: A Blueprint to Increase Civic Engagement*, City of New York, Michael R. Bloomberg, Mayor; NYC Service website at http://www.nycservice.org/; Suzanne Perry, "Bloomberg and 16 Other Mayors Announce Coalition to Promote Volunteerism," *Chronicle of Philanthropy*, September, 10, 2009; and Cities of Service website at http://www.citiesofservice.org/html/.

Chapter 6 Digital Citizenship

Robert D. Putnam quotation beginning "The culprit is television": "The Strange Disappearance of Civic America," *The American Prospect*, 1995, online at http://xroads.virginia.edu/~HYPER/DETOC/assoc/putnmtv1.html.

Benedict Anderson on *London Times* as unifying force: Cited in Henry Jenkins, "What Is Civic Media?" September 19, 2007, Center for Civic Media website at http://civic.mit.edu/blog/henry/what-is-civic-media.

American teens as "media creators": Pew study cited in Henry Jenkins, *Confronting the Challenges of Participatory Culture: Media Education for the 21st Century*, The John D. and Catherine R. MacArthur Foundation, p. 6.

SeeClickFix story: Interview with Ben Berkowitz by author, September 10, 2009. Also see SeeClickFix website at http://www

.seeclickfix.com/; Ben Berkowitz, "Government as Vending Machine?" September 4, 2009, online at http://seeclickfix .blogspot.com; and Erica Schlaikjer, "See. Click. Fix. Repeat," March 18, 2009, online at http://thecityfix.com/see-click-fix -repeat/.

Information on Center for Future Civic Media at MIT: Interview with Ellen Hume by author, April 21, 2009. Also see Center for Future Civic Media website at http://civic.mit.edu/.

Comments by Jimmy Wales about Wikipedia: Noam Cohen, "Wikipedia to Limit Changes to Articles on People," *New York Times*, August 24, 2009.

Information about Many Eyes: Stephen Few, "Many Eyes Can Be Better Than Two," online at http://www.perceptualedge.com/ blog/?p&equals$84; and Many Eyes website at http://manyeyes .alphaworks.ibm.com/manyeyes/.

Information about Snopes.com: Website at http://www.snopes .com.

Henry Jenkins quotation beginning "On August 29, 2005, Hurricane Katrina": Henry Jenkins, *Confronting the Challenges of Participatory Culture*, p. 41.

Quotation from Micah Sifry ("Anybody can now commit an act of civic engagement"): Panel, "Why Is Social Media Important for Civic Engagement?" National Conference on Citizenship, Washington, D.C., September 9, 2009.

Information about Jared Cohen and the role of Twitter in the Iranian uprising: Interview, Scott Simon, "State Department Guru Talks Twitter Diplomacy," on NPR, October 17, 2009. Online at http://www.npr.org/templates/story/story.php?storyid& equals$113876776, and Mark Landler and Brian Stelter, "Washington Taps into a Potent New Force in Diplomacy," *New York Times*, June 17, 2009.

Chapter 7 Doing Well by Doing Good

Loews Hotels Good Neighbor Policy: See website at http://www
.loewshotels.com/. Also see Irene Korn, "Hotels with Heart,"
MeetingsNet, May 1, 2007; Dorinda Elliott, "The Power of
Travel," *Conde Nast Traveler*, May 2007; "Hospitality Shared,"
Tucson Lifstyle; "Loews Hotel to Renovate Historic Church
Building," *New Orleans CityBusiness*, April 28, 2006; and Sandi
Beach, "Hang 20 at Loews Coronado Surf Dog Competition,"
San Diego Sun Coast, June 23, 2009.

FedEx story: *Global Citizenship Report 2008*, Memphis, TN:
FedEx Corporation, online at citizenshipblog.fedex.de-
signcdt.com/fedex_citizenship_2008.pdf.

Benefits of pro bono work: Raymund Flandez, "Pro Bono Work
Helps Firms Fight Economic Slump," *Wall Street Journal*, September 1, 2009; Richard C. Morais, "Pro Bono Spreading with
the Recession," *Forbes*, August 24, 2009; Rachel Breitman,
"Law Firms Scrambled to Place Deferred Associates in Volunteer Posts," *The Am Law Daily,* March 19, 2009, online at http://
amlawdaily.typepad.com/amlawdaily/2009/03/desperately-
seeking-public-sector-jobs.html.

Rubicon Programs story: "45 Social Entrepreneurs Who Are
Changing the World," *Fast Company.com*; Rubicon Programs
website at http://www.rubiconprograms.org/.

Pioneer Human Services story: Athima Chansanchai, "Game Not
Over: Pioneer Human Services Gives People a Second
Chance," *Seattle Post-Intelligencer*, December 19, 2007; "45 So-
cial Entrepreneurs Who Are Changing the World," *Fast
Company.com*; and Pioneer Human Services website at http://
www.pioneerhumanservices.org/.

One Laptop Per Child story: John Markoff, "For $150, Third-World
Laptop Stirs a Big Debate," *New York Times*, November 30,
2006, p. 1; Matt Warman, "One Laptop per Child: How

Technology and the One Laptop Per Child (OLPC) Movement Have Become Key Factors in Rwanda's Economic Growth," *Telegraph,* October 1, 2009, online at http://www.telegraph.co.uk/technology/6247728/One-laptop-per-child.html; Geoffrey York, "One Laptop Per Child Program Collides with Reality," *Toronto Globe and Mail,* October 15, 2009, online at http://www.scrippsnews.com/node/48312; and One Laptop Per Child website at http://laptop.org/en/.

KickStart story: Martin Fisher, "Income Is Development: KickStart's Pumps Help Kenyan Farmers Transition to a Cash Economy," *Innovations,* Winter 2006, p. 9; Annelena Lobb, "How Innovative Devices Can Boost Poorest Farmers, Entrepreneurs," *Wall Street Journal,* May 18, 2007; KickStart website at http://www.kickstart.org/; and "45 Social Entrepreneurs Who Are Changing the World," *Fast Company.com.*

Bottom-of-the-pyramid business opportunities: C. K. Prahalad, *The Fortune at the Bottom of the Pyramid: Eradicating Poverty Through Profits* (Upper Saddle River, NJ: Wharton School Publishing, 2004).

Procter & Gamble Pur story: Website at http://www.pg.com/company/our_commitment/drinking_water.shtml.

Patient capital: *Finding Capital for Sustainable Livelihoods Businesses* (Geneva, Switzerland: World Business Council for Sustainable Development, 2004), online at http://www.wbcsd.org/web/publications/sl-finance.pdf; and John Tozzi, "Social Entrepreneurship: Resources for 'Patient' Capital," *Business Week,* April 3, 2009, online at http://www.businessweek.com/smallbiz/content/mar2009/sb20090330_647056.htm/.

Social business concept and Grameen Danone story: Yunus and Weber, *Creating a World Without Poverty.*

Chapter 8 Bridging to Act Two

"As long ago as 1968": "Second Acts in American Lives," *Time,* March, 8, 1968, online at http://www.time.com/time/magazine/article/0,9171,899981,00.html.

Dave Nelson story: Interview with Dave Nelson by author, May 15, 2009. Also see article, "Dave Nelson: Scaling the Wall into the Sector," Bridgespan website at http://www.Bridgespan.org/Resources/Library/Explore/PractitionerNelson.aspx.

Bridgespan story: Interview with David Simms by author, April 21, 2009. Also see Bridgespan website at http://www.Bridgespan .org/; David Simms and Wayne Luke, "Fulfill the Dream of Leading a Nonprofit," *Harvard Business Review,* January 2009, p. 26; The Bridgespan Group, *Finding Leaders for America's Nonprofits* (Boston: The Bridgespan Group, 2009).

Chapter 9 Revitalizing Our Democracy

Information on the Partnership for Public Service: Interview with Max Stier by author, May 20, 2009. Also see John D. Donahue and Max Stier, "The Next FEMA," *The Washington Monthly,* November/December 2008, p. 19; Service to America Medals website at http://servicetoamericamedals.org; Tony Dokoupil, "C'mon and Be a Bureaucrat," *Newsweek,* March 1, 2008; *The Best Place to Work in the Federal Government, 2009 Rankings* (Washington, DC: The Partnership for Public Service, 2009); *Where the Jobs Are: Mission Critical Opportunities for America,* 2nd ed. (Washington, DC: The Partnership for Public Service, 2007); and *Roadmap to Reform: A Management Framework for the Next Administration* (Washington, DC: The Partnership for Public Service, 2008).

Information on America Forward and federal support for social innovation: Interview with Deb Jospin by author, May 20, 2009. Also see *America Forward: Invent, Invest, Involve* (Washington, DC: New Profit Inc., 2008); Nathaniel Whittemore, "Digging

Deeper on the Social Innovation Fund," May 8, 2009, online at http://socialentrepreneurship.change.org/blog/; Clayton M. Christensen, "The White House Office on Social Innovation," July 1, 2009, online at http://www.huffingtonpost.com/; and America Forward website at http://americaforward.org/.

Alan Solomont story: Interview with Alan Solomont by author, May 7, 2009. Also see Alan Solomont, "Opportunities for Action," speech at AmeriCorps National Best Practices Conference, May 5, 2009; and *Truth Shall Grow from the Earth, Justice Shall Look Down from the Heavens* (Boston: Combined Jewish Philanthropies, 2004).

Acknowledgments

It is now the beginning of winter in 2009, and in New York City there is the annual sense of excitement as we are in the heart of the holiday season. The stores, restaurants, and theaters are thankfully busy with New Yorkers, as well as out-of-towners, getting ready to exchange gifts and holiday cheer with family and friends.

Amid the joy of the season, though, there is the constant reminder in newspapers and on television that the economy of our nation—and much of the world—has only begun to step away from the precipice of collapse. With official unemployment hovering around 10 percent, it is impossible to ignore the challenges and struggles that so many of our family members and neighbors face, especially during this time of year when we hope for so much more for so many.

As someone who has a lot to be grateful for, I have continually tried to lead a life that demonstrates my gratitude and appreciation for those that have passed before me, and for the people that I love, work, and interact with on a daily basis. Not only have I been blessed with a family that through tremendous hard work, discipline, and a little luck along the way, has been able to accomplish so much, but my life has also been fulfilling on so many levels due to my friends, colleagues, and associates.

In my first two books, I shared some thoughts that hopefully have helped others achieve success in their lives. And now, with *Citizen You: Doing Your Part to Change the World,* I am excited to lay out a road map for you to learn and understand how important it is, especially in today's world, to be an engaged and active citizen.

For me, family continues to be at the center of my existence, so I must acknowledge, thank, and express my appreciation to so many relatives who in fifty-six years have made me who I am. In the acknowledgments section of my last book, I made reference to Lizzie and thanked her for her friendship and ability to listen to my rants and raves. Now some three years later, I must also add to that list my unending love and appreciation for her, as she is now my wife and partner. Lizzie and our three kids provide me with unconditional affection, support, and humor. We laugh a lot, and occasionally cry, as we, like everybody else, have to face the realities that we experience when we see people that we care so much about deal with health issues, and sadly, death.

It has now been four years since the passing of my father, Bob Tisch, but not a day goes by that somebody does not mention his name to me or tell a charming tale about a man who did so much for so many. My mother, Joan, continues to be the strong matriarch that she always has been, creating an environment for my siblings, Steve and Laurie, our children, and our families to do what we think is important for the betterment of the communities where we live. I thank them all for their never-ending love and support.

The company founded by my late father and late Uncle Larry continues to strive for success while remaining true to its values thanks to the hard work of my partners in the business, cousins Jim and Andrew, as well as the dedication of thousands of other talented individuals throughout the company. My thanks also to Jack Adler, president and COO of Loews Hotels, and his team for their leadership of the founding subsidiary of what is today Loews Corporation. While taking care of our guests and team members, they also maintain our basic belief that it is our responsibility to be good neighbors—and active citizens—in the communities where we operate our hotels.

As you have read, the core themes and values of *Citizen You* have been born out of a lifetime conviction that we not only can always do more for our community and neighbors, but indeed it is our responsibility. In today's world, the challenges we face are so vast that the only way we are going to solve them is by each of us taking our skills (and, yes, we all have something to offer) and putting them to work in a meaningful way. These goals and aspirations are currently being taught to the next generation of leaders at colleges and universities like my alma mater, Tufts University in Medford, Massachusetts. When I was asked to endow what is now the Jonathan M. Tisch College of Citizenship and Public Service at Tufts, I was honored and humbled to support this important mission in a consequential way. I am so pleased that there is a committed faculty and administration that focuses on the values that my family has lived by for more than three generations.

The president of Tufts University, Larry Bacow, is a man of tremendous intelligence, integrity, and humility. He has done a superb job this decade of leading this institution to educate and prepare the students for a life of giving and commitment. I would also like to thank and acknowledge the dean of Tisch College, Robert Hollister, for his dedication and passion for the cause.

We are fortunate in life when we can find people who we enjoy working with, admire for their skills, and respect for their many contributions. That is certainly the case as it relates to the team that I have had by my side for now three books. First and foremost, let me thank my cowriter, Karl Weber, for another superb literary journey. Once again, Karl has used his myriad talents to help tell a tale that hopefully you will find interesting, compelling, and motivating. He is the consummate professional who listens, interacts, and writes, all the while being my partner as we tell this story.

Jeffrey Stewart, who I have mentioned in years past, is now running a business we started, which is making investments in various media platforms. Even with his new responsibilities, he continues to be a dear friend and invaluable advisor. And my literary agent, Wayne Kabak, also has been invaluable and does so much more than just "making the deal." Without these two gentlemen, this book would not be in your hands.

And I would like to thank the team at Crown Publishers. This is our first effort with them, and they have been nothing but professional and supportive. Their ideas and inspiration have only made this book more readable and relevant, and we look forward to a very long-lasting relationship. Accordingly, let me thank my editor, John Mahaney, publisher, Tina Constable, and the many others at Crown that made this book possible.

Another survivor of all three books is the gentleman who manages our press effort, Mark Fortier, a man with great ideas and relationships. Adding to the team this time are the creative and forward-thinking people at Blue State Digital and the unflappable Jen Farley of Walnut Hill Media. My thanks also to Vicki Alfonzetti and Susan Shannon, who keep me on track and on schedule and make sure nothing falls through the cracks.

The inspirational and meaningful foreword that starts this book has been authored by my dear friend, Mayor Cory Booker, of Newark, New Jersey. Cory has dedicated himself to improving the lives of the residents of this great American city through inspired leadership, hard work, and discipline. As Newark regains its stature, which had been lost during the past few decades, Mayor Booker continues to manage by example and work with those active citizens in his community, who like him, believe there is a very bright future for their city. I thank him for his leadership and friendship.

In addition, I want to thank the many individuals who agreed to be interviewed and who provided valuable information, ideas, and insights about their work and about the important trends our book illuminates. These individuals—Citizen Engineers, Citizen Teachers, Citizen Entrepreneurs, Citizen Businesspeople—each a Citizen You, have inspired me. They give me energy and optimism and reinforce my belief that each of us truly can do our part to change the world. They include: Malek Al-Chalabi, Kim Alter, James Anderson, Lawrence Bacow, Ben Berkowitz, Ann Bevins, Diahann Billings-Burford, Kristine Brown, Stephanie Brown, Lee A. Coffin, Stephanie P. Coplan, Melissa DeFreece, Tai Dinnan, Daniel Friedman, Nicholas Gerry-Bullard, Stacey Gilbert, Scott Harrison, Sofia Hart, Robert M. Hollister, Ellen Hume, Deborah Jospin, Vanessa Kirsch, Piyali Kundu, Peter Levine, Aaron C. Miner, Krista Grace Morris, Marzuq U. R. Muhammad, David Nelson, Nitzan Perlman, Kent Portney, Amanda M. Rey, Eric Schwarz, David L. Simms, David B. Smith, Alan D. Solomont, Robert J. Sternberg, Max Stier, Christopher W. Swan, Rachel Szyman, Alice Tin, Ekaterina Titova, Kelly Ward, Nancy Wilson, and Pam Zelaya. My thanks to one and all.

As we face challenges in our lives, our communities, our nation, and our world, it is my sincere hope that the ideas and themes discussed in *Citizen You* will help you in your own journey, with your own family, within your own community. And it is with that hope and trust that I say thank you, in advance, for your years of dedication and service as you become an "active citizen."

JMT
New York City
December 2009

Index

About the Authors

JONATHAN M. TISCH is cochairman of the board and a member of the office of the president of Loews Corporation, one of the largest diversified financial holding companies in the United States, and is also chairman and CEO of its subsidiary, Loews Hotels. For six years, Tisch served as chairman of NYC & Company, the city's tourism and marketing agency, and as chairman of New York Rising, he helped lead the drive to rebuild the economy after the attacks of 9/11. Additionally, Tisch holds positions as chairman emeritus of the United States Travel Association, trustee of Tufts University, treasurer of the New York Giants football team, and boardmember of the Tribeca Film Institute. He is the author of two best-selling books, *The Power of We: Succeeding Through Partnerships* and *Chocolates on the Pillow Aren't Enough: Reinventing the Customer Experience*, as well as the host of television's *Beyond the Boardroom*. He lives in New York City.

KARL WEBER writes about business and current affairs. His books include *Creating a World Without Poverty*, coauthored with Nobel Peace laureate Muhammad Yunus; *The Triple Bottom Line*, with sustainability expert Andrew W. Savitz; and *Food Inc.*, the companion to the award-winning documentary. He lives and works in Irvington, New York.